Investigative
Reporting

David Anderson & Peter Benjaminson

Investigative Reporting

Indiana University Press   *Bloomington & London*

Published in Canada by Fitzhenry & Whiteside Limited, Don Mills, Ontario
Manufactured in the United States of America

Library of Congress Cataloging in Publication Data

Anderson, David, 1942—
Investigative reporting.

Includes index.
1. Reporters and reporting.   I. Benjaminson,
Peter, 1945–   II. Title.
PN4781.A59   070.4′3   75–23896
ISBN 0–253–33164–1
ISBN 0–253–20196–9 pbk.   2 3 4 5 80 79 78 77

To Albert and Florence Benjaminson
and Marvin and Juanita Anderson

Contents

Preface

This book has been written with two goals in mind—to help the beginning or student journalist understand some of the techniques basic to investigative reporting and to inspire journalists, whether novice or experienced, to undertake more investigations.

We have sought to illustrate the realities of investigative reporting: the evasiveness of subjects, the anxiety of editors, the numbing frustration of repeatedly running down bad tips and unworthy hunches. We have also tried to show that such problems are routine and should not be cause for disappointment. We have also sought to convey some of the satisfaction felt by a journalist who has done a difficult job well. Although our print backgrounds have undoubtedly influenced our perspectives, this book is meant for all reporters. We want to encourage more of the careful, thorough, dogged journalism that has come to be known as investigative reporting wherever it might appear: in newspapers and magazines, on radio and television.

Work on this book began in early 1972 and most of it was written during and after the Watergate experience. As the book goes to press, Hollywood is making a movie based on *All the President's Men,* the account by two *Washington Post* reporters of their discovery of much of the early Watergate story. The glamour of Watergate coverage—something all journalists must now live with—is bound to be both a benefit and a burden for the profession. Temporarily at least, editors have been emboldened to encourage their reporters to cast a more searching gaze at the world around them. Undoubtedly, more young journalists will be attracted to the field, and their competition will do seasoned reporters no harm. But we suspect as well that many people more interested in glamour than in gritty reality will be drawn to journalism. Finally, because nothing good comes from an inaccurate or superficial news story, throughout this book we have stressed the importance of accuracy and thoroughness in investigative reporting.

In writing the book we have received much encouragement and many helpful suggestions from professionals and laymen alike. We have also been inspired by the work of many investigative reporters across the country, some of whose stories appear in the appendix. We are particularly indebted to Duane Lindstrom, who gave much time to the original outline, and to Jay Brant, who wrote the section on legal research. We are also indebted to Susan Rossen and Nancy Heusted who patiently read the entire manuscript in its many drafts and who are largely responsible for making it intelligible. We would like to thank Ladd Neuman, Dave Johnston, Nancy Hartman, Deborah Burgess, Louis Heldman, Ellen Grzech, Edward Boyer, Joel Dreyfuss, Philip Meyer, Carl Levin, Ron Dorfman, Melvin Mencher, and Pete Steffens for their help and inspiration. Thanks also to Walter Jacobson, Terrence Gorman, Roger Flaherty, Rone Tempest, Jim Neubacher, Ellen Hume, William Schmidt, Gary Blonston, Walker Lundy, Larry Jolidon, Judy Diebolt, Jo Thomas, Brownson Murray, Alison and John Oppedahl, Fred Morris, the *Free Press* library staff, and the many reporters and editors at the *Detroit Free Press* with whom we have worked and who have taught us much.

In addition, there are a number of investigators whose work we sought to emulate years ago and who, although they do not know it, are largely responsible for the book, among them: Pete Waldmeir, Art Petaque, William Clements, Donald Barlett, Morton Mintz, Morton Kondracke, Henry DeZutter, Lois Willie, Seymour Hersh, Jack Nelson, Mike Royko, and, of course, Robert Woodward and Carl Bernstein. We would suggest that the beginning journalist could do nothing so profitable as to spend some time watching these men and women work and reading their stories.

D.A.
P.B.

Investigative
Reporting

Part I

Basics

1
The Investigative Reporter

Everybody knows what an investigative reporter is. He's the guy with the dangling cigarette, the grim visage, the belted trench coat, and the snap-brim Fedora. He slinks in and out of phone booths, talks out of the side of his mouth, and ignores other, lesser reporters.

He never had to learn his trade. He was born to it. He sprung from his mother's womb clutching a dog-eared address book and a set of pilfered bank records. He has an interminable list of contacts. His job consists largely of calling the contacts and saying "Gimme the dope." The contacts, of course, always have the dope at their fingertips and are only too glad to part with it. He has all the time in the world to pursue sleazy characters through seamy intrigues. He appears in the city room only every two or three months to drop his copy on the desks of his astonished editors, mumble a few words, and disappear again into the night.

This book is written in the belief that there is no such person. For one thing, he may be a she. For another, many general assignment reporters, political reporters, and feature writers—in print and broadcast journalism—wind up doing investigative reporting from time to time. In fact, any reporter who does the job well is already part investigator. Those who merely record the public words of people powerful enough or clever enough to attract the media's attention are publicists or stenographers; they are not journalists.

The only workable definition of an investigative reporter is a reporter who spends a lot of time doing investigations. But uncovering information, particularly information that has been deliberately concealed, requires a certain type of personality. According to conventional wisdom, that personality consists mainly of extraordinary patience, or, put another way, an extremely high threshold of boredom. We think, however, that in addition, investigative reporters share a certain abiding faith in human nature:

a faith that someone, somehow, is working against the public interest.

While this may seem the epitome of cynicism, it is a useful attitude for an investigator. Suppose an investigative report reveals that a governmental agency is hiring civil servants because, and only because, they worked in a political campaign. In most cases, when this sort of abuse is reported, it is discovered to have been going on for years. During those years, it is quite probable that many persons in that city or state believed that the government officials involved were perfectly honest. If the investigator had shared that attitude, the story would never have been written. We sincerely doubt that there is a decent-sized city in the country where right now some public officeholder, private businessman, or foundation official is not engaging in a practice that will result in an investigative story in the months or years to come. It is basic human nature. The opportunities for personal profit in public and corporate life are so great that some officials will always succumb to temptation. For example, they may know for days or weeks in advance when important decisions about buying and selling land will be made, and often capitalize on their advance knowledge.

But even reporters cynical enough to see plots where others see only plans do not always take the time to do the necessary digging. A third trait, therefore, common to most good investigators, is the belief that many illicit acts cannot be covered up forever—or even for very long. Powerful officials and institutions are often corrupted, and the people involved are frequently careless with evidence. They brag to their friends, file incriminating documents in public offices, and trust people they have no reason to trust. The investigator also knows that these people can be led to blurt out their misdeeds in a moment's befuddlement.

Just as there is no such thing as the perfect crime, there is no such thing as the airtight conspiracy. The clues are always there. If a reporter digs hard enough, long enough, and with enough intelligence, the clues will be found. Often, what separates the investigator from other reporters is a willingness to dig. The challenge of unraveling, say, a very complicated land scheme will drive many investigators to spend weeks on end closeted with dusty real estate records. In fact, the more difficult the investigation, the more involved the scheme, and the more clever the people or organizations behind it are, the longer an investigator will want to spend researching the story.

The work ultimately involved in investigative reporting is not unlike the work involved in many other professions. It's painstaking, careful, logical, and complete. Good lawyers do it in preparing for trial, archaeologists do it in examining the ruins of ancient civilizations, and historians do it in analyzing the past. Unlike most historians, however, investigative reporters do their work while the subjects of their research are still around to see the results. Although historians face problems of incomplete and lost records, investigators must face outright hostility and obstruction. Generally, the corrupt do not fear the judgment of history as much as they fear exposure, prosecution, conviction, and disgrace. That is why they conceal their activities, and why reporters often must go to unusual lengths to uncover them.

Investigative reporting, then, is simply the reporting of concealed information. Some investigations concern the activities of public officials, such as corrupt politicians; others concern activities of corporations, political organizations, charities, and even foreign governments. Often, investigations uncover some sort of financial fraud. In subsequent chapters, we will attempt to show the novice investigator how to uncover concealed information using a variety of methods, none of which involve any magic and none of which require any special abilities. Obviously, some reporters have personalities more suited to dealing with certain kinds of people than do others. Charm, however, is not half as important as a willingness to work hard and think carefully.

2
Ethics of Investigative Reporting

Many fundamental techniques of investigative reporting involve actions some would label dishonest, fraudulent, immoral, and perhaps even illegal. Since investigative reporting aims at bringing corruption, hypocrisy, and lawbreaking to public attention, it is reasonable to expect the newsgathering profession to act as ethically as possible. And if all the information a reporter ever needed for investigations was on file, in legally available public records, there would be no problem: reporters could be completely candid in dealing with people under investigation. But the major fact of investigative reporting is that people frequently will go to great lengths to conceal damaging evidence.

Public officials, for example, tend to conceal ownership or interest in any company doing business with their agency. It is unlikely that a reporter, suspecting such an arrangement, would be able to prove it by knocking on the official's door and saying, "Hi. I'm here to uncover malfeasance. Any cancelled checks you'd like to show me?" Generally, before confronting the subject of an investigation, the reporter would seek confirmation of the official's financial links to the company, perhaps by posing as a businessman. That, of course, is dishonest. The reporter is often left in the classic ethical dilemma: he's damned if he does and damned if he doesn't. By lying to the double-dealing official, the reporter will shock many people's ethical sensibilities. But if the story doesn't appear, that corrupt official will continue to enrich himself at public expense.

Most reporters use deceptive methods to gather information—on the theory that in a democracy the public's right to information outweighs a public official's right to expect complete candor from journalists. Deceptive methods are justified, however, only when greater harm will be done the public if the information remains concealed than the harm done individuals by its publication. A reporter should never resort to questionable methods if the information can be obtained in any other way.

In those cases which are difficult to judge, most reporters tend to err on the side of dishonesty to obtain the information. The underlying assumption is that society has more to gain from an accurate, thorough reportage of events than it has to lose from the discomfort of the corrupt. Most professional journalists would prefer not to find themselves in a position of withholding important information from their readers simply to avoid worrying about their own personal ethics. Their overriding goal is to inform the public. Nevertheless, at some point, every investigative reporter who is in the least bit sensitive questions the ethics of the profession.

In spite of the burden of glamor which Watergate has given the profession, most investigative reporters take tremendous criticism from the friends and families of people they expose. They are accused of "sensationalism," "trying to sell newspapers," "bias," and "irresponsibility." Sometimes the subjects of newspaper investigations have nervous breakdowns, are jailed, hospitalized, or even attempt to commit suicide. After a few such experiences, even the most jaded reporters begin questioning their motives, their methods, and their fitness to sit in judgment of others. What accolades most investigators receive—whether pats on the back or lucrative prizes—come primarily from other journalists or from partisans who see their own cause being advanced by the reportage.

Even more disturbing than purely ethical considerations are the illegalities involved in many investigations. Reporters have been indicted, convicted, and jailed for stories they wrote, for acts they committed in gathering their information, or for refusing to answer judges' questions. In at least one case an investigative reporter had to find work in another state to avoid prosecution. In all probability, a much greater percentage of investigative reporters would find themselves afoul of the law were it not that many prosecutors fear the consequences of a hostile press on election day.

In 1972, two of the Pulitzer Prizes were awarded over the protests of some Columbia University trustees who were offended by the winners' methods of gathering evidence. The trustees were upset about the awarding of Pulitzers to columnist Jack Anderson, for publishing secret government memoranda revealing the United States' pro-Pakistani tilt during the Indo-Pakistan War,

and to the *New York Times,* for publishing the Pentagon Papers.
The trustees were quoted as calling the methods involved in obtaining these documents "stealing or robbing."

Since former President Nixon did not give his income tax returns to the *Providence Journal,* presumably the Internal Revenue
Act was violated when information from those returns was given
to the newspaper, which subsequently printed the story about
Nixon's low tax payments for 1970 and 1971. Many reporters,
most frequently columnist Jack Anderson, have obtained and reported the contents of classified information.

Consider for a moment Section 793 of Title 18 of the U.S. Code.
Commonly known as the Espionage Act, this law provides a wide
and sometimes fatal range of penalties for anyone who ". . . having
unauthorized possession of, access to, or control over any . . .
information relating to the national defense, which information
the possessor has reason to believe could be used to the injury of
the United States or to the advantage of any foreign nation, will-
fully communicates . . . the same to any person not entitled to
receive . . ." Clearly, a lot of newspapers have violated this and
other laws, particularly in covering foreign affairs. Yet the stories
made possible by these and similar criminal acts have been good
journalism. To say that the *New York Times* and other media
should not have revealed the contents of the Pentagon Papers is
to say that employees of those newspapers have the right to decide
what the public should know and what it should not know.

While many journalists and their attorneys have argued that
because of the First Amendment laws such as the Espionage Act
do not apply to newspapers, many prosecutors have argued otherwise. The final authority on whether a law has or has not been
broken is the judge hearing a particular case. If the judge rules a
reporter has broken the law, then the reporter has broken the law.
Other journalists have argued that when they break the law it is
justified because laws which result in censorship of the news are
bad laws and journalists have a moral obligation to break them.
Enough has been said about the morality or immorality of breaking "bad" laws that we feel no need to add to the debate. We
would only say that some laws, particularly those written by
politicians to protect politicians—what we would term antidisclosure laws—fairly beg to be broken.

A few years ago in Michigan, for example, the state senate went
so far as to begin construction of a glass booth for the press corps

in which the volume of floor debate heard might have been subject to control by the senate leadership. Would reporters be acting properly in attaching a suction microphone to the partition to hear debate without the senate's permission? We think they would be. Or, consider an Illinois law which permits land to be owned in secret trust. Under this system public officials can buy, sell, or rezone land without public disclosure. Consequently many Illinois public officials have made fortunes in real estate, often at the taxpayers' expense. Would a reporter be acting properly in using deception to uncover and report on the ownership of such trusts? We think so.

Regardless of the questionable ethics of such antidisclosure laws, the reporter is left in the position of attacking public officials for breaking one body of law—conflict of interest, for example— while having broken other laws—stealing documents, perhaps— to prove the conflict of interest. The argument that hypocrisy is excused for reporters, or that the ends justify means only in journalism, is a hard one to uphold. The longer one is in journalism, or any position to observe social processes close up, the more apparent it becomes that there are no such things as "ends." Nothing is ever ended, there are no final solutions. If the "means," meaning the methods by which people try to reach ends, are immoral, then there is only immorality. It has been argued that despite good intentions, the dishonest journalist is only adding to the general immorality. But the argument that means never justify ends presupposes ethical absolutes in which all acts are either good or bad, and there are no greater and lesser evils.

Suppose, for example, a city seems unable to enforce the building code in a particular tenement and a reporter is informed that the building is secretly owned by a building inspector. The owner listed in the tract index says the building was sold to someone else and says that the purchaser's identity is none of the reporter's business. To what lengths should a reporter go to find out who currently owns the building? Should he or she lie? Should it make a difference if the building is dangerous? Should it make more of a difference if someone, perhaps a child, was killed falling through a rotted porch railing?

In their book *All the President's Men, Washington Post* reporters Bob Woodward and Carl Bernstein reported that they lied to employees of the Committee to Re-Elect the President (CREEP). They told the various campaign officials, generally in late-night visits to their homes, that other, unnamed officials said they might be willing to talk. It wasn't true. But it was, according to the two, an effective door opener.

The facts of Watergate, like so many other investigations, could not be dug out of publicly available records. In many such cases, the only recourse to ignoring the story is to trick those involved into revealing the facts. These tactics often create great animosity between public officials and journalists: only a small minority of public officials either welcome or appreciate aggressive reporting. Most would prefer that reporters "let public officials carry out the mandate they were given by the voters"—which is another way of saying, "Look, they elected me, so who are you to question what I do?"

As a result, most state and local governments have adopted a substantial body of law designed to keep reporters at arm's length. Public policy is regularly hammered out behind closed doors in what are known as "executive sessions" and many records that could be used to spotlight corruption or mismanagement are kept from reporters and from the public. The effect of these laws is to make good reporting difficult and sometimes even illegal. Budgets are drawn up, land is rezoned, and civil servants are hired and fired behind closed doors. In our opinion, reporters who do not do everything possible to halt such practices, or find out what happens in such meetings, concede too much of the public's right to know—a right that is not theirs to give away.

In cases where enterprising reporters unearth genuinely harmful information—perhaps plans that compromise the national defense—one could argue that if a reporter found the information, it's probably nothing new to the enemy. *Washington Post* publisher Katherine Graham makes another good point, we think, when she argues that it is the government's responsibility to keep genuinely harmful information secret, not the newspapers'.

The problems of method are not the only ethical questions that confront investigative reporters. Questions range from matters of personal integrity to the choice of appropriate language when it comes time to write. Unfortunately, reporters sometimes make errors, sometimes exaggerate or fabricate, and sometimes engage in conflicts of interest themselves.

Some pass on quotes from anonymous but always articulate "observers," whose views happen to coincide with their own. Almost every journeyman reporter has, at one time or another, cleaned up a person's grammar, particularly when quoting less-educated people. Phrases tend to become complete sentences, whereas people rarely speak in complete sentences. But too often the clean-up results in the person quoted saying something more akin to what the reporter wants to hear than what was originally intended. Sometimes, however, the reporter is not at fault. A copy reader will clean up a verbatim quote and slightly alter the meaning, without consulting the reporter. Except in cases where an awkward or ungrammatical quote would subject someone to unwarranted ridicule, reporters should strive for absolute accuracy. If a public official's meaning is not clear from his statements, that's his problem—or perhaps his intent. What goes inside the quotation marks should be a quote.

As more and more reporters investigate subjects which lend themselves to feature writing, many are adopting the use of "composite" subjects. They fabricate a person who says or does all the things that the many people interviewed have said or done. Though the device has been overused, and often does little but cover up for a lack of thorough research, it is not dishonest as long as the subject is clearly identified as a composite. But when a reporter writes about a composite without the necessary disclosure, the result is misleading and, therefore, dishonest. Inevitably, the composite subject comes across as having a wider variety of experiences or insights than anyone actually interviewed. And with a composite subject, the tendency is to play down or leave out altogether the opinions or the experiences that do not fit the reporter's preconceptions. Gail Sheehy wrote about a composite prostitute, in an article that appeared in *New York Magazine* in 1973, and got caught. Sheehy described in great detail the various financial and sexual escapades of what must have been the most prolific hooker in New York. A short time later, however, the *Wall Street Journal* revealed that Sheehy's whore was not a person but a composite.

All reporters, at one time or another, come across stories in newspapers, be it their own or a rival newspaper, that they know are untrue. Unfortunately, it is a custom among journalists to look the other way; a kind of I-won't-embarrass-you-in-print-if-you-won't-embarrass-me-in-print ethic. In the late sixties and early seventies, there were over a dozen journalism reviews around the country and for a while it looked like the old-boy era of journalism was coming to a close. But by the mid-seventies, many of the reviews had died off and all but a few were just barely limping along. The *Columbia Journalism Review* and [MORE] are both published in New York and both concern themselves primarily with the east coast. The *Chicago Journalism Review*'s circulation dropped from over 9,000 in 1970 to less than 3,000 in 1975 and it collapsed.

This means that unless a newspaper outside New York or Washington makes a serious mistake, it is unlikely to come to the public's attention. Newspapers do not cover themselves, or each other. One reason newspapers rarely investigate each other may be the fear that they would destroy each other's credibility. The excuse most commonly advanced, however, is that the public is not interested in the media's problems. By ignoring one of the country's major institutions, however, investigative reporters are in another hypocritical position. They'll take on almost anybody, it seems, but another reporter. (For an exception, see appendix, "Ethics in Journalism.") If a major newspaper or TV station reports something falsely, it is just as newsworthy as if the governor tells a lie and as such it should be investigated and reported. Catching an errant reporter or newspaper is no more difficult than any other investigation and generally much easier. An investigator can almost always find someone on the inside who is willing to cooperate.

The most common, if not the most dangerous, form of media corruption is what is euphemistically termed a "freebee." Freebees are little bribes. They include everything from free meals to liquor at Christmas time to all-expense-paid junkets. When public officials go on trips paid for by local businessmen, particularly businessmen regulated by the officials, good newspapers howl. When journalists go on similar junkets little is said. While it is usually illegal for politicians to engage in conflicts of interest, there is, and rightly so, no such law governing reporters. But journalistic conflicts of interest are just as unethical as the political ones.

Reporters, particularly investigators and political reporters, should be somewhat cautious about how they handle their private affairs to avoid even potential conflicts of interest. That doesn't mean journalists can't go out carousing and tearing the tags from pillows, on occasion. But it does mean that a reporter about to inherit a half-interest in Volkswagen shouldn't write stories complaining about the high tariffs on foreign autos.

Obviously, reporters live in the same world as everybody else.

They are susceptible to charges of being pro-homeowner if they own homes, or being anti-homeowner if they rent apartments. Labor writers are occasionally damned by one faction or another depending on whether or not they are members of the Newspaper Guild. One businessman speaking before a group of publishers complained that because the publishers paid their employees so little, reporters were invariably biased in favor of the poor.

A reporter who gets too close to sources by taking handouts or lying on their behalf in print is not only unethical but stupid. Even if he or she doesn't get caught, the reporter may wind up so compromised that blackmail is risked. Even the most harmless freebee can hurt. One of the authors lost the grab for the bill at a restaurant while seeking to bluff his luncheon guest into admitting taking a bribe. The author had eaten a tuna salad sandwich. The bluff hadn't worked (the official had been an investigative reporter himself), and a story never appeared. But for the next two years, whenever an investigation was dropped or fell behind schedule his editors wanted to know how much tuna salad was involved. But most importantly, it is only human nature to be affected by a public official who gave you a gift at Christmas or the businessman who sold you a new car at or below cost. A reporter may go a little easier on such benefactors than the evidence warrants, or may even go a little too hard in attempting to compensate. It is better not to get into such a position in the first place.

The most difficult problems that arise in investigative reporting are the everyday decisions about what is or is not newsworthy, what facts should be included in a story, whether certain actions really are unethical or illegal, and in what perspective the facts should be reported. In most instances, on important stories, these problems are discussed at length by the reporters and editors involved. The debate generally centers around whether the paper has a molehill or a mountain on its hands. Reporters seem most often to overplay their own discoveries, and editors to downplay them. Reporters are defending their egos, seeking better placement of the story in the paper, and perhaps overly impressed by the difficulties they surmounted in obtaining the information.

Editors tend to attach little weight to attempts to cover up a story and must worry about how articulately they could defend the story to an irate publisher. Obviously, it is good for a reporter's career to win major prizes, and at many newspapers, it is better for an editor's career to remove as much controversy from a story as possible. Serious charges against powerful people can bring all kinds of trouble for a newspaper: charges and countercharges, threats of lawsuit, lawsuits, and even arousal of the advertisers. On the theory that reporters are not infallible, most newspaper editors take a decidedly devil's advocate role to test a story before publishing it. A reporter who has done careful research and is certain of the information is not bothered by hard questions.

The problem becomes most difficult, however, when the two sides disagree on whether certain actions taken by a person or institution warrants exposé treatment. Sometimes editors will ask questions like, "Why are we singling out this guy when everybody does it, it's common practice?" The reporter is likely to answer, "Because he's the one we caught and that's his tough luck." Obviously, if the person in question has done something wrong and it's important that the public know, the story should be printed. If the paper has information that the practice is common, that should be printed also.

Sometimes there is a difference of opinion among professionals as to whether certain kinds of behavior are wrong and, therefore, in the public realm. Perhaps an editor will ask a reporter to investigate a public official's drinking problem or other behavior that borders on the personal. The reporter may feel such conduct does not warrant a story. Should the story be given to another reporter who believes drinking is an abomination? Should the story idea be dropped? What about that percentage of the readers who think a public official's drinking habits are somehow important? Should they be ignored? Don't they have as much right to information as anyone else? Most journalists would agree that if the official's public decisions are affected by excessive drinking, it should be reported. But what about a public official's sex life? Does the public have a legitimate interest in that? The authors know of one reporter much given to covering a bachelor mayor's love life. The reporter once followed the mayor and his date on a short vacation in pursuit of a scandal. The reporter, we are told on good authority, left his wife at home and took his girl friend on the trip.

Reporters must also exercise great care not to draw conclusions, or even make inferences, which can't be directly supported by the facts at hand. That sounds fairly simple but a lot of otherwise good stories have been wrecked, or almost wrecked, by a reporter trying to stretch the evidence just a little bit too far. If a reporter charges, on good evidence, that a person has committed terrible act A and also hints that he may have done horrible thing B, the culprit is in an excellent position to deny B, denounce the investigator as an overzealous moron, and walk away more or less unscathed. On the other hand, if a reporter is certain a person committed both A and B, but neglects to mention B, then he has given that person a privilege that is not his to give. People in a democracy have a right to learn everything they can about actions that affect their interests.

Many good investigations are killed or watered down for one of the following reasons:

"So what if he's a partner in a business with guys who are breaking the law, that's guilt by association."

"How can we say he's guilty of conflict of interest (or anything else) when he hasn't been convicted. After all, a man is innocent until proven guilty."

The guilt-by-association dogma holds that a newspaper shouldn't say a man is a thief just because he hangs around with thieves. In a strictly logical sense, this is true. Were it not, one could accuse all prison guards, probation officers, and judges of murder because they hang around with murderers. But when it comes down to cases, the guilt-by-association homily prevents a lot of newspaper readers from learning that the county prosecutor spends time at the race track with syndicate types, or that a county judge is a partner in a real estate business with city commissioners who are rezoning their own land. Obviously, these are facts to which the readers are entitled.

That judge may be conspiring with the commissioners if he knows they are voting on their own land. Depending on the relevant conspiracy statute, however, the judge may not have committed any crime. But his strange sense of ethics ought to become a matter of public record anyhow. The same is true of a state legislator, for example, who campaigns on a platform of Victorian morality, votes for long jail sentences for drunks, and yet drinks heavily once out of the sight of constituents. While we don't think an active vice life should disqualify a person from public office, blatant hypocrisy is certainly newsworthy.

A lot of reporters are also slowed by the dictum that a person is innocent until proven guilty. Many take that to mean a newspaper can't say a person did something unless a court has concurred.

However, since a good investigation leads to direct knowledge of the events, a journalist should feel free to report them whether or not a judge has agreed. The only caution here is language. The word "murder," for example, is a legal term. It cannot accurately be said that a man murdered someone unless he has been convicted of that crime, and even then it should be said he was "convicted of murder." But, if a reporter clearly sees a man shoot, he or she can accurately report what was seen—a shooting. By the same token, if it is established that a city councilman owned a parcel of land on January 28, 1976, and voted to rezone that land that same day, it can be said he had conflicting interests when he voted. If, however, one wishes to go a step further and ring in the conflict of interest law, it should be said only that the councilman was "in apparent violation of the state conflict of interest statute."

Any editor who really believed that a person could not be said to have committed a reportable, scandalous act until proven guilty of it would have investigative reporters do little more than gather their evidence, present it to the local prosecutor, and sit back awaiting a verdict. "Innocent until proven guilty" simply expresses common law's intent to afford defendants due process. What it says is that a man cannot be punished by a policeman or prosecutor. It does not say a newspaper cannot report events without the prior approval of the courts, even if some of those events may involve a person's breaking the law.

A final word on newspaper ethics. We think almost all of the mistakes, dishonesties, and indiscretions of journalists can be traced to a single cause—furthering their own careers. That is what has fostered the "scoop mentality": reporters competing not to better inform the public, but to beat the competition to a story that is about to break anyhow. That is why widows are informed of their husbands' untimely deaths by reporters masquerading as cops. That is why investigations are overplayed or underplayed. And, that is why a lot of advertisers are still able to edit newspapers.

The profession would be a lot better off if those who are in it for their financial advancement would find some other career. There's a lot more money in real estate than in investigative journalism. If a reporter starts worrying too much about money or about becoming executive editor, he or she should do the readers a favor and quit.

3
What to Investigate

There is no institution of any standing, anywhere, that wouldn't be improved by a bit of investigation. After all, in 1974 Boy Scouts of America, Inc. was found to be lying about its membership figures in order to qualify for federal aid. Other malfeasances have been unearthed at Boys Town in Nebraska, a health charity, and in the fund-raising techniques of an organization set up to aid widows of policemen. Presidents, senators, congressmen, governors, federal judges, cops, and even investigative reporters have all been caught violating their public trusts.

American citizens are oppressed, in some small and in some not so small ways, by clogged and archaic criminal justice systems, by outmoded and degrading bail bond systems, by wasteful government subsidies to giant corporations, by school systems that graduate illiterates, by health care systems that care miserably for millions while ignoring millions more, by inadequate and unfair taxation systems, and by acts of corrupt officials. This is not to say that everyone in America is miserable. Far from it. But it does mean that opportunities for investigation are often staring the reporter in the face.

In fact, there aren't nearly enough investigative reporters to go around. As a result, choosing subjects to investigate is one of the most crucial aspects of investigative reporting. The correct choice of an investigative target could mean not only professional satisfaction for a reporter but a more healthy community at large. Also, no matter how good a job of investigation a reporter does, if the topic is boring or trivial, the story will be boring or trivial.

Too often, reporters choose their investigations not because of the scope or significance of the story they hope to produce, but because information on the topic is easily obtainable and the need to expend great labor on the story minimal. This causes too many reporters to wait by their telephones for the right "tip" or for an "insider" to come along and hand them an all-but-written story.

True enough, a reporter is hired to write stories and if a story presents itself, there's no reason why it shouldn't be written. But the most useful stories are usually those originated by a reporter. A "tipster" turned away by the press will often take the inside information on criminality in high places to a prosecutor or police agency, and the story will come out eventually.

In our opinion, it's the stories about those institutions everyone takes for granted—the Federal Aviation Administration and how it sets air fares, the local probation department and how it supervises parolees—that are the most rewarding. They would never appear without original research by reporters. For example, in Chicago it had long been understood that control of the Cook County assessor's office was a political necessity for the Democratic machine—not only for the large number of patronage jobs in the office, but also because a hard working and sufficiently dishonest assessor was a very effective campaign fund raiser. For decades the matter lay untouched by the press, save for the usual gossip by reporters in bars. There would be a great story if only a link could be shown between the machine's fund raising and the campaign contributors' property tax assessments. But it seemed too many contributors and too many buildings were involved, the contributions were too well hidden, and the assessment process was just too complicated. At least it seemed that way until the spring of 1970, some months before the fall election.

Two reporters for the *Chicago Daily News,* William Clements and Charles Nicodemus, sent out form letters to the Cook County sheriff, clerk, assessor, and to other county officers saying that as part of their election coverage preparation they wished an appointment and an in-depth explanation of how each office worked. Naturally, the assessor didn't think he was the target of an investigation and didn't try to impede or sidetrack the reporters until it was too late. The assessor, P. J. "Parky" Cullerton, released one of his top assistants to give the reporters a three-day course in assessing. After that Clements and Nicodemus did their own assessments of over two dozen of the biggest buildings in downtown Chicago.

While this was going on, WMAQ-TV commentator Walter Jacobson managed to talk his way into a fund-raising party for Cullerton where the camera recorded the presence of many of the biggest property owners in the city. Why, Jacobson asked his six o'clock news audience, were all those people there and what did they want? Although Jacobson could not say for certain that the big realtors were benefiting from the assessor's magnanimity, the implication was clear. When the facts came out several months later in the *Daily News,* they were even more appalling. Clements and Nicodemus had spent three months in the assessor's office. They found a skyscraper, two years old, being assessed as if it had depreciated for nearly a hundred years. The assessors claimed they were given information by the building's owner that justified the low taxes, but refused to let the reporters see it, saying the information was "confidential." When all the stalls were over, the reporters were able to conclude that no such information existed, in fact, that no kind of information would have warranted that kind of tax break, and finally, that the average Chicago taxpayer was paying for taxes not levied against influential owners.

Clements estimated that the taxpayers were making up for somewhere between $5 million and $20 million annually—just on the buildings he and Nicodemus investigated. Since that represented only about 10 per cent of the new high rises in the city, the loss to the city coffers was considerable. Furthermore, a number of the underassessed buildings were owned or operated by men serving on Assessor Cullerton's campaign committee, and other major building owners were in regular attendance at a wide range of Democratic Party fund-raising functions. Following the *Daily News* story, other papers ran some excellent recovery investigations detailing even more abuses. For example, a suburban community newspaper found a number of posh country clubs assessed at only six cents a square foot while land around them sold for as much as ten dollars a square foot.

A number of other major investigative stories in Chicago stemmed from a decision by a public interest law firm to examine all recent major land transactions in or near downtown Chicago. There was a large urban renewal project on the near West Side where a city official was found to have received about $15 million in suspicious payments, although he had invested no money in the renewal project himself. Then there was the railroad, tax exempted by state law, found selling off surplus land to developers who continued not paying taxes, even though they were not exempted. There were large parking lots on land slated for other uses by government contracts, there was city-owned land being sold to aldermen's friends in return for bank stock. In fact, in all but a few cases of private land sales, the law firm found either conflict

of interest or violations of law. Perhaps the most appalling case
was one uncovered by Ralph Whitehead and Duane Lindstrom,
two former investigators for the law firm, who were then working
for Lerner Newspapers in Chicago. They found that a large hotel
on land near the downtown area had negotiated a 99-year lease on
the land from the city's continually bankrupt school board in
return for three per cent of the hotel's drink revenue. A realtor
friendly to those who negotiated the lease was president of the
school board.

Some people claim that Chicago is exceptionally corrupt. We
would point out that it's possible that Chicago has a reputation
for corruption not necessarily because it is more corrupt than
other big cities, but because until quite recently it supported four
fairly independent newspapers with large numbers of competing
investigative reporters.

A most fertile field for investigation is land purchase, real estate
speculation, and other business dealings by public officials. Since
the dawn of this republic, when, according to some historians,
delegates to the constitutional convention used inside information
to deal profitably in bond markets, public officials have been in a
peculiar position. On the one hand, they are charged with doing
what they think is best for the public in formulating public policy.
On the other hand, like most red-blooded Americans, they do not
shun financial gain. In many cases, not only would they like
money above and beyond their salaries for their personal satisfaction, but they desperately need those funds to finance the ever-
growing expense of public campaigning. Again and again, their
financial needs, coupled with their privileged position at the helm
of society, lead them into conflicts of interest: the illegitimate
meshing of their own needs with their concept of what is for the
public good.

The best place to begin searching for such conflicts is in the
various campaign contributor lists now kept by most states and in
most counties. In some presidential and other elections, people
who are not self-interested often become excited enough to give
generously to campaigns of their choice. But when a low-level
official receives large contributions, it's time to be suspicious and
try to find out what the official gave or will give in return. Some
gifts to politicians come in forms other than campaign contributions, such as stock deals, limited partnerships, cut-rate houses
and cars, consulting fees, real estate commissions, finders fees, and

even legal fees. Public officials who run businesses on the side can easily disguise such payments.

Persistent rumors that a person is a crook of some sort also bear looking into. The rumors may have been started by political enemies, but they may be true. Journalists should watch too for signs of government employees living beyond their means. One reporter spent so much time riding in a Chicago squad car that the cops, accustomed to his presence, spoke openly in front of him. The reporter learned that one of the cops, a patrolman, owned a second home in Florida, a camper, four automobiles, including a Ferrari and an Alfa Romeo, and a jewelry collection of undetermined size. A revelation of this kind, of course, does not make a story—at least not yet. Perhaps the government employee married well or inherited a fortune. (Married and inherited money can be verified in probate court, by marriage licenses, and with business records; see chapter 6.) Or, perhaps the money came from gambling. Lobbyists have been known to regularly lose large sums at the poker table to favored politicians.

But, we repeat, the most fruitful investigations will often be of those institutions which function so unobtrusively and with so little fuss that the public assumes that they are doing their job as well as it can be done. A careful look at any long-established institution will often reveal a dense bureaucracy, grown up by custom and accretion, that is no longer doing the job it was set up to do or is actually doing a job that most people, if they thought about it, would not want performed at all. The concerned reporter, who is interested in his long-run as well as his short-run journalistic reputation, will attempt to dig into the operations of these agencies and let the public know how they can be reformed or improved.

One of the most popular ways to do this is for a reporter to get on the receiving end of one of these institutions and write about what it's like. One reporter, who passed for an eighteen-year-old, enrolled herself in a big city high school and wrote a series that had school administrators and bureaucrats explaining themselves for months afterward. Another had herself committed to a federal mental institution and wrote a revealing series about conditions there. Reporters have taken jobs in automobile factories, driving ambulances, working for various government agencies, and helping drug dealers prepare dope for distribution, to name but a few. But such participatory journalism is not always either necessary or desirable. In most cases, the non-participatory techniques of investigative reporting, which this book describes, can be employed to investigate both institutions and individuals. After all, institutions are merely groups of people, and no reporter has ever been able to investigate an institution without investigating the people involved and their official or unofficial activities.

A final note: The responsible investigator should avoid trivial sensationalism, or, at least, follow it up with some thoughtful investigation in the same field. For example, while the sun bathing habits of a single garbage truck crew might make an interesting story and photo layout, a reporter could spend time researching and writing a more valuable story comparing sanitation costs and contracts in various cities, drawing the relevant conclusions for local public policy.

Part II

Sources and Records

4
Attracting and Evaluating Sources

Although a reporter may spend day after day searching out a clue important enough to justify beginning a full-scale investigation, it is possible to chance upon a prize-winner by picking up a city room phone to order a pizza and having a heavy breather at the other end of the line announce that the price of anchovies was fixed by an international cabal of fish-firm executives meeting in the back of his shop. The reporter wasn't exactly straining any investigative skills by picking up the telephone, but with any ambition at all he or she is off on the next investigation.

This is the easiest way to receive tips—unexpectedly. Attracting and encouraging tips, however, as well as developing and cultivating sources, and evaluating and using the information they provide, all require forethought and preparation. Once the source is whispering sweet somethings in a reporter's ear, the reporter has, by definition, already attracted him. Unless the reporter's name came in a dream or the phone number was dialed at random, it is likely that the source had a specific reason for calling that particular newspaper or that particular reporter.

In spite of the populist pretensions espoused by most media outlets, a great many are popularly regarded as house organs for various established interests. These papers and stations rarely print or broadcast investigations aimed at those they favor and often kill even straight news stories that might be damaging to those interests. If a source has some information that would tend to discredit an institution a certain newspaper protects in its news columns, it is unlikely that the information will be given to a reporter for that paper. The Republican party employees who allegedly leaked reports of Democratic vice presidential candidate Tom Eagleton's electric shock treatments to the press apparently avoided feeding the story to the "elitist" East Coast media—a favorite Republican bugbear—and instead saturated the Midwest news media with their tips, finally hitting pay dirt with the *Detroit Free Press.*

Sources appear to differentiate among reporters as well as among newspapers. Journalists who defend the oil companies during an "energy crisis" are not likely to get calls from tank farm attendants telling them where badly needed heating oil is being secretly stored. Real estate writers who are virtual public relations agents for the home building industry are not going to learn of massive scandals in federally subsidized housing programs. Even unsophisticated readers may realize intuitively that tips given to such writers would not result in news stories. (Although this rule is generally accurate, some tips go to whatever reporter is near the telephone when it rings.)

Once a reporter becomes well known, there is no problem encouraging sources to call. Neal Sheehan of the *New York Times* probably didn't know much about the Pentagon Papers until someone—probably Daniel Ellsberg or one of his helpers—handed Sheehan a box with papers inside. Sheehan's "investigation," incidentally, consisted of reading the papers in the New York hotel room where he closeted himself with some editors and a typewriter.

Even if a reporter has a big name, though, it has to be the right kind of big name. It's possible that columnist William Buckley, at least until a few years ago, was almost as well known as columnist Jack Anderson, but Anderson probably received a hundred or more solid tips for every dollop of information phoned to Buckley. That's because Anderson is seen by many as a champion of the little man, a friend of the griper, and an avenger of evils perpetrated by officialdom. Buckley—although he may not deserve his public image—is seen by many as a representative of, and spokesman for, that officialdom.

Doing investigative stories is one way to attract sources. But there are other ways to indicate to potential sources that a reporter is in the market for information. If a journalist is interested in tips relating to a particular person who is suspected of wrongdoing, it may be possible to convince an editor to okay profiles, features, or hard news stories about that person. It doesn't matter—as long as the reporter's byline appears on all of them. These bylined stories invariably attract sources who have information about the person. (That is why it is so common to read newspaper stories charging someone with committing illegal acts A, B, and C, then to pick up the paper two days later and read that he also committed illegal acts D and E. Either other sources not contacted by the reporter came forward or sources who had known about D and E but withheld their knowledge from the reporter were cajoled by the stories about A, B, and C into coming forward.) Reporters are rarely concerned about alarming the subject of an investigation with this approach. Most well-known people are egotistic enough to believe that even their routine movements are worthy of public notice; so much so that it would be unlikely they'd spend much time wondering about a spate of stories about them. Experienced investigators, however, are careful not to produce paeans of praise about the person they're pursuing for fear they'll scare off the sources they're trying to attract.

Another effective method of attracting sources is to appear on a television talk show. Viewers who hear a voice and see a face are much more likely to contact the reporter than if he or she remains merely a byline. If reporters project an interest in investigative stories, they often find that people are so anxious to get in touch that they'll forward information not only about the subject discussed on the air, but about a variety of other matters as well.

Landing a beat assignment is another effective way to attract sources. A reporter's byline on stories that appear month after month about a particular institution will readily suggest the author's name to the general public as a potential recipient of information about that institution. Tips come also from the members of the institution the reporter is assigned to cover. According to Woodward and Bernstein, the *Washington Post*'s night police reporter was the recipient of such a tip, without which the *Post*'s Watergate investigation might have been sidetracked or delayed. As a veteran beat reporter, Eugene Bachinski was so trusted by his sources on the District of Columbia police force that one of the officers told him that two address books confiscated from the Watergate burglars contained the notations "W. House" and "W.H." next to a phone number.

Perhaps the easiest way to attract tips, though, is to act like a human being instead of the stereotypical reporter of late-night movie fame. Experienced reporters attempt to meet as many people as possible in all walks of life and to be as charming as possible when meeting them. They avoid dogmatism if drawn into arguments with sources and let sources know they are open to new ideas, especially new story ideas. They don't begin scribbling notes the first time a source mentions a well-known name. They attempt to act as casual as possible while remembering as much as possible. They talk less and listen more. Most important, they treat with special courtesy those people who usually are treated curtly: waitresses, clerks, countermen, low-level bureaucrats. It pays when the favor is returned in the form of a news tip. Good reporters are not born with a long list of contacts; they make them.

Sources, of course, may have varied motives. Often the source is simply a conscientious public servant who sees a wrong being committed and thinks the public ought to know about it. This person usually turns to the press only after unsuccessful attempts to interest superiors in ending the wrongdoing. As the case of New York City Policeman Frank Serpico illustrated, the press is often the only effective outlet for civil servants who wish to remain honest and still do their jobs. Other sources may reveal information to revenge themselves on one of their superiors or colleagues who they feel has done them an injury. Although their motives are less pure than those of public servants who wish to right a wrong, the information they provide need be taken no less seriously, just more cautiously.

Some information is provided inadvertently by people in government or private industry who like to gossip. When talking to reporters about their work, these inadvertent sources may not realize that the information they provide may result in a newspaper investigation which their employer will not appreciate. Sometimes, sources are just average citizens who stumble across interesting information. Because these people are unused to bearing important secrets, or because they're unused to talking to reporters, or perhaps because they have been disbelieved and are frustrated by the burden of information they carry, their words often spill out in a confused rush to the first reporter polite enough to listen to them.

All these sources are in marked contrast to informants who, after providing a reporter on one or two occasions with leads that result in stories, come to consider themselves "inside dopesters." Having adopted this self-image, they begin to look for more tips to sustain it. In some cases, they become volunteer adjuncts to a reporter's investigative effort, all the more valuable from one perspective because they are unpaid, highly motivated, and probably not as well known as the reporter they are voluntarily assisting. They are valuable not only for the information they are able to provide from their own store of knowledge, but also because in a pinch a reporter can often call on them to dig out a specific piece of information. Their names should be kept on file, with one caution. These people are not necessarily ethical, by definition not professional, and every one of their tips must be thoroughly checked out, especially if the reporter senses that the newly discovered journalistic egos of the volunteer aides are driving them to exaggeration. It's the reporter, not the source, who is responsible for reportorial inaccuracies.

Whatever the motives or aspirations of the source, it's the information, not the source, that should most concern the reporter. Tips should be judged on their individual merit, rather than on the motives of the person who conveys them. For example, when rumors began to circulate in Washington, D.C., regarding possible payoffs to Vice-President Spiro Agnew, reporter Saul Friedman, a Knight Newspapers Washington correspondent, was provided with information reflecting badly on Agnew by a most unusual source—a lawyer for one of the companies that had bribed Agnew. The company itself had at least one unsavory motive for directing attention to its own bribee: to divert attention away from itself. If it continued to attract attention, the company feared it might lose some lucrative federal contracts. So a junior partner in the Washington law firm representing the company advised Friedman to "take a careful look" at the Baltimore grand jury investigating local corruption for information on the vice-president. Friedman interviewed some sources in the Justice Department who knew what information was being presented to the grand jury and wrote a story which reported that people close to Agnew allegedly were involved in payoffs and kickbacks during the time Agnew was governor of Maryland and later vice president of the United States, and that Agnew himself might be involved in such practices.

This first story attracted little attention when it was published because it appeared on one of the days former White House counsel John Dean was testifying before the Ervin committee. So Friedman went on, attempting to squeeze the rest of the story from people whose motives were even less pure than those of the junior law partner: the senior partners in the firm and the Maryland contractors under investigation for paying off Agnew. But before Friedman could write another story, Jerry Landauer of the *Wall Street Journal* reported definitely that the target of the Bal-

timore grand jury investigation was Agnew himself. Although in
the first story he had not linked Agnew directly to the payoffs,
Friedman was able to use his research to write a story for next
day's paper detailing the alleged payoffs and the mechanisms of
their delivery and receipt, including a number of details not contained in the *Journal*'s account.

There are numerous other examples of self-interested sources
providing useful tips to investigators. Self-interest is almost invariably the motive when, for example, campaign aides to a candidate
inform a reporter of alleged misconduct by their opponent. During the 1972 primary election race for Cook County (Chicago)
state's attorney, an aide to a reform candidate told a reporter that
the Daley machine candidate had been active in partisan politics
while serving on the bench. Such activity was a violation of the
ethics rules laid down by the Illinois state supreme court. In
addition, the charge was damaging to the machine candidate's
campaign; self-interest obviously motivated the tip. But the reporter began to check out the story, despite the source. Interviews
with a number of recently fired or disgruntled machine election
workers enabled the reporter to establish specific dates when the
judge presided over affairs at party headquarters well before he
became a candidate. Interviews with machine functionaries in
adjacent wards indicated that the judge had issued formal invita-
tions to neighboring machine politicians to attend party meetings
in his ward, a rather blatant sign of partisan activity.

The reporter checked his newspaper's photo file on the judge—
a good way to discover surprising things about who someone's
associates are without leaving the office—and found a year-old
picture of the judge with his arms extended horizontally, suggesting that two people had been cropped out of the picture. The
reporter spent another hour in the photo library and eventually
found the missing parts of the same picture in the separate photo
files kept on the other two politicians. When contacted by the
reporter, the photographer who had taken the picture remembered where he had taken it—at a party fund-raising luncheon.

Confronted, the judge was successfully bluffed (a technique
discussed in chapter 12) into revealing other improper partisan
activities. Unfortunately, however, the story was killed when the
judge successfully persuaded his friend the publisher to do him a
favor.

But as often as not, partisan leaks don't hold water. For example, when a black Wayne County (Detroit) circuit court judge launched a mayoral campaign in Detroit in 1972, rumor-mongers insisted he was linked to gangland drug figures and was a crook himself. A month-long investigation of the rumors ensued. The reporter assigned to the story traced each rumor back to its source and in each case the alleged source denied authorship of the tale. Checks of public records indicated that the judge was living no higher than his salary warranted. Although he had been associated with drug figures before being named to the bench, in each instance he was acting as an attorney for those figures. And although his shady clients had indeed contributed to his successful campaign for a judicial seat, the judge listed their contributions on the required campaign reports.

One of the most persistent rumors about the candidate was that when asked why he wanted to run for mayor, although the mayor's salary was lower than a judge's, the candidate reportedly had replied that he would "make a lot more money" as mayor. This was taken to mean that he planned to accept payoffs as the city's chief executive. Months later, when Michigan State Senator Coleman Young entered the mayor's race, rumor-mongers began attributing the same story to him. So perhaps both men, both black, had been victimized by racially biased tipsters. In any case, since no evidence was ever found to support the rumors about the judge, no story was written.

Whatever its apparent initial worth, however, no tip should be completely ignored. Reporters shouldn't fly off the handle when someone calls and says, "I read your story today and see you don't like Senator X," or, "It's pretty clear you agree with me that Mayor Y is trying to pull a fast one." The person who volunteers such remarks is probably not just making small-talk. It is more likely an attempt to feel out the reporter's attitudes. If the reporter can possibly agree with whatever the source blurts out (or at least remain silent), the source, feeling comforted by what seems to be ideological fellowship, may tell the reporter something useful. Experienced investigators ignore whatever may annoy them about a tipster's small talk, manner, or appearance. None of these is necessarily relevant. Some people act crazy yet have accurate information. Others look, act, and dress like bankers yet spout third-hand nonsense.

Perhaps the classic example of this is a self-styled Chicago "legal researcher" named Sherman Skolnick. Skolnick sees a lot of conspiracies among the powerful to do harm to the powerless. He has told newsmen that the altimeter in the cockpit of the commercial airliner in which Mrs. Howard Hunt, wife of the Watergate figure, died was sabotaged so that her plane would crash and she would be silenced. Skolnick is widely regarded by journalists in several states and Canadian provinces as an endless source of unproveable stories. He will tell you, for example, that one of the authors of this book is a Central Intelligence Agency spook (untrue) and that two of the reporters whose work appears in the appendix were trained by the CIA (also untrue, as far as we know).

The problem with Skolnick, however, is that every once in a while he is absolutely right. For a long time he insisted on repeating to various reporters that former Illinois Governor Otto Kerner, then a federal judge, was a crook. Eventually, a jury agreed.

Skolnick also repeatedly charged that two Illinois supreme court justices (one of whom former President Nixon was reportedly considering for the U.S. Supreme Court) were crooks who had taken shares in a bank which had a case before their court. Much laughter ensued. He said that none of the Chicago newspapers would print the story because officials of both newspaper chains had been given stock in the same bank. More laughter. A short time later both judges were removed from the bench for conflict of interest and investigators for the *Chicago Journalism Review* unearthed public records showing that, indeed, a dozen members of the media—newspaper publishers and editors along with radio and television station owners and news directors—had been given stock in the bank.

Reporters who took Skolnick seriously wasted a lot of time; reporters who ignored him missed many excellent stories. Old time newsroom hacks would automatically have dismissed Skolnick as a nut. They would also dismiss all the old ladies who walk into newsrooms with shopping bags full of aging records, and all the people who telephone slurred stories to newspaper city desks. Some of these people may indeed be a bit insane, but they often have stories to tell, often surprisingly well-documented and detailed stories, and they shouldn't be rejected out of hand by news hawks too busy rewriting handouts to spare the time to listen to them. After all, prize-winning stories sometimes begin with what seem to be off-the-wall tips.

A Detroit reporter, for example, was once visited by an immigrant from Barbados who took an hour of what the busy reporter considered precious time to tell him a patently ridiculous tale. The man alleged that one of the Wayne County (Detroit) commissioners, a woman, had picked him up on a Caribbean beach while she was on vacation. They became lovers, he said. She brought him back to the United States, where they were married. During the few months their marriage lasted, he told the reporter, she had attempted to start a prison riot in Ohio, had tricked him into perjuring himself, and had threatened him and others with a pistol. The immigrant's self-interest in the dissemination of this tale was obvious; the commissioner was suing him for divorce and federal immigration agents were attempting to deport him. Even worse, from the reporter's point of view, the man could produce no evidence in support of his version of his love affair with the commissioner. Now what could be more ridiculous than listening to his story? But the bemused reporter, fancying himself a humanitarian, waited patiently through the entire tale and walked back to his office with an indulgent smile on his face.

Within a matter of days, Detroit Police Commissioner P. G. Tannian accused the county commissioners of refusing to fund an inter-governmental police agency because accusations against one of the commissioners were being investigated by that agency. It became evident that it was the immigrant's wife who was being investigated. The reporter who had listened condescendingly to what he had thought were insane ramblings suddenly found himself the sole possessor of enough background information to write a good story about the reasons underlying the squabble between the cops and the commissioners. Not devastating reporting, but informative nevertheless.

No two tips, of course, are of equal value. A reporter who answers the telephones in any newspaper's city room for half a day will converse with perhaps a dozen callers who will tell him that giant grasshoppers are eating every house in the neighborhood or that myopic martians are molesting the water heaters. But the reporter who answers these phones often enough will eventually be contacted by some startled businessman who picked up the wrong briefcase on a visit to city hall and now possesses a copy of an agreement between the mayor and the local Mafia don to split rakeoffs from crooked contractors. The problem, of course, is to separate the substantive tips from the creations of an often malicious imagination.

Columnist Jack Anderson failed miserably in this task at a crucial juncture in the 1972 presidential campaign. Without adequately checking the facts, he reported on national radio an unverified tip that had been telephoned to him: that Democratic vice presidential candidate Tom Eagleton, who had already admitted a history of mental distress, had also been ticketed for drunk driving on several occasions. No evidence ever materialized to support this report. Later, Anderson alibied unforgiveably: He said he couldn't take the time to check the report because he might have lost his scoop if he did.

What Anderson didn't have—documentation—is what most often separates good tips from bad. Any tip is incalculably stronger if it can be verified or at least corroborated on paper. A document indicates that a third party, and usually an official third party, is involved in the case. In addition, possessing a document will probably help get the story published. It can reassure an editor and the newspaper's lawyers that there will be something more solid than a few whispered words to rely on if and when the story must be defended in court. In the absence of documentation, identical or corroborating accounts of the same facts from different sources—if possible, with different biases—are of roughly equal value. Best of all, of course, is an admission by your investigative subject that the deed was his. (Securing such confessions will be discussed in chapter 12.)

In his investigative account of the My Lai massacre, *New York Times* reporter Seymour Hersh, a free-lance journalist at the time, showed how a convincing story can be put together with little documentary support. Hersh constructed his account more than two years after the massacre occurred by touring the U.S., interviewing discharged G.I.s who had been at My Lai, and carefully stitching together their complementary accounts.

Even before seeking out corroborating evidence, however, the reporter should try to put the source in a position which will force documentation or verification of his own account. The reporter should take the source over the same ground two or three times to see if the story changes with the telling. Or, the reporter should attempt to wring from the source a detail which can be checked with a second, preferably neutral, source. For example, if the source is encouraged to mention a specific street corner or address at which some incident took place, or to state firmly what the weather was like at a particular time, then the information can be checked against street maps or old weather reports. If the source's account is verified initially, detail by insignificant detail, the reporter can begin to check out the more significant allegations.

Some sources, especially professional bureaucrats who are accustomed to collecting paper and are protected by civil service statutes, are able to provide reporters with massive documentation. For example, a Detroit reporter was approached in 1973 by an employee of that city's auditor-general. The auditor's assigned task was to prevent other city officials from misspending public funds or falling into conflicts of interest. The employee, protected by his union and by civil service regulations, felt free to tell the reporter that the auditor had engaged in just the sort of folly he was charged with preventing: he had hired his own son, with city funds, to teach his employees "report writing." The employee buttressed his account with copies of letters from the auditor to the city civil service commission and to a local university arranging for the course, an invoice from the university for the course cost, a city voucher indicating that payment had been made, and a diploma from the course signed by the auditor's son. The signature would have been especially useful to the reporter had the auditor denied the existence of the arrangement, since another copy of the son's signature could easily have been obtained, and the two compared. But as it happened, the auditor-general admitted all after the reporter confronted him with the information.

After this story was printed, the auditor began to harass his talkative employee. He restricted the employee's telephone calls, cut his vacation time, and so on. The reporter, in part because he did not want it said around city hall that his sources would be mistreated, wrote a story about the mistreatment. The harassment ended, and the auditor took early retirement.

If a reporter finds that documentation is vital to a story, and the source, on initial contact, doesn't provide it or an indication of where it might be found, there is no reason why the reporter can't ask the source to get it. The reporter can tell the source that without documentation or verification there won't be any story. Some reporters specialize in pep talks that will convince their sources to take the risks necessary to obtain the crucial documentation.

For example, suppose an assistant city assessor calls a reporter to say that the chief city assessor is ordering the underassessment of buildings owned by the chief's cousins. (A lower assessment means lower property taxes, of course.) But the assistant won't provide the reporter with copies of the relevant paperwork, explaining that if he did the boss would find out and fire him. At this point, the reporter could accept his demurral and begin a laborious check of birth and marriage certificates, telephone books, and city directories, in an effort to identify and locate the assessor's cousins and the properties they own. The reporter could prepare an evaluation of the worth of the buildings owned by the cousins and then compare that assessment to the official city assessment. With some effort, a good story could be produced this way. But it would be much easier if the reporter had the work sheets setting out the assistant assessor's appraisal of the worth of the buildings, the chief assessor's veto of that appraisal, and substitution of a lower figure. It would be a much stronger story as well, because it would show the assessor's role in the tax favoritism.

The reporter's task is to give the timid tipster a course in investigative journalism that will convince him either that any participation in the story can be successfully concealed or that his job is safe in any case. The reporter can appeal to his sense of righteous indignation: "You mean you have a Harvard doctorate in assessing gas stations and some dingbat who doesn't have the brains to be a janitor, much less your boss, tells you to forget all you know so that his relatives can cheat on their property taxes?" Thus, the reporter gives the source a way to vent his anger and help the reporter at the same time. If the source is afraid that by copying only his own assessment work sheets the boss will know who to blame, the reporter can suggest he copy the work sheets of the other assistant assessors as well, thus involving them and protecting all. If the reporter has a personality and a reputation that are sufficiently forceful and convincing, it may be possible to persuade even the most timid bureaucrat that he need not worry because publication of the story will put the boss in the spotlight and preclude any revenge or harassment.

Once information from a source has been solicited and evaluated, the reporter must decide if that potential story is worth the time it will take to document and write. Perhaps a reporter is informed that a certain contractor, now dead, bribed a certain city official, also now dead, in Madrid, in cash, ten years ago. The only witness was a slow-witted, near-sighted towel attendant in a Spanish bordello whose mother is head of the secret police. Chances are the reporter will never prove that story. Of course, if the bribe was substantial, if by giving it the contractor illicitly secured the contract to pave every park in the city, and if, since the paving, skinned knees have become the number one crippler of local schoolchildren, the reporter may wish to start hunting up the official's heirs, friends, enemies, and tour guides in an attempt to verify the story. But in the time it is likely to take, the reporter may be able to discover, research, and write two other stories of greater importance.

In deciding if a story is worth the time, a reporter should talk to other reporters. Maybe they have already heard, researched, and debunked information similar to what the reporter has received. Maybe they know the source. Maybe they're already writing the story. Nothing is quite as discouraging as working for days on a top-notch investigative piece only to discover that another reporter is typing out a final draft while you're still looking for the phone booth your source called from.

Experienced investigators know that they'll have to produce stories if they're to continue to attract sources. They try to avoid disappointing sources by not using their information. If a reporter's publisher routinely kills investigative stories for reasons unrelated to good journalism, the reporter should either quit investigating or quit the paper, because the flow of tips will soon dry up. Reporters need not worry, however, about disappointing those sources who inadvertently provide them with what we choose to call "overheard tips." Reporters are often alerted to potential investigative stories by public officials and ordinary citizens who inadvertently tip off a reporter to the need for an investigation in a specific area while they publicly discuss another, perhaps less newsworthy, issue. Alertness is essential in recognizing the importance of such offhand assistance.

For example, a reporter covering the deliberations of the Detroit Common Council in 1971 was startled to hear the councilmen talking about the complaints of their constituents that relatively new cars, legally parked, were being towed away by a firm under contract to the police department's abandoned auto section. By talking to the irate citizens and by digging in public records, the reporter was able to determine that the police inspector in charge of abandoned cars and an associate of organized crime bosses had been owners of the towing firm. The reporter discovered that numerous cars had been falsely designated as abandoned and then towed away, sold, or stripped for profit by the firm. The reporter also learned that the towing firm, managed by a former felon, had been illicitly granted a city license by police detectives who were later indicted in other bribery cases. The resulting stories caused the reorganization of the abandoned auto section of the police department and an end to city contracts for the towing firm involved. It also meant fewer official car thefts on the streets of Detroit. And it was all inspired by offhand chatter among councilmen about complaints from the folks back home.

5

An Introduction to Records

There are three kinds of records. There are those the law entitles the public to see, those the law prohibits the public from seeing, and those not mentioned by the law. Good investigators do not admit the existence of a category of records that they will never see. As far as they are concerned, the only important distinctions among the three kinds of records involve the methods best suited to getting them and the relative difficulty in doing so. Income tax records, for example, are very hard to get. Property tax records, on the other hand, are easily obtained. For some reason a person's income tax is confidential, but his property taxes are everybody's business.

With a few exceptions, records-keeping is fairly consistent from state to state and from city to city. Which kinds of records are public and which are not, however, varies widely. The recent push for political ethics, disclosure, and campaign reform legislation means that the amount of information available to reporters is likely to increase substantially within the next few years. Whenever any ethics bill is signed into law, reporters in that state should study it carefully to keep abreast of which records are available.

Unfortunately, most public information acts are vaguely worded and too many bureaucrats are quick to exempt the records in their custody from the law. Others impose such restrictions on the use of the records by reporters as to make them virtually unusable. For some time the Chicago police permitted reporters to view arrest reports but not to photocopy them or even take notes from them. Some agencies charge as much as $2.50 for the first page and $1.25 per page thereafter for photocopies. Other agencies insist that reporters fill out a form for each record they wish to see. In many cases, a copy of the form is then sent to any politicians whose records are viewed, to alert them to a possible investigation.

Beyond these petty hindrances, however, reporters are sometimes told that the records are not for public view even if the law clearly says otherwise. The records clerk can simply say, "Get me a court order, Mac. I'm not taking your word for what the law says." For these reasons, the distinction between public and non-public records is often of little practical use. The truth is that even within the same government office, the accessibility of the records often depends on which clerk is approached first, how he or she is handled by the reporter, and whether the clerk (or his boss) is mad at the newspaper that day.

Of course, a newspaper can force the release of improperly held documents if it is willing to go to court. In some jurisdictions, a lawsuit or two may greatly enhance the situation by softening up bureaucratic resistance. It is certainly better to litigate the matter than to take "no" for an answer. Once a city's police department has lost a suit seeking access to crime statistics reports, for example, it is unlikely that the fire department would bother to prevent reporters from reading fire or arson reports. But filing suit is, obviously, an impractical solution to the everyday problem of gaining access to records. In addition to the enormous cost and time involved, a lawsuit can damage the chances of an entire investigation by prematurely alerting those under scrutiny. If a reporter needs a court order, however, to get certain records and wants to avoid tipping off those under investigation, the wisest course is to sue for a similar but different set of records. For example, if the reporter is looking for a record of all the narcotics arrests by a certain policeman, the newspaper or broadcast station could sue for access to records of all the gambling arrests of another policeman.

Beyond avoiding court fights, there are a number of other very good reasons reporters do everything they can to get the records clerks on their side. They can show reporters the short cuts. They can also help with the digging and once they have joined in, are not likely to alert the people being investigated. Furthermore, they are in an excellent position to provide needed information in the future. Presidents, governors, mayors, and department heads come and go with the political tides. But bureaucrats, now mostly under civil service and union protection, remain. When a newspaper's reporters are good to them, they come to view that newspaper as a shield to protect them from marauding politicians and as an outlet for their own grievances. As such, they can be invaluable to investigators. Besides, working among friends is easier on one's nerves. After publishing a few investigations, a reporter usually has an ample supply of enemies.

Gaining access to public records is only part of the battle. Knowing what kinds of information are kept on record is even more important. Too often, reporters presume that because they have not previously heard of a certain type of record, it does not exist. Fortunately, ours is a society of paper shufflers: there is hardly a deal made, an action taken, or an official statement uttered that is not committed to paper and filed somewhere. Who knows how many Pulitzer Prize stories are scattered in file cabinets all over the country?

Discovering what kinds of information are recorded and where they are kept is not as difficult as it sounds. Just as society abounds with people who fill out and shuffle forms, it abounds with people whose job it is to know what records are kept and who has them. If the information a reporter seeks is on paper, somebody put it there and knows how to retrieve it. Knowing who these people are and talking to them is a substantial part of most investigations. People who regularly deal with records of interest to reporters include:

Lawyers, particularly public service lawyers who tend to specialize in ecology, civil rights, housing, fraud, and corruption. Certain defense lawyers also know how to work with a variety of public records and some of them can be helpful on stories dealing with organized crime.

Court clerks, city clerks, county clerks, and legislative clerks are all very knowledgeable about what kinds of things are a matter of accessible record, where they are kept, and how to read them.

Federal prosecutors (assistant U.S. Attorneys), state attorney general's staffers, local prosecutors, and lawyers working for the vast number of federal and local regulatory agencies are also experts on records available in their own and related fields. Often, they can be persuaded to obtain information for reporters that reporters could not obtain for themselves.

Federal Bureau of Investigation agents (many of them accountants and lawyers), Internal Revenue Service agents, Federal Strike Force agents, U.S. Marshals, and local police investigators are sometimes helpful. They are more likely to disclose what is available and how to get it than to help reporters directly, but sometimes they will, if they are certain it will not compromise their job security.

Librarians at public, law, and school libraries can be very helpful in explaining indexes and directories, and many are adept at locating government studies quickly.

Politicians can be very helpful. In the course of mudslinging campaigns, they come across a lot of mud but also some useful and accurate information. They know where the bodies are buried and the records kept. Experienced investigators know it's often fruitful to mention the name of the subject of an investigation to some politicians of the opposing party.

Legislative aides, city council staff researchers, law clerks, and researchers for various city, state, and federal agencies spend lots of time doing the same sort of research required of investigative reporters. A reporter working on a story about why the river is yellow downstream of the local varnish factory should talk with staffers at the Environmental Protection Agency or the state department of conservation. They may know of reams of information about the varnish company already on the public record that could dovetail nicely with what the reporter can find elsewhere.

Lobbyists will often help with investigative research, as long as it's not aimed at them. They, too, are paid to know what's going on.

Researchers for labor unions, consumer groups, community organizations, and special interest groups also deal regularly with public, and sometimes not-so-public, documents. Because a lot of these people tend to move in and out of government work, they often have excellent contacts in many agencies. Persons active in the many Public Interest Research Groups (PIRGs) across the country can also be very helpful. Without the power of the press or the terror of subpoena behind them, they have to rely heavily on public records research and have become quite adept at it.

Academicians, professors, and graduate students often accumulate vast information, either from records or on their own. Sometimes they get information that reporters can't get because their sources aren't worried about it turning up in a newspaper. Every now and then some graduate seminar studying, say, community power, sets off to investigate why the construction of a local interstate highway resulted in the condemnation of only certain parcels of land, and comes up with some interesting findings.

Last, and probably most important, are other reporters and editors. Suppose a reporter has spent a week working on persistent reports that the local circuit court judge, who convicts blacks four times as frequently as whites, is a member of the National Socialist White People's party. The reporter spends days in the county clerk's office going through old records but can find nothing linking the judge to any right wing groups. He mentions it to the reporter at the next desk who suggests calling the Anti-Defamation League in Washington. He does, and they offer to send a pamphlet written by the judge entitled, *Never Hit a Nigger on the Head When You Can Kick Him in the Shin Instead.* The point is that no one reporter knows as much about where to find things as all other reporters put together. An experienced investigator who is stumped on a story starts talking to colleagues. If they can't help, the reporter might seek aid from absent predecessors by thinking through investigations from years past.

It is unlikely that talking to a dozen or more persons in the categories mentioned above would not turn up something useful or at least encouraging. There is not a public record available on the subject of property, for example, that an experienced real estate lawyer does not know about. Too many reporters begin investigations on topics new to them without spending enough time talking to experts in the field.

Even those documents the law forbids reporters or the public from seeing can be obtained. We doubt that there is a large newspaper in the country whose reporters at one time or another haven't written stories based on classified military documents, personnel records, inter-office memos, or federal income tax returns. The Pentagon Papers and records obtained in the burglary of the FBI office at Media, Pennsylvania, were passed between newspapers like so many press releases. Yet it is not necessary to work in Washington or for a major media outlet to obtain even the most esoteric documents. For example, the Lerner chain of community newspapers in Chicago obtained U.S. Army Intelligence bulletins which set out the policy on civilian spying and gave agents instructions on techniques.

A good investigator never forgoes an investigation because it can only be documented by inaccessible records. It is simply a matter of comparing the importance of the story to an estimate of the time required to obtain the records, and then deciding whether or not to go ahead. Without trying to get certain information, the reporter will never know what is available.

One reporter, desperate for the names and addresses of recent immigrants to Chicago, went to a regional office of the U.S. Immigration and Naturalization Service. He was told that the records were confidential, by law. Before giving up, the reporter gave a half dozen immigration officials a low-key pep talk on how long he had worked on the story, how much it meant, and how the lists could help clear up a major scandal. For all he knew, either the director or one of the department heads sitting in on the meeting was a part of the scandal. But, he continued, if the list came to him in the proverbial plain brown wrapper he would obviously have no idea who sent it. The director leaned back in his chair, laughed, looked out the window and said, "Listen, son, I'm afraid you've been watching too much television. We don't break the law here; we don't even bend it in this office." A few days later the list arrived at the reporter's newspaper, in a plain pink envelope, not a brown one.

There are more public records available in various government offices and private files than most journalists realize. Many reporters tend to ignore these files because mucking through them can be tedious and because they mistakenly believe that stories flowing from file cabinets are duller than stories flowing from people. On all but the most complicated stories, however, file cabinet research seldom lasts more than a few days. And it's only tedious when a reporter is working a dry hole; relevant documents are rarely dull. Even more important, documents are used mainly to prepare for interviews. If the records prove an iron-clad case, a reporter must still interview the people involved to get their reactions, retractions, and explanations. Properly written building code stories, for example, are not about building codes or even buildings, but about the people who own them, the people who must live in them, and the officials who find it convenient or profitable to look the other way.

6
Public and Private Records

People are born, go to school, get married, get divorced, receive salaries, give to charity, buy and abandon automobiles, travel, buy goods on the installment plan, change their names, open businesses, join professions and armies and governments and churches, borrow from museums, acquire guns, buy stocks, and die. It is a rare person who goes through life without signing papers and creating documents that an investigative reporter might look up in some office someday. The following paragraphs contain capsule descriptions of documents most people produce, where they can be found, and what an experienced investigator can do with them.

Airline manifests: Although they often deny it, airlines do keep records of the passengers on most flights. A public relations person is more likely than a counter clerk to show such a manifest to a reporter. The clerk will probably suspect the reporter is another employee of the company and is checking up on him. The public relations person may be an ex-reporter and may understand how crucial it sometimes is to be able to write that two particular persons were on the same flight to, say, Jamaica. Reporters sometimes ask others—a government agent with subpoena power, for example—to obtain manifests for them. If a reporter's ethical standards are low enough, it's often possible to find out where the subject of an investigation is going by calling the airline's reservation office, posing as the subject, and asking for reconfirmation of the subject's reservations.

Audits and consultants' reports: Every now and then some public agency decides to hire an outside consultant to check its efficiency. If the consultant reports back that the agency has been doing a good job, a press release is issued. If the consultant says the agency was wasteful, inefficient, stupid, lax, and criminally negligent, nothing is said.

The Wayne County Road Commission hired a consultant to study its operations in the early 1970s and when the consultant came back with a report saying that area roads were getting four to eight times as much salt as snow and ice conditions warranted, the board quietly accepted the report. Had the beat reporter covering the meeting not burned himself with a stray cigar ash and jerked awake at the moment the report was accepted, no one except the board members would have known of its existence.

When the reporter asked for the consultant's report, the board secretary said it was not a public document because it had not been formally accepted. The reporter argued that it was a study of a public agency, paid for by public money, and was discussed at a public meeting. After much arm waving and yelling the reporter got the document. It wasn't a great story, or even an investigative story, but it illustrates two principles. First, that covering a beat and waking up at the right moment often leads to good discoveries. Secondly, if all else fails, threaten to go berserk.

Birth records: For most persons, birth records are usually on file in a public office: the health department, or the county clerk's office with jurisdiction over the area in which the person was born. One problem with birth certificates is that the reporter usually has to know where a person was born before he can check the birth certificate. Since many people wish to obtain copies of their own birth certificates for such purposes as school registration, most jurisdictions have made the retrieval of the certificates relatively easy. If a reporter is looking for someone else's birth certificate, however, it may be more difficult since some bureaucrats consider birth information private. But a friendly smile or the right contacts can do wonders.

Birth certificates come in handy when a reporter is following the nepotism trail and wishes to find out if a certain official has in-laws on the payroll. By obtaining the official's birth certificate, the reporter may find the official's mother's maiden name on it, and then be able to search for public payrollers with the same last name. Some jurisdictions, however, do not include parents' names on birth records issued to second parties.

Business records: If Joe Smith wants to open Smith's Candy Store, he has several choices available to him. All the routes, however, require filing signed forms with public officials. In most states, Smith can go into business under what is called an assumed name. That is, he assumes the name of "Smith's Candy Store" for business purposes. In some jurisdictions, assuming a name for business purposes is called "doing business as" and the forms involved are called "dba" forms.

To assume a business name, Smith must get the approval of the county clerk in the county in which his store will be located. The clerk will check the files to see that no one else is operating a business under that name. If the check shows the name is free, Smith will pay a small fee and file for the name as his own. His application, as approved by the clerk, will be kept on file so that others—including reporters—will be able to see who operates Smith's Candy Store. If Smith wants to run the store under a partnership agreement with someone else, he will file a copartnership agreement with the county clerk. That form will contain information about both Smith and his partner and will be signed by both.

Smith could also run the store as a corporation, in which case he would go through the process of incorporation and then file papers with a state office, usually the secretary of state. In many states incorporation would require Smith to reveal the names and addresses of all the incorporators and directors of the firm, the amount and type of stock issued by the firm, the number of shares held by each incorporator, a description of the work the firm intends to engage in, and the name and business address of its local representative. Although salary figures for officers and directors are not found in incorporation papers, that information is often found in proxy solicitations sent to stockholders, since adjustments of these figures must be approved at stockholders' meetings. Non-profit corporations are also required to file similar reports.

Both profit and non-profit corporations in most states are also required to file annual statements. In some states, these annual reports are even more detailed than articles of incorporation. Most of the information originally submitted is repeated and updated, and a complete corporate balance sheet is filed, detailing corporate assets and liabilities. Parent and subsidiary corporations often must also be listed, along with the name and address of the person or firm which helped the corporation prepare its annual report.

The information provided on such forms varies greatly, however, from state to state. In some states, in fact, annual reports are neither required nor filed, and in others, they are called franchise reports and may be filed with the state's franchise tax agency. (In legal jargon, a franchise is a government-granted right to do business, and certain business taxes are known as franchise taxes.) In some of the states in which annual reports are filed as franchise tax reports, the papers are not available for public inspection, allegedly because they contain tax information.

Since attorneys must know who runs what in order to know who to sue, access to and copying of business records has been routinized in most states where the information is available at all. In some states, all the forms are on file with each county clerk. In others, the files have been centralized at the state capital and are available by mail or phone, usually for a small fee.

The only problem is that in most states business forms are not cross-indexed by the name or names of the people involved. In other words, a reporter can't find out what firms someone is connected with simply by looking up that person's name. Another problem is that out-of-state companies do not always register in all the states where they do business, so a reporter often must write or call another state's capital to obtain the records. (When in doubt, start with Delaware, since it is the most popular filing state among multi-state corporations.) What this country needs is a cross-referenced, national corporate index, which would allow an investigator to look up information about a firm, no matter where it did business, as well as look up individuals and discover what companies they were associated with, wherever those firms happened to be located.

Even a reporter not engaged in a particular investigation involving business records finds it wise to make a friend or two in the office where such forms are filed. Occasionally someone will take out an assumed business name that trades on the name of a public agency or better-known corporation. Perhaps a high pressure book-selling firm will register the name Official New York School Books, Inc. in hopes that its salesmen can confuse people in door-to-door sales pitches.

Cab company records: In most cities, cab drivers are required to note the pick-up times and destinations of each fare they take.

This makes cabbies relatively reliable sources if they can remember which face went with which trip on their manifest.

Campaign contribution and expenditure records: Campaign finance records are filed by law with election officials or county clerks in most jurisdictions. In some jurisdictions, statements must be filed during the campaign; in others, by a certain date after the campaign. On most forms, the candidate must list expenses and specify how much each person contributed in the primary, the general election, or both. Reporters often find it fruitful to compare lists of campaign contributors against lists of those awarded government contracts and political appointments. (Information on firms receiving contracts is usually available from the purchasing unit of the jurisdiction involved.) Since the occupations or businesses of campaign contributors are often not listed on the financial records, reporters are often reduced to calling the contributor's home during business hours and obtaining his office telephone number from his wife or children. If no one at the business will say what business it is, the number can be looked up in the telephone company directory which lists telephone numbers in numerical order followed by the address, firm, or person to which it belongs. (See *Criss-cross phone directories,* below.)

Unfortunately, many candidates raise a lot of campaign money at fund-raising dinners or parties at which contributions take the form of ticket purchases. Most campaign reporting laws do not require that ticket purchasers be listed. All that may appear in the records is "fund-raising party, $20,000." A savvy reporter will attend campaign fund-raising parties if possible, or at least interview the persons who attended or gave them. It is unlikely any big shots would have bothered to attend if they had not given money or bought some tickets. It will be very difficult for everybody who attended to forget who else was there.

Charity records: Many charities and non-profit organizations are frauds of one form or another, and even some fairly legitimate charities make questionable decisions about raising and spending the public's money. Fortunately, investigations of charities are fairly easy because their books must be filed annually with state agencies and are open to public inspection. Furthermore, in most charities there are likely to be a number of people who are in it solely for the public service involved and whose cooperation is not

difficult to obtain. The main difficulty with investigations of charities, non-profit organizations, and other good works occurs when
it comes time to publish the story. Even the most corrupt charities
can easily drape themselves in the flag, motherhood, and apple pie.
Most have taken great pains to cultivate widespread public approval of their activities.

Charity fraud usually consists of one or more of three standard
elements: some of the money raised is not spent for the purposes
listed; the funds are raised through deception or coercion; or some
of the money collected is not reported. Shady charities often overlook laws requiring them to file their books with the appropriate
state agency. A reporter can sometimes pressure that agency to
requisition those forms if the charity has not filed them. The
income tax returns of tax-exempt foundations are also available
for public inspection. Blue Cross and Blue Shield organizations in
various states are also required to file voluminous information
annually with the appropriate state agencies in the respective
states.

Legitimate, honest charities and non-profit corporations rarely
have qualms about showing reporters their books or answering
questions beyond the nervousness that normally greets journalists'
hard questions. Even some of the crooked outfits will make a
display of happily showing their books on the theory that the
average reporter couldn't understand them anyway or because
they are inaccurate. Don't let all the numbers scare you. Looking
at a set of books is not difficult once you understand the basics of
accounting. A quick aid is a booklet published by Merrill Lynch,
Pierce, Fenner and Smith, Inc.—*How to Read a Financial Report*
—available without charge at their brokerage offices.

In dealing with a charity, a reporter needs to find out how much
money the charity collected over a set time period, how much was
spent raising the money, and how much went to the charity's
cause. Then he or she must do whatever spot checking is possible
to see if the figures are accurate. The reporter should obtain the
names and addresses of some of the larger donors and contact
them to see if their personal records correspond to the entries in
the charity's books. The same should be done with some of the
named recipients. It is important that the reporter choose the
names; the charity's officers may select only a sample they know
is bona fide. The reporter is not checking to see if the books
balance—that the credits equal the debits. Books always balance.

He or she is checking to see that the reported income and outgo are accurate and will also be looking at such things as officers' salaries and expense accounts.

Among the most common charity frauds are the myriad police and firemen's benefit funds. Generally, they claim that the money raised goes to widows, orphans, retired firemen or policemen, and other worthy groups. They sell meaningless advertisements in magazines that either don't exist or are not well distributed. They also sell window decals to shopkeepers for anywhere between $15 and $100 apiece. The purpose of the decals is to ward off arsonists, robbers, and burglars, encourage the fire department or cop on the beat to watch the store, and, not incidentally, ward off rival police charities. As such, these so-called police or firemen's charities are but thinly disguised protection rackets. They may advertise that they give $1,500 to the widow of each policeman or fireman killed in the line of duty. Typically there are six such widows a year but the charity raises hundreds of thousands, if not millions, of dollars.

Many charities keep up to 80 or 90 percent of what they collect for administrative overhead. We know of one charity designed to promote the culture of a certain ethnic group that kept 100 percent of what it raised in Chicago over a five-year period. Stories about such charities are made even more interesting when the reporter takes the trouble to ask the responsible authorities why they have permitted the abuses to continue unchecked. The reporter may find the authorities take a harder line on consumer and ecology organizations than on more "patriotic" charities. It is wise to remember that investigating charities may hit close to home. Many newspapers support local United Fund or Red Feather drives and many publishers have pet charities.

Chattel mortgage records: These forms are filed for the benefit of private businesses—collection and lending agencies. If such records are kept in a reporter's jurisdiction he need only know the name and address of the person being investigated and he can request copies of a form the person filled out and signed each time he or she purchased something wholly or partially on credit. The forms are useful in obtaining a copy of someone's signature or in comparing a person's assets to his income. For example, if the person lives in a $150,000 house, paid $100,000 cash, financed the other $50,000, and is only a deputy assessor, he may be on the take. If he lives in a $35,000 house, put $5,000 down, and financed the other $30,000, he may be honest after all. Or, suppose a reporter investigating the city treasurer discovers that the official was granted a 7 percent mortgage at a time of 8½ percent mortgage interest rates. If the city deposit records indicate the treasurer deposited a lot of city money in that same bank, at the same time, at a low interest rate, the reporter may have uncovered a very clever and sophisticated bribe.

Interest-free deposits are a popular medium of exchange. In 1972, Illinois Blue Cross-Blue Shield was found to be putting members' money in interest-free accounts in the bank of one of its board members. No interest had been paid on the deposited funds since 1943. When the board heard that the *Chicago Journalism Review* was about to expose this practice, the first interest payment was made on the millions of dollars on deposit.

City directories: Not to be confused with telephone directories, these handy books list city residents alphabetically as well as by street address and by telephone number, and are published for most cities. The directory gives the spouse's first name, the employer's name and business address (or a description of the kind of work an individual does), and notes if someone is a member of the armed forces. Most large newspapers buy the latest editions of city directories, and they are used constantly.

City licenses: In many cities, people who engage in a variety of occupations—fruit peddlers, junk yard owners, sidewalk florists, etc.—must pay a city tax and carry a city license. They are usually required to file detailed applications for these licenses and the applications are available, on request, to the public. The range of occupations covered by license bureaus is vast. In New York City, for example, a person must have a license to hold a block party, be an able seaman, embalm, exterminate, grade hay and straw, smoke on piers, establish a seaplane base, store rubber cement, make sausages, transplant hard shell clams, and open a deli. Each license application contains personal and occupational information which could be useful to an investigator.

Congressional records: Congress investigates more subjects than newspapers have the time or space to cover. A call to a local congressman or the Library of Congress is the fastest way to obtain a copy of a congressional hearing report. Going through a local congressman is also the quickest way to obtain various studies produced by the executive branch. For both types of reports it is wise to get the names of staffers who did the leg work on the reports, since the final document is often a watered-down abbreviation of the original investigation. The staffer who spent a year investigating the topic is likely to have some strong feelings about the material that was left out and be quite willing to pass it on.

Congressional hearing records are used by many newspapers and broadcast stations when they want to call someone a Mafioso and don't want to be sued for libel. The paper or station merely reports that the person was identified as a Mafioso in a hearing held by one of the House or Senate committees that looked into organized crime. The problem with this practice is that not everyone so identified was proven to be actively involved in organized crime, and it is also possible that not everyone who, ten years ago, was in the Mafia or associated with Mafiosi, still is.

Criss-cross phone directories: Primarily for the benefit of salesmen, criss-cross phone directories have been printed for most major population areas. In these directories, persons are listed, not by the alphabetical order of their names, but by the alphabetical and numerical order of their street addresses. This enables salesmen to plot out their door-to-door routes, knowing in advance the name of the person in each house. With this kind of directory, a reporter can easily obtain the names and phone numbers of a person's neighbors and interview them over the telephone. A reporter can also survey a neighborhood and see who the subject of an investigation lives near. There are also directories published by the telephone company which list an area's phone numbers in numerical order, each number followed by the name and address of the person or firm to which it belongs.

Death records: Death certificates, especially in interesting cases involving foul play, can be obtained from the county medical examiner in the jurisdiction in which the death occurred. The primary value of death certificates, of course, is that they indicate the time, place, and cause of death. Obtaining a death certificate is easier when the deceased left a will and real estate is involved, because copies are often filed in the grantor-grantee index (see chapter 7, Property tax records) along with the deeds and mortgages.

Expense account vouchers: A lot of people serving in paid and unpaid public positions, such as on school boards or park commissions, come to feel quite strongly that the public owes them something more than gratitude or their salary for their efforts. So before building the new high school, they find it necessary to inspect Hollywood High School—in January. They take their husbands or wives along, they fly first class, and they put the whole bill on their expense account. Boards and commissions also tend to hold meetings in good restaurants and let the taxpayer pick up the tab.

Financial information: If a newspaper or broadcast station is willing to spend the money, the reporter can request a Dun and Bradstreet report—a rather complete, commercially prepared financial and credit report on a firm through the news organization's business department. A journalist can also gather financial net worth information by checking the local assessor's office for the worth of the house owned by the subject of the investigation, and by snooping around and finding out how many cars the subject has, what kind of clothes he wears, and what he does on his nights on the town. The reporter can also find out if the subject has a boat or an airplane because both must be licensed in most states.

Be careful about drawing hasty conclusions from net worth studies, however. Simply showing that a person is wealthy beyond his public salary does not show that the extra money was made illegally or immorally. We know of a Cook County sheriff's policeman who legally inherited a multi-million-dollar fortune. When he drove a Corvette to the police station nobody said anything. But a few years later when he traded it for a Jaguar E-Type, he was told it would have to go because it looked too much like he was on the take. So he bought a ratty Dodge station wagon.

Government directories: The *U.S. Government Manual,* issued annually, lists all federal agencies, officials, and branches. Most states issue similar manuals, some of which include biographies of officials and legislators.

Gun registration: In one sense, at least, right-wing organizations opposed to gun control are right. Requiring people to register their guns does tell the government where those guns are located and thus allows greater government surveillance of the life of its citizens. But these laws also allow investigative reporters to find out which public figures own guns—since gun registration records are usually available for the asking—or which of those people who say their guns are registered have actually purchased permits.

Income tax records: Getting somebody else's tax records from the Internal Revenue Service is considerably harder than getting one's own, but it can be done. The *Providence* (R.I.) *Journal* published information from President Nixon's tax returns in 1973. Obviously, there are people who work for the IRS who are willing to supply tax returns, or information from them, under certain circumstances. The problem lies in finding those people. A number of IRS agents in the Chicago Strike Force are reliably reported to have threatened to arrange for the publication of former U.S. Attorney General John Mitchell's tax records unless he stopped obstructing their investigation of former Federal Court of Appeals Judge Otto Kerner. The same sources said the threat worked.

Even the IRS agents who will not show a reporter a certain person's tax returns can be helpful in other ways. Many of them will gladly tell a reporter which are the more corrupt government agencies in the jurisdiction and provide hints on where corruption can be found. Tax forms are most easily available from the taxpayer himself, but if this approach is barred by investigative circumstances, other sources exist. One, as mentioned above, is the IRS. The others are people the taxpayer may have provided with copies of the forms, such as an accountant, or those persons or organizations the IRS may have provided with copies. Even post-Watergate, these could include:

The President and some members of the White House staff.

Other governmental agencies. These agencies claim they use the returns primarily for statistical purposes.

Police and other law enforcement agencies. These agencies claim they use the returns for tax prosecution as well as for the prosecution of other crimes.

Congressional committees. Members of these committees have

a ready-made excuse for demanding tax returns. They can say they study them to more intelligently prepare future tax legislation.

State governments, which, as a result of some controversial laws, receive the federal returns so they can determine if their residents are paying the proper state taxes. Critics have argued that the federal government should give the states only that information relevant to this task rather than forwarding entire returns to state bureaucrats.

Some reporters demand income tax information from the taxpayers themselves as a cudgel to force other admissions or viceversa. For example, a reporter confronting someone with an allegation of bribe taking should ask to see his income tax forms to prove no bribe was taken. If the person refuses, the reporter should say that a refusal suggests guilt. Then the reporter should pull the same stunt with the alleged briber, but accuse that person of taking rather than giving the bribe. The law requires that illegal income be reported on tax forms, so the alleged briber may turn them over to prove no bribe was received. Then the reporter should check to see if the alleged bribe was reported as a business expense.

In an age of steadily expanding international business transactions, tax forms are interesting for another reason. Americans must declare their holdings in foreign firms and pay a 15 percent interest equalization tax on those firms at the time they acquire them.

Legal newspapers: In most major cities, a commercially published legal newspaper lists the day's name changes, business bankruptcies, suits filed, assumed names requested, births, marriages, divorces, etc. A quick glance at this publication every day often pays off.

Legal notices: Most public agencies are required by law to publish legal notices in newspapers of general circulation in their area when they, for example, solicit bids, issue bonds, begin public projects, hold hearings, etc. Copies of legal notices are generally on file with the newspaper that published them and with the government agency that arranged for publication. Official collusion and conflict-of-interest stories can be buttressed by the omission of legal notices with the intent of aiding particular individuals involved in the collusion. In some jurisdictions, it might be wise to find out how the papers in which the notices appear are chosen. Find a small newspaper publisher who's benefitting from $400,000 a year in legal advertising and you'll probably find a newspaper not all that critical of the government or government agency tossing that business its way.

Marriage records: Applications for marriage licenses are also usually on public file in the jurisdiction where the marriage took place. As with birth certificates, the reporter must know the approximate date of the marriage and the jurisdiction in which it occurred in order to see the marriage license application. As with birth certificates, a suspicion of nepotism is the major reason for going after a marriage license application. If a reporter suspects an official of having in-laws on the payroll, and if the official has no children, there won't be a birth certificate on which to find his wife's maiden name. But, her maiden name will appear on the couple's marriage license application. The reporter will also have to look up the official's sisters' marriage certificates for complete in-law information.

Military records: Records of active service personnel are available from the Pentagon. Former service personnel can be located through local Veterans Administration offices or through the U.S. Army Personnel Center in St. Louis. The *Army* and *Air Force Registers,* and the *Register of Commissioned and Warrant Officers of the Navy and Marine Corps,* list each commissioned officer by name, serial number, date and place of birth, and induction. These directories also list retired officers and are helpful when a reporter wants to locate people who are no longer in the service.

Classified military records are sometimes available from friends in the Pentagon. In the early seventies, a number of former Army Intelligence officers, disgruntled by the Pentagon's snooping on civilians, were able to get friends still on the inside to give them classified documents which they passed on to Senator Sam Ervin and some selected reporters. Classified records are also available from friendly congressmen or from the employees of congressional committees. Classified records are also occasionally available from unexpected sources. One Chicago reporter was able to verify earlier reports that the Nike missile bases in the city's lakefront parks were, or had been, armed with nuclear warheads when he was unexpectedly provided with evidence by a band of wandering Indians. The Indians, whose leaders had been trained by urban organizer Saul Alinksy, had occupied an abandoned missile emplacement to protest a housing shortage. In one of the abandoned underground silos, they found a technical manual on how to install and activate the missiles' nuclear warheads.

Museum records: Museums are public or quasi-public institutions in many cities, and itemizations of their collections are usually available through the museum's registrar. This information might be considered of interest only to art critics except that in some jurisdictions, museum officials—seeking bigger budgets—lend out works of art to public officials with pull. A Detroit reporter discovered that a museum-owned Diego Rivera watercolor, susceptible to damage from overexposure to light, had been hanging for eleven years on the sunlit wall of the office of an assistant county clerk whose boss had once been influential; that a former Detroit mayor, on leaving public life, had taken two of the museum's paintings with him to his new out-of-town residence; and that the city's current mayor, Coleman Young, had stacked a valuable statue lent by the museum among a pile of dirty coffee percolators and cups in the process of redecorating his office. The story also pointed out that although the ostensible purpose of the lending program was to increase public access to art, many of the works were in the private, inner chambers of judges where only a few attorneys got to see them. As a result of the story, many of the art works were recalled to the museum.

The minutes of a museum's board of directors are also interesting—in part because they list contributions to the institution, which are often strategically timed to serve as tax write-offs for well-known, wealthy contributors.

Newspaper libraries: Obviously, this is the most convenient place to begin an investigation. Reporters have discovered that it's wise to check the paper's library for the names of everyone even peripherally involved in an investigative story. Clippings or photographs, innocuous in themselves, may link the subject of the story with people who were, for example, convicted of fraud after the picture was taken, and may add whole new dimensions to an investigation.

Payroll records: Personnel departments at most firms will confirm or deny—often over the telephone—that a certain person is on the payroll, unless, of course, that person is secretly employed as part of a corrupt arrangement. Civil service departments in many cities will provide similar information. Reporters sometimes encounter resistance when they try to photocopy payroll records, but remember that a public payroll is a public record, exact salaries included. (The only exceptions might be the payrolls of agencies like the CIA.)

Once a reporter has obtained a copy of a public payroll, it can be used to begin a number of investigations. City payrolls are nice to have around to compare with police arrest blotters, business fraud indictments, and lists of people seen hanging around with known criminals. (The ordinary investigative story about almost anything is much improved if it can be discovered that its subject is also, say, a city attorney.) Payrolls can also be checked against lists of campaign workers. Or, a reporter might check the various departments to see if there are as many people working there as are listed on the payroll. If eighty are listed, and the reporter can only find seventy-seven, it may be that the department is paying a few party stalwarts who never work, or it may be that somebody is signing phony names to phony checks and cashing them. The next step is to look at the cancelled payroll checks and see who's cashing them.

In 1973, *Detroit Free Press* reporter Jim Neubacher heard rumors that a woman named Glenda McGuire had a job with Michigan Governor William Milliken's administration but that no one ever saw her or knew what she did. Checking the payroll was easy. Roger Lane, a *Free Press* Lansing staffer, called the state civil service and asked where Miss McGuire fit in. He was told that she had been hired by the governor's office as part of the governor's unclassified personal staff. Lane then called the governor's office and was told that Miss McGuire served as one of the governor's eight personal aides at a salary of more than $18,000 per year.

Neubacher's first task was to find out where, if anywhere, Miss McGuire worked. He went to the governor's Detroit office and asked to see her. He was told she worked in Lansing. In Lansing

he was told she worked in Detroit. Finally, a governor's aide told
Neubacher that Miss McGuire did interviews for a research report
which would give Milliken "insight on public attitudes," particularly among blacks. Neubacher was told that Miss McGuire
worked out of her Detroit home and had no office, desk, phone,
or state car. (Neubacher had seen no trace of Miss McGuire in
either the Lansing or Detroit office.)

Neubacher asked to see any preliminary reports or memos—or
any scrap of paper—pertaining to her project. No scrap of paper
could be found. But the aide to the governor said he talked with
Miss McGuire regularly. Neubacher asked who Miss McGuire
was interviewing, and the aide couldn't come up with a single
name. Neubacher asked the aide to ask Miss McGuire for a representative list of 15 or so names of persons she had interviewed.
Eventually, Neubacher was given the names of eleven alleged
interviewees, including Miss McGuire's sister's boyfriend, a
young man Miss McGuire grew up with, and the principal of the
school where her sister taught. Neubacher contacted them; none
of them remembered any interview, although six other persons on
the list did remember brief telephone conversations with a woman
from the governor's office. When Neubacher finally interviewed
Miss McGuire, she had a Lansing office, which appeared all of a
sudden because she said she had finished interviewing and was
ready to write her report.

In his April, 1973, *Free Press* story, Neubacher reported that
Miss McGuire was being paid more than $18,000 a year by the
taxpayers to do practically nothing, and that she was given the job
because her boyfriend, a Detroit Recorder's Court judge, had
helped Governor Milliken during the 1972 campaign. Neubacher
was able to substantiate the latter part of his story by linking Miss
McGuire to the judge through motel registrations and real estate
records (Miss McGuire had lived in a home owned by the judge),
and also by linking Miss McGuire's hiring to a closed-door meeting between a Milliken aide and the judge. As a result of the story,
Miss McGuire lost her job.

Private organization records: Among the private agencies with
extensive files are public service law firms, Ralph Nader-type
groups, ecology and consumer organizations, trade associations,
political parties, the League of Women Voters, and civic watchdog
organizations. Also, many community, ethnic, and even ecclesias-

tical organizations keep voluminous information on their enemies. Many such groups have full-time investigators. Most of these groups will routinely cooperate with a reporter who can convince them their enemies are the same. In doing a story about the glue magnate who bribed the zoning board, it would be just as foolish to overlook the ecology groups, glue workers' unions, and public interest law firms involved as it would be to ignore the city planning and zoning records.

Professional, business, and trade directories: The *Dictionary of the American Medical Association* supplies a state-by-state listing of medical schools, hospitals, and physicians, including the date of birth and the medical school attended by each doctor. The *Martindale-Hubbell Law Directory* lists lawyers by area and includes a biography of each, sometimes listing the law school each lawyer attended and major clients represented by individual law firms. This could lead to some important stories if a lawyer has taken stock or part-ownership in a firm in return for legal services —a common practice—and later accepts a judgeship or a regulative agency position without ridding himself of that stock. What if a case involving the firm comes before him or her? The directory also sometimes comments on the competency of the lawyers it lists. A copy of the original bar exam application of every laywer, complete with background information, is on file with the supreme court clerk in the state where the exam was administered. Notaries public must also file personal information with state officials, usually either the secretary of state or the governor. Many business and trade organizations also publish directories of their members.

Religious directories: Many religious organizations publish directories of their members.

School directories: Most schools will tell any caller, even over the telephone, whether a certain person was ever a student there, the dates of entrance and departure, and the degree awarded. Although a vast majority of America's schools are publicly supported or aided, school administrators seem to consider all other information on their students confidential. It's even difficult to find out who has applied for admission to a particular school, although politicians sitting on academic boards of directors have been known to help unqualified but intimate associates be admitted without public notice being taken. If a school refuses to reveal even the most basic information about its students, a quick look at the appropriate yearbook will close the information gap, and most schools keep their old yearbooks on file in their own libraries, which are often open to the public.

Securities and Exchange Commission records: The SEC has a long list of do's and don'ts for those who buy and sell stock, and reporters investigating stock fraud find that they must familiarize themselves with these rules. The SEC also regularly records a large number of stock transactions. It publishes a *Directory of Corporate Ownership* and a monthly summary of major stock transactions. By looking through current and back copies of the monthly summary, a reporter can often discover who controls many corporations and the names of the front men or nominees used by stock owners for stock purchase. If, for example, a reporter flipping through a monthly SEC summary finds that the mayor has purchased a large block of stock in Amalgamated Consolidated in the name of his lawyer, Harold DeComing II, it may be a good idea to see what local property is also listed in DeComing's name. Perhaps it's the land the mayor wants the new city hall built on.

State regulatory records: State regulatory boards keep up-to-date files on all of the members of the profession or trade they are charged with regulating. Most of these records are public; others may be pried from recalcitrant officials or from sources. In various states, realtors, physicians, attorneys, nurses, architects, funeral directors, hairdressers, barbers, TV technicians, and others are all regulated by state boards. If a person is not listed with the appropriate board, he or she is probably practicing illegally.

Telephone company records: Although most telephone companies will seldom give out unlisted telephone numbers or disclose the amount of someone's telephone bill, phone officials will sometimes tell reporters in what geographical area an unlisted number is or is not located. (Maps showing the location of all numbers beginning with the same three-digit sequence are printed in the front of most telephone directories.) Although they don't give them out to reporters, phone companies do keep records of telephone calls made; if they didn't, they couldn't bill their customers. Therefore, it is possible to obtain these records, or bills, from cooperative employees inside the company or through a government agency with subpoena power.

It is also possible to obtain these records by trickery. At least one reporter we know would stoop so low as to call the telephone company business office, and, posing as the person being investigated, claim that he didn't recall making certain long-distance calls that had been charged to him. He would then ask the phone company to check the numbers and dates of the calls and report back. (The same gambit is sometimes used by reporters who wish to check on the money a person has borrowed. They simply call the credit company to "reconfirm" the loan. A similar technique can be used to check on someone's airplane reservations; see *airline manifests,* above.) Obtaining such information from the phone company, however, works both ways. So, if an experienced investigator is intent on protecting a source's identity, he or she may call from a remote pay phone or from the paper's subscription department rather than from a home or desk phone.

Remember also that if nobody knew an unlisted phone number, nobody would ever call that person—and there would be little reason to have a telephone. The trick in getting an unlisted phone number is to find the person's friends and persuade one of them to provide the number. Some reporters will tell the friend, especially if it's the truth, that a possibly damaging story is about to be printed or broadcast and that the reporter needs to talk to the unlisted person immediately to find out if the story is true. At worst, the friend may call the unlisted person and relay the information.

Trade publications: Since the editors of these publications assume that their readership is restricted, the publications are often loaded with inside information. Duane Lindstrom, former research director for Citizens For a Better Environment in Chicago, unearthed a number of major land use scandals by regularly perusing local real estate trade publications. Every now and then a rather brazen developer would indicate that an upcoming project had investment advantages others lacked, such as exceptionally low, or non-existent, property taxes.

Vanity directories: Unplumbed depths of personal information on thousands of prominent and not-so-prominent people await the enterprising reporter who looks in the latest editions of any of the vanity directories, on file in most major libraries. They include the *Social Register, Burke's Peerage, Who's Who* in its various versions *(Who's Who in America, Who's Who in the West), American Men of Science, Contemporary Authors,* and others. The value of such directories, however, is limited in that usually only information furnished by the listed person is printed.

Vehicle records: There are two ways of obtaining vehicle records: either through a contact at the secretary of state's office or through a police agency such as the local police, state police, or county prosecutor's office. Many newspapers and television stations attempt to maintain a reliable contact with access to vehicle information for help tracing license plates and for verifying residency in election and residency rule investigations. Vehicle records are also necessary in tracing autos that are towed away as abandoned.

Some secretary of state's offices (and chattel mortgage offices in other jurisdictions) also record purchase agreements on new cars. That information can be useful in a number of ways. Perhaps those records will indicate that the city purchasing director got a price break on a personal car from the auto dealer who always seems to be the low bidder, by a small margin, on city contracts. A reporter can find out the dealer's true cost on a car with options by calling the relevant auto firm's public relations department.

Voting records: In most jurisdictions, when a person registers to vote, he must give his full name, his present and previous address, and his mother's maiden name. This information is stored on file cards with the jurisdiction's election officials. Whenever that person votes, an "x" is marked on the file card next to the date of the particular election. Reporters will find it easy to become friendly with the election officials who control these files by encouraging their newspaper or station to play up stories about voter registration deadlines and other matters important to the officials. Once on friendly terms, it is easy to persuade them to give a reporter access to the voter record file cards.

The information gleaned from these files is frequently of use in non-election-related investigations. However, election stories can result from a perusal of these file cards when, for example, a reporter knows someone's real address and discovers that he or she is claiming a false address for voting purposes—a crime in almost every jurisdiction. Reporters have taken the trouble to go over the voter registration records for one precinct, and then interviewed the people whose records indicate they voted in the previous election. If a significant number of voters say they didn't vote in that election, but were marked present and voting on their registration cards, somebody may have been voting for them. Voting in someone else's place is both a crime and a tip-off to a very good story.

Welfare records: In many jurisdictions, a reporter can find out informally from the local welfare office if a particular person has been on welfare and for how long, but other information—such as the levels of payments, the reason the person went on relief, etc. —must be pried out of a case worker willing to talk. If a reporter finds a talker, it is useful to remember that welfare records are also a good way to find out who's related to who, and often, where people previously lived, and where they were born—information a reporter needs to locate birth, marriage, or criminal records.

A surprising number of journalists are of the opinion that nothing genuinely derogatory can be found in records available to the public. But the fact of the matter is that most corrupt persons, like potential automobile accident victims, feel they are fairly safe in believing it won't happen to them—that with all the crooks in the world the press won't take the time to come after them. In most instances, they are right.

Federal Communications Commission records, for example, contain a case of a lawyer advising a corporate client that even though he had to file potentially damaging information, he should so overload the file with trivial information that reporters would be loath to sort through it all. A certain Chicago tax assessor believed that his assessing system—based on factors involving a building's original cost, age, occupancy rate, and relative profitability—was so complicated that no reporter would have the nerve to charge that it was being applied unfairly. His presumption proved accurate for thirty-six years: from 1934 until 1970, the story went unwritten.

Experienced reporters realize, however, that evidence of wrong-doing often is contained in public records simply because the persons involved have no alternative but to file it in public record offices. So, although public records research is often fruitless, on some occasions every record touched reveals something relevant to an investigation. Take as an example the Detroit reporter who, in 1971, was investigating allegations that the Detroit Police Department's auto recovery bureau, and a towing firm on contract to the bureau, were falsely designating relatively new cars as abandoned, then towing them off, and selling them for the towing firm's financial benefit. The reporter's first step was to look up the company in the assumed names office. The firm was incorporated, so the names and addresses of its officers and directors were on record, as well as the names of some of the stockholders in the firm. Earlier annual reports, filed in the same office, provided the names of earlier officers, directors, and stockholders.

The names on the forms didn't mean anything to the reporter, so he looked them up in his newspaper's library. The old clippings he found indicated that one of the firm's founders had been indicted by a federal grand jury for conspiring with an alleged Mafia leader in an illegal gambling operation. Another clip indicated that the alleged Mafia leader had been identified as such before a U.S. Senate committee. Another old clip indicated that the towing firm's president had been convicted years before of receiving stolen property, a felony.

Knowing that in Detroit towing firms are required to hold city licenses, the reporter looked up the firm's license application in the city license bureau. On the application filled out by the convicted felon, the president of the firm, the question, "Have you ever been convicted of a felony?" was left unanswered. But the form had been approved anyway, in writing, by two Detroit police detectives. At this point, the reporter should have been sufficiently suspicious of the policemen to check the names of the firm's officers against the police payroll, but he didn't think to do so.

After his check of the towing firm's incorporation papers, but before writing his story, the reporter went back to the assumed names office for a re-check. There, he discovered that the records he had previously examined were out on loan to two persons who had left their business cards where the records had been. Those cards identified the two as agents of the IRS and of the police department's own self-investigation unit. So, the reporter was able to write in his first story that the firm was alleged to have misdesignated cars as abandoned and towed them away for profit; that it was owned by a former felon who, in violation of city ordinances, had submitted an incomplete license application; that one of the founders of the firm had been indicted for conspiring with a man named as a Mafia leader at a U.S. Senate hearing; and that the towing firm was being investigated by the IRS and the police department.

After the story came out, the reporter, working on a follow-up, called all the current officers of the firm to get their reaction to the first story. One of them, apparently not the most crafty person in the world, blurted out over the telephone that he had been on the police department's auto recovery bureau (which designated cars as abandoned) when he bought part-interest in the towing firm, and that the firm had not been contracted by the police department to tow away cars until after he became one of its owners. He also said he saw nothing wrong with his course of conduct because the superintendent of police had known all about it all along. When questioned, the superintendent said he didn't remember anything about it, but the follow-up story made interesting reading nevertheless.

It made especially interesting reading because the reporter, acting on a tip, did what he should have done before writing his first story: he checked the names of the two detectives who approved the towing firm's license application in the files of his newspaper's library. There he discovered that one of the detectives, after approving the application, had been indicted for accepting a bribe in another auto case. This information was duly noted in the follow-up story. After a second follow-up, the auto recovery section of the police department was reorganized and the towing firm lost its city contract. (See appendix, "The Auto Towing Caper.")

The reporter's only regret about these stories was that they incorrectly identified the Detroit Police Department's self-investigation unit as the Special Investigation Bureau. The correct name for the unit at the time the stories were written was the Internal Affairs Bureau. The name of this unit may have been the only fact that the reporter didn't check several times, because he blithely believed himself familiar with the names of the various police units. In investigative stories, it's almost always the fact you think you know and don't bother to check which comes out wrong.

7
Zoning, Land Use, and Property Tax Records

Zoning

Zoning is a strange and wondrous thing. The value of land can be made to rise and fall like a roller coaster simply by changing the little numbers on a zoning map. Zoning was conceived earlier this century to prevent commercial structures from being built in residential neighborhoods. Some say it was popularly adopted to keep the poor and the black out of "good" neighborhoods. Houston, Texas, however, which has no zoning ordinances, looks just like any other American city. The rich live in one neighborhood, the poor in another. The drawing rooms of the mansion district have not been remodeled into taco stands.

One of the effects of zoning has been the creation of a class of wealthy zoning officials and land speculators. When the uses permitted on the land go up, so does its asking price and value—until, of course, the zoning is changed again. The possibilities for graft in zoning are one of the major marvels of modern malfeasance. According to Dan Paul, a Miami attorney who wrote the Dade County (Florida) Metropolitan Charter some 18 years ago, "Zoning is the single biggest corrupter of the nation's local governments."

Zoning is a very complex subject and its jargon consists of no household words. We suspect that for these reasons most reporters are leery of getting into it. With all the land use symbols involved, such as B3 and R2A, zoning stories are generally unread by anyone, except perhaps the family that finds itself living next door to a new cyanide plant.

But there are great and good stories in zoning, to be had almost for the asking. In some zoning scandals, reporters may find no money changing hands. Often, well-intentioned city fathers are bullied into bad zoning decisions by the relentless pressure to increase the city's tax base. Public officials are very susceptible to corporate threats to build in "friendlier climes" if they are not granted the zoning variance necessary to build their sulfur dioxide factory upwind of the tuberculosis sanitorium. Municipalities are played off this way, one against another, and wind up bargaining away either their tax base or their environment.

The term "zoning variance" should make the alert reporter take notice. What it means, generally, is that despite the advice of the professional planners who felt an area should be restricted in use or building size, the politicians in power decided to permit different, sometimes even incompatible, uses and structures. The questions to be asked are: Why was the area zoned one way in the first place, if variances were to be granted? How is it decided who gets the variances?

In a lot of zoning changes, it appears that lightning has struck. The numbers on the zoning map are changed and land that was worth a dime a square foot on Monday is worth $2 a square foot on Tuesday. Consider the case of the peon's assistant who spends his entire life plowing 80 acres with his fingernails and wakes up one morning to discover that encroaching suburbs have raised his property taxes to the point where he can no longer afford to farm. Two days later, someone offers him four times what he thinks the farm is worth and, happily, he sells the land. But the developer who bought it has the connections, energy, and nerve to get the little numbers on the maps changed, and in a short time the farm is rezoned from R1A (single family residence) to C5A (which permits limited nuclear wars.) It is then worth four times what the developer paid.

Reporters interested in zoning stories don't have to wait for the local "inside dopesters" to tip them off. They can just look at recent major zoning changes in their areas. If they go back any farther than recent zoning changes they will find themselves conducting their interviews in Miami, Palm Springs, and Rio De Janeiro. Wherever a large upgrading occurred, someone has made a fortune. To start a zoning investigation, the reporter first needs to find out who owned the land and benefited from the variance. (If the zoning variance has not yet been granted, the same information will be vital to the story.) Whose campaign did the owner support? The reporter also needs to find out who was on the various boards that recommended or approved the change, what they did for a living, what land they owned, who they bought it from, who their relatives are, and who their relatives worked for.

Next, the reporter should interview the people who were, or will be, adversely affected by the zoning change. The best approach is to simply knock on doors in the affected neighborhood, let people know about the investigation, and enlist their aid against a common enemy. It shouldn't be hard to get them to ask around and call if they hear anything. There is no such thing as an airtight conspiracy: someone has talked; tracks have been left. Secretaries not party to the action know about the deal and whatever secret alliances may be involved. So, probably, do various municipal employees, real estate brokers, tax assessors, or even the local bartender. Perhaps a hundred people are in a position to provide important information. Surely one of them will talk about some part of it. Then it is only a matter of using that information to deduce the broad outlines of the deal and bluff the various officials and developers into admitting the details.

In most communities, proposed zoning and city plan changes must be discussed at one or more hearings where the public is invited to voice support or raise objections. In such cases, an advance notice is usually published in a general circulation newspaper describing the proposed change. Sometimes, however, zoning officials neglect to run the notices. In at least one case in suburban Detroit, a legal notice said a small shopping center was proposed when, in fact, the zoning board had planned to approve, and did approve, a large shopping center. (See *legal notices,* chapter 6.)

Land Use

In some communities, the practice of planning future land use has as much (or even more) effect on corruption as zoning. As planning becomes more widespread, reporters will have to study proposed changes in land-use plans as well as in zoning. Planning is simply what is done prior to zoning. A plan amendment, or a new plan for a certain area, records the local public body's statement of intent for future zoning. By planning an area for high rise offices, officials are saying that when a developer actually comes along and requests that the zoning in an area be changed to permit high rise offices, the request is likely to be granted.

Recently, planning has come to wield the force of law because the courts are tending to hold city commissions or planning commissions to the plans they set out. If a developer buys land planned for high density residential use, yet is denied high density residential zoning when he is ready to begin development, he can sue for the requested zoning and, in some jurisdictions, win in nine cases out of ten.

That being the case, the replanning of land has a substantial impact on its value. Yet, we know of no state where an upgrade in the planning designation alone increases the taxes. This presents unscrupulous public officials the opportunity to increase the market value of their own land, or that of their associates, without increasing the taxes on that land. Consequently, while good planning is a definite aid to the orderly and aesthetic growth of an area, it presents great temptations. The power of planning encourages shady public officials to perform any one of a number of dishonest acts:

Public officials—including mayors, city councilmen, planning commissioners, planning staffers, assessors, and city attorneys—may participate in the rezoning or planning of their own land. They may openly announce they own the land, or they may own it (or shares in the companies that own it) secretly. Either way, their participation in the redesignation is a conflict of interest. They should not participate in any decisions affecting the value of or taxes levied on the land. This includes discussions of or votes on zoning, planning, sewer assessments, street lights, utilities, roads, zoning variances, or site plan approvals.

Public officials may accept campaign contributions, gifts, stock options, stock, or money from developers favored by their votes. It should make no difference to a reporter whether the vote comes before or after the money is paid.

Public officials may use their votes or influence to increase the value of land owned by their business partners, relatives, or friends. The scrupulously honest official will abstain from all such votes or discussions.

Public officials may rezone or replan land for developments in which they later come to hold a direct or lease-hold interest. For example, a developer who plans to lease back part of a shopping center to a local businessman, who is also a city commissioner, is in an excellent position to encourage favorable zoning by offering a more lucrative lease arrangement.

Public officials may benefit from inside knowledge. Most commonly, they buy land, or advise associates to buy land, in an area they expect to be upgraded by zoning or planning changes. Before the expected changes are publicly known, the land can be purchased for a fraction of its future value. Secondly, corrupt officials can purchase lands or buildings they know, or have good reason to believe, are about to be purchased by a public agency. This practice also produces healthy profits for the officials involved at public expense.

In 1974, the U.S. Attorney for the Northern District of Illinois indicted over a dozen suburban Chicago officials for these and similar practices. In Troy, Michigan, a suburb which enjoyed a land speculation boom for years after the 1967 Detroit riots, numerous city officials benefitted from the rapid increase in land values. One group of land investors included three city commissioners, the city attorney, two members of the city commercial and industrial development committee, a member of the property tax review board, a school official, and two local realtors. They did not register the deeds they accumulated, and they filed their realty copartnership agreement in a county where none of them lived and where none of the land was located.

All of the thirty-seven parcels of land the group purchased were either within or immediately adjacent to an area which went from single family residential use to a higher density, under a new city plan discussed and approved by the members of the group who were city commissioners. One elderly man who sold four acres of land to the group in 1968 told *Detroit Free Press* reporters he had first inquired at city hall to see if the land could be developed commercially. He was told it couldn't and sold the land a short time later. Soon after the sale, the city commission amended the master plan and the old man saw a "For Sale, Commercial" sign go up on his former property. What he didn't know when he sold the land was that many of the purchasers were city fathers, and that prior to the sale date they had already commissioned an outside consultant to replan that section of the city.

The existence of the land-buying partnership among the city officials was discovered, incidentally, only after the *Free Press* had written a story about how James Damman, one of the former Troy city commissioners who was running for lieutenant governor, had received huge campaign contributions from developers aided by his rezoning votes. A few days after the story was published in October, 1974, *Free Press* political writer Remer Tyson met Governor Milliken for breakfast and successfully pressured him into asking his running mate to make his tax returns public, as the governor and his opponent already had.

On Damman's tax returns were deductions for interest payments and property taxes on the land he and his partners owned. From there, it was only a matter of determining that the group's land was within the area upgraded by city plan changes, and then of comparing the dates of the various purchases with the dates the plan changes were initiated and approved. Once that was done, reporters interviewed former Troy city commissioners who were not partners in the land firm. They established that Damman had a good commission attendance record and had taken an active part in the various non-public "study sessions" at which the new land use plan was shaped. (See appendix, "Land-Use Planning.")

A cautionary note: When doing zoning and planning stories, reporters should take extreme care to read the fine print in the local zoning ordinance. In one township, R1 may permit up to fifteen housing units per acre and in another, the classification may make no mention of density at all. We are told that in some exclusive suburbs, a person must own an acre of land for each bedroom planned in a new home. Obviously, a reporter must be very certain of these nuances before accusing someone of engineering the grandmother of all boondoggles. Good sources for interpreting the detail of zoning machinations are law professors who teach zoning, urban planning firms, and the zoning staffs of nearby, honest cities.

Property Tax Records

The property tax section may be the most boring place in the hall of records, but consider for a moment some of the things a reporter can learn there:

Who pays the taxes on a certain parcel of land (and hence who owns it or at least knows who the real owner is);

The past and present zoning of the land;

Which $30,000-a-year public officials live in $150,000 homes;

Whether a person's tax-paying address is the same as his voting address;

Who someone bought a house from and, often, at what price;

Who the real estate broker and lawyers were and who holds the mortgage on the house;

Whether the local bowling alley is listed as a public school and is thus exempted from paying taxes;

The approximate value of urban renewal land before and after the bulldozers got to it;

If the county assessor is paying his or her own taxes;

If big campaign contributors are being fairly taxed.

As we said, property records and property tax records are easily inspected. Such offices are generally swarming with lawyers and real estate agents, and reporters often go unnoticed in the shuffle. The main difficulty lies in correctly converting street addresses or intersections into the appropriate parcel numbering system or legal descriptions, and vice versa.

Legal descriptions of land, always highly abbreviated, read something like this:

Lot 3 or parcel 12 of the NW Sec. of the SW quarter of
Eyesters Beaver Gardens, T2N, range 11E, Hapless Twp.

That's if the reporter is lucky. Some legal descriptions are a series of surveyor's notations that ramble on for hundreds of words and delve into arcs, tangents, secants, and all the horrible things the average reporter has forgotten since flunking high school trigonometry. He or she either has to call for help or buy a tract map and a degree wheel and carefully trace the lines described. Until a reporter gets good at this, it is wise to have one of the clerks demonstrate how it's done, or even to visit the house numbering offices established in many jurisdictions which convert legal descriptions into street addresses for a small fee.

Assessors' offices, treasurer's offices, and tract indexes all have an elaborate system of maps, cross-indexed "binders," and, on occasions, electronic filing systems, to help researchers locate land. The maps bear land identification numbers which refer to pages in tax books and to individual lots. Some offices charge a fee for their help, but most will get the information without charge, particularly for reporters. But relying on the clerks without checking their work can be risky. If a reporter gets just one of dozens of numbers wrong, it is possible to wind up describing the wrong property or accusing the wrong person of property manipulation.

The first time a reporter delves into property tax matters, it usually takes a few hours to learn how the whole system works. After that, it becomes fairly routine. In general, property is "assessed" at some fraction of what it is really worth. Generally, what it is "really worth" is determined by its "fair market value" (what it would sell for). For a building, the assessment is based on its replacement cost (how much it would cost to build another structure like it), or some multiple of the annual income it produces if it's a commercial building, or some combination of the two.

The single most common mistake reporters make in mentioning a property's value is confusing the assessed value with the real value. In some states all properties—houses, factories, stores, and vacant land—are all assessed at the same fraction of the fair market value. In other states the fraction varies with the type of property assessed. Houses may be assessed at 50 percent of market value and office buildings at 20 percent while land is assessed at 10 percent, for example. Then, in some states, the market value is further reduced by various depreciation factors. An office building that is half-abandoned, for example, will have its assessment further reduced by, say, 40 percent. The way to avoid any possible confusion is to call an assessor over, point to the number, and say "What is that?" Then, attribute the value of the land to the assessor's office.

The opportunity for corruption and unfair taxation in different states is directly proportional to the complexity of the assessment procedure. In states that do not set a fixed percentage of real worth as the basis for assessment, little more than the assessor's discretion decides a property's taxes. The opportunity for corruption usually manages to overwhelm at least a few assessors. But even in states which require that all property be assessed at half of market value, for example, it is still the assessor who determines what the market value of the property is, and that leaves enough room to permit corruption. In most states, a state agency also applies an equalization factor to the assessments made by various county officials. This is to prevent a county from paying less than its fair share of taxes if its assessors set unrealistically low values for the property.

The formula for determining a property's taxes, then, is:

$$(Vm)(Va)(Ef)(R) = T$$

Vm is the market value. *Va* is the fraction of market value used or imposed by law. *Ef* is the state equalization factor. *R* is the tax rate. *T* is the amount of taxes due on the property. For example, suppose a house under investigation sold two years ago for $48,000. Last year, a house down the block, almost identical, sold for $49,000. It would be reasonable to estimate the current market value *(Vm)* at $50,000. Either state law or current assessment practice in the jurisdiction specifies that homes are assessed at, say, 60 percent of fair market value. That means the assessed value *(Va)* of the home in question is 60 percent of $50,000 or $30,000. Since the state has decided that assessors in the county or township where the house is located assess property too low, there is a state equalization factor *(Ef)* of 1.2. The $30,000 assessed valuation is then multiplied by the equalization factor for a $36,000 state equalized value. That figure is then multiplied by the tax rate *(R)* to determine the amount of taxes the property owner should pay. If the tax rate *(R)* is $70 per $1,000 assessed valuation, the tax liability should be $2,520. If the local assessor has arrived at a substantially different figure, something is wrong.

In most large cities, private companies publish books showing land values in the city and suburbs. It is often useful to compare what these books say property is worth against what the local assessor says. These books, like the blue and red used car price books, derive their prices from surveys of recent sales. Wide discrepancies in the assessment of selected parcels may show that an official is underassessing friends or overassessing enemies. If the book is not available at the city hall or county building's reference library, a copy can often be borrowed from any large real estate firm, bank, or savings and loan.

The assessment of buildings is more complicated than the assessment of land, making it more time consuming for reporters or prosecutors to arrive at an accurate, independent appraisal of a building's worth. For that reason, the crooked assessor is more likely to negotiate building assessments. What the reporter must do first is learn the complex formulae assessors use to value buildings. The formulae include such factors as replacement cost, square feet of floor space, gross annual rent, age, condition, and the recent sales prices of similar buildings. It means little to say that an assessor is assessing everything in the county too high or too low, since the state will lower or raise the taxes by the appropriate equalization factor. What the reporter is seeking to find out is if the assessor is breaking his or her own rules in favor of, or to the disadvantage of, particular buildings or land parcels.

Experienced investigators take extreme care with the basic research underlying such stories because, in essence, the reporters involved are making their own assessment of the worth of the buildings, a fairly brazen enterprise, and a single mistake could invalidate the whole story. If possible, the wise reporter convinces a disgruntled employee of the assessor's office to help with the investigation or even convinces the publisher to finance an independent appraisal of at least one of the buildings the reporter thinks is underassessed.

Since property transfers are often used to conceal or disguise bribes, tax records are helpful insofar as they constitute a sort of government-approved property valuation. For example, if a businessman sells his home to a politician for $50,000 and the assessment records value the house at $70,000, it's a story. If the assessor's records show only a vacant lot or row of small buildings where someone built a large factory two years ago, something newsworthy is happening.

The tract index, or record of deeds, in each jurisdiction is the means by which citizens are provided with a record of property ownership. Mortgages and partnership agreements are also often recorded. In most jurisdictions, these records reveal the approximate amount of money involved in the various ownership transfers of each parcel. Reporters and realtors can compute these prices by counting the tax stamps on each deed in the record of deeds and working backwards. If each stamp represents $1,000 of purchase price and the deed transfer shows forty-five stamps, that means the property sold for between $45,000 and $45,999.

Experienced property researchers usually commute between the office where the deeds themselves are stored and the tract index. The information in the two offices is complementary, but the differences between the services provided are quite important. For instance, to find out who owns a certain property, the reporter can look up the address or legal description in the tract index and find the entire history of that plot: sales, purchases, mortgages, and all. The tract index, however, may not give indications of the amount of money exchanged in each transaction, nor copies of the legal papers, deeds, divorce papers, and death certificates involved. For that information, the reporter must take the index number of each transaction listed in the tract index to the deed room, where the various papers can be found and the tax stamps on the deeds translated into purchase or sale prices.

The deed room is especially helpful if a reporter wants to find out what land a person or company owns, rather than who owns a particular piece of land. By looking up their names in the grantor-grantee index, the reporter can check a person's or a firm's past and present land ownership—information crucial to planning and zoning investigations. The grantor-grantee index also directs an investigator to the relevant deeds, so that if forgery or misrepresentation is suspected, a check can be made on the signatures of the principals involved, including notaries, lawyers, secretaries, spouses, perhaps even associates or friends acting as witnesses.

Tract index listings are sometimes surprising. In 1974, a real estate company headed by Detroit Mayor Coleman Young owned some apartment buildings on the city's east side. A Detroit reporter checked those buildings in the tract index and discovered that the mortgage on the properties had been transferred from the life insurance company which originally held the mortgage to the U.S. Department of Housing and Urban Development (HUD), which insured it. The reason was that the mayor's company had not made any mortgage payments for months. In other words, a company headed by the mayor himself was facing foreclosure on its property in a city plagued with foreclosed and abandoned HUD-owned houses.

A secret of Chicago Mayor Richard Daley's—that his one real estate holding was protected by a secret land trust, run by an accountant who had received hundreds of thousands of dollars worth of city business—was also revealed through tract index research. The reporter involved, Ed Pound of the *Chicago Sun-Times,* was curious about Daley's life style. Daley lives modestly, almost humbly. He has put a number of his sons through school, but shows no signs of affluence other than a summer home in Michigan. So Pound went to the Michigan county where Daley has his summer home and looked it up in the tract index. He found that the title to the house was listed under the name of an Illinois corporation, Elard Realty ("El" from Daley's wife's name, Elanore, and "ard" from Daley's first name, Richard). The corporation, a secret land trust aimed at concealing the real ownership of the property, was run by an old friend of the mayor's, the accountant who had received city business. Illinois and Florida are apparently the only states which allow secret land trusts; Michigan does not, so Daley couldn't bill his taxes to a trust number at a bank as he could have in his home state.

In addition to the public tract index and deed room, a number of private firms—mostly banks—keep similar records for much of the country. The title transfer records these firms retain will often show the name of the broker or salesperson who handled the transfer. When contacted, the broker will often reveal additional details about the purchase, how long the property was on the market, the asking price, how long the buyer was in the market, and perhaps even some financial information on both the buyer and the seller. If the broker balks, or if there is no reason to think he or she will talk, a reporter may be able to convince someone at the assessor's office to make the call instead. Assessors do make such inquiries routinely to keep abreast of changes in property value. Some reporters, finding both these options closed, are not above calling the broker and pretending to be "from the assessor's office." Sometimes they even place the call from a phone in the assessor's office.

One thing to remember is that real estate and insurance brokers are licensed by the various states. An unusual number of public officials are real estate brokers and insurance salesmen, not because people with these vocations are attracted to public service, but because people attracted to public office soon learn that their many contacts can be profitable if they are in a position to get brokers' commissions. The commissions not only conceal bribes, but allow the officials to report them as income (thus keeping IRS investigators off their backs) and explain them away to nosy reporters. Taking bribes in the form of commissions also can reduce any potential charges from bribery to conflict of interest.

For example, if the Grave Stone Company wants the contract to pave all the parks in the city, the company president may buy his next home through a broker who happens to be the park commissioner. The park commissioner will then recommend that the company be awarded the city's contract on the grounds that the low bidder, if there is one lower than Grave, lacks experience in park paving. When caught, the company president will deny it was a bribe, saying that he didn't even decide to buy the house until after the parks were already paved. He will say that if he never bought anything from anyone even remotely connected with his business, he would not be able to buy anything. Likewise, the park commissioner will deny it was a bribe. He will say that the reporters are just trying to sell newspapers through sensational stories that ruin people's lives and do irreparable harm to their families. He'll say he obtained a broker's license to have additional income, so he wouldn't be tempted to wheel and deal with the taxpayer's money and, therefore, the reporter has the story backwards. He will say that he has been paid commissions from lots of people who never did business with the parks department and that, therefore, he is a legitimate real estate broker. He may even offer a reporter a commission to show that they aren't such bad things.

Something else to watch for when mucking about in real estate records is if a utility or a state-controlled or non-profit corporation sells or leases any of its land, air rights, or rights-of-way. The land should be traced back to its original deeds, which are usually on microfilm, because in many cases the land was given or sold on the condition that it be used for specific purposes only. Such deeds or legislative acts generally contain a "reverter clause" which requires that the land be returned to the public when no longer used for the purpose specified in the deed. Many states gave land to railroads and utilities (to "foster commerce and industry") with the proviso that the land revert to the state anytime the railroad or utility ceases to use it. At a time when many railroads are going out of business and closing down inner-city switching yards and rights-of-way, they often sell the land illegally to developers. Most of the reverter deeds were drawn up a hundred years ago or more, and who remembers? Certainly not the railroad's lawyers.

The Illinois Central, caught in such a sale by a Chicago ecology organization, argued that the reverter clause no longer applied, because it was so old, but that the part of the deed exempting the land from property taxes still held, and applied even to the new office and apartment buildings planned for the site. The judge hearing the case commended the railroad attorneys for their nerve and ordered the railroad to reimburse the state the sale price of the land.

In the preceding pages we have discussed records of "real" property: land and permanent improvements to it, such as paving, swimming pools, or buildings. Personal property is what sits inside the buildings or out in the driveways. It includes plant machinery, mink coats, DeSotos, and all the Little Liver Pills stored in the Carter warehouses. Some states tax personal property and others do not. (Florida, for example, taxes and lists bank accounts.) If a reporter is investigating taxes in a state which assesses personal property as well as real property, it is important to avoid confusing the two. If, for example, the total of property taxes paid by the owner of a certain lot is $5,000 and the assessment is $100,000, a reporter would not want to report that the building is assessed at $100,000 until finding out if the assessment figure included the $50,000 diamond stored in the building.

Because so much of what is taxed as personal property is portable, taxpayers are often tempted to transport it somewhere else when tax time rolls around. When the county treasurer is asked why the county commissioner did not pay taxes on the diamonds in his jewelry store, the treasurer may say it's because the jewels were in the commissioner's other store, across the state line, until last week. Personal property taxes are very hard to collect equitably. In Illinois, the county sheriffs downstate sometimes resort to snatching cars from driveways to enforce the tax collection, but in the Chicago area, the tax is not enforced at all.

8
Court Records, Police Records, and the Law Itself

Court Records

Most of the subjects a reporter investigates are also dealt with by the courts on a semi-regular basis. If a reporter is trying to find out what someone is worth, for example, it may be that a judge has already asked and compelled an answer to the question, and it has all become a part of the public record. People and corporations are charged with crimes and/or sued every day. When lawyers and prosecutors go after each other or each other's clients they are often quite thorough and develop much information that reporters find extremely useful. This information is contained in court records.

Court records—consisting of the suits, indictments, other civil and criminal actions, and all the documents relating to them—are readily available to the public. The court clerks will usually explain anything confusing, and the court reporters and judge's law clerks are also, as a rule, very helpful. This is particularly true in jurisdictions where judges are elected. Should a reporter run into the occasional clerk who is recalcitrant, a talk with the presiding judge, who actually controls the records, will generally straighten things out. Should the judge also balk, the reporter need not give up. A complaint to the local bar association should bring the whole lot of them—judges, clerks, and file cabinets—to a quick attention.

In investigating a slumlord, for example, the records of the court which handles tenant eviction cases would be an important source of information for a reporter. The names of people the slumlord has evicted can be found there, along with the names of their lawyers and their witnesses. If the reporter wants to find what property or companies a man may own, he or she could check the court records to see if that man has been recently divorced. Whether or not his wife contested the property settlement, he will have to file a statement of assets and liabilities with the court or with a court agency such as friend-of-the-court. If he secretly owns land he is rezoning, or embezzeled money when he was county treasurer, his ex-wife may even tell the reporter about it when contacted. The federal government may have sued someone for unpaid taxes or even brought criminal fraud charges. Corporations are regularly sued by customers, competitors, or even governments. Often corporations and land developers hire public officials who happen to be lawyers to handle certain matters for them as a way of repaying official favors.

People inherit money as a result of probate court hearings. Checking probate court records of such hearings is not only a good way to find out what people inherited, but who their relatives are. Since changing one's name is an effective but illegal way to escape debts and other unpleasantries, our nation's probate courts keep careful records of the petitions and court orders that effect such changes. (A judge's permission is required for a legal name change.) Various officials in various jurisdictions have been known to change their names, assume official posts, and then award contracts to relatives who did not change their names, or even to firms bearing their old names and still owned by them. A check with the probate court records, in the county in which the name change was approved, often provides what the reporter needs: the old and new names and the date the name was changed.

Petitions for, and court decisions ordering, the commitment of people to mental institutions are also available in court records, as are bankruptcy petitions, and the records and transcripts of bankruptcy hearings. Bankruptcy records are especially interesting because they almost invariably contain a listing of the complete assets and debits of a firm going into bankruptcy, thus allowing an alert reporter to discover what individuals hold what interests in the firm. The bankruptcy proceedings may also indicate any organized crime participation in the ruination of the firm.

No matter what kind of information a reporter seeks from court records, however, a quick reading of the pleadings is rarely enough —no matter how simple or innocent the matter may seem. The thorough investigator uses briefs and transcripts, if transcripts were made, to obtain the names of other litigants, witnesses, and lawyers involved, and then interviews them. Information that might be useful to the reporter's investigation may have been ruled inadmissible in court and not appear in the transcript. Some of what was ruled out may have been hearsay, or the judge may have felt that, while true, it did not pertain to the matter at hand. The information may be useful nonetheless to a reportorial investigation. Even the hearsay may be useful, so long as it isn't immediately printed but treated as an unproved tip to be further researched and documented. Beyond that, any of the parties involved in a court action may have discovered additional information pertaining to the case since appearing in court.

Court records yield information not only about people and corporations who may have been plaintiffs or defendants, but can also be used to evaluate the performance of judges, prosecutors, and police agencies. Buried in those records are statistics that will show which judges give twenty-year sentences for minor crimes and which judges found 85 percent of the defendants who came before them not guilty. The records will show how many cases were dismissed because the arresting officer didn't appear to testify and which robbery detectives have the best conviction rate. They will show if the county prosecutor, campaigning for re-election on a "law-and-order" platform, has as good a conviction rate as his predecessors. Careful scrutiny of the records will show whether blacks are convicted more often than whites, and whether the race of the victim seemed to have significant bearing on how justice was done.

Two investigators for the *Philadelphia Inquirer*, Donald Barlett and James Steele, ran records of the Philadelphia justice system through a computer and found inconsistent sentencing, inefficiency, laziness, and racism at all levels. Their series of reports was best summed up by a cartoon showing a judge throwing a dart at a board divided into areas labeled "bail," "re-trial," "10–25 years," "probation," "life," and "summer camp."

Reporters should also look into the hundreds of different kinds of quasi-judicial hearings held by local, state, and federal agencies. It is at these hearings that utilities apply for rate increases, haulers apply for permits, corporations apply for permission to pollute, quacks apply to continue practicing, and civil service violators seek to keep their jobs. Insurance companies, banks, and utilities are all licensed by state boards which hold public hearings. Crime commissions, hospital licensing boards, environmental protection agencies, water quality boards, tax commissions, public utility commissions, and intrastate commerce commissions also hold quasi-judicial hearings, complete with competing lawyers, and most of them keep publicly available records of those hearings. If a reporter wants to find out how many doctors, nurses, druggists, and veterinarians have been licensed or prosecuted in the state, the various licensing boards probably have the information on file.

Police Records

The lack of a criminal record does not necessarily mean that someone has never been arrested or convicted. (To be certain, a thorough reporter tries to convince a police friend to check with the FBI.) Perhaps the arrest took place in another jurisdiction. If the city police don't have a record on someone, the county or state police may. Frequently, calls to neighboring states or to a suspect's home state uncover outstanding warrants. Sometimes, too, people are able to get their criminal records expunged in court or have them removed by bribing a clerk. In at least some police stations, the expunging of records involves nothing more than crossing out entries with a pencil. One enterprising reporter we know persuaded a friendly records clerk to hold a criminal court judge's criminal record up to a light to read the "expunged" arrests.

Experienced reporters, however, are careful in drawing conclusions from arrest records. Arrest does not mean conviction; and if a person grew up in the "wrong" neighborhood, particularly if he or she is black, it is not unusual—and not always an indication of criminal activity—to have an arrest record. Also, given the amount of plea bargaining that goes on in most courts, reporters are aware that a conviction for a misdemeanor may have precious little connection with the gravity of the crime actually committed. Finally, just because someone is sentenced to five years, a reporter cannot assume, without further checking, that he or she served the full term. Parole may have been granted after only a year.

The Law

There are often occasions when a reporter needs information about the law itself. The law is kept in law libraries, generally associated with a local law school, run by the local bar, or even a governmental unit. Most law libraries admit only lawyers or law students, even though many of them are supported with tax money. Cynics have theories about that practice, but let's suppose those rules are there simply to keep bums from sleeping on the carpets. It means a reporter either needs a note from a lawyer saying the reporter is doing research for the lawyer or must bring a lawyer along while doing legal research. Until a reporter is thoroughly familiar with the process of checking statutes (laws made by legislatures) and case law (interpretations and rulings by judges), it is probably a good idea to have a patient, competent lawyer as a tutor.

The kinds of law most frequently used by investigative reporters can be found in one or two conveniently indexed volumes referred to as "codes" or "compiled laws." In general, these are hardcover volumes with "current inserts"—paperback pamphlets that are regularly published to keep the volumes up to date as the local legislative body adds, amends, or repeals laws. At the local level, the codes also contain the charters granted by the state or adopted and amended by the electorate under a grant of "home rule" power from the state. Charters function for cities much like constitutions function for states and the federal government. Most charters are quite specific, and public officials are often caught violating specific charter provisions.

At the federal and state levels, the codes include annotations of relevant court decisions and attorney general's opinions, along with the federal and state constitutions. These compilations at the federal level are the *United States Code Annotated* and the *Federal Code Annotated.* Both contain the same law; they are simply published by different companies and use different organizing methods. Federal administrative regulations are contained in the *Code of Federal Regulations.* On the state level, titles of codes vary somewhat from state to state: *Alabama Code, Colorado Revised Statutes Annotated,* and the *Michigan Compiled Laws Annotated* are some examples. Regulations issued by state agencies are sometimes available in a single set, and sometimes are not available even in well-stocked law libraries. In such circumstances, reporters must request the most recent regulations from the secretary of state or the responsible agency itself.

To locate law in a code, compilation, or administrative code, the subject word or descriptive word index should be consulted under all the possible headings. Indexes are often fallible; just because nothing appears under the most logical heading, a reporter should not assume there is no law on the point. Conflict of interest, for example, may be listed under the heading "adverse pecuniary interest." Also, be sure to consult the current inserts which update the index. Once a reporter has found what appears to be relevant laws, they should be looked up in the accompanying volumes of the set. Before spending too much time reading long sections of laws, however, the current inserts and any other published pamphlets of recent laws should be checked to make sure the reporter has the last word on the subject. Current inserts are organized in the same way as the bound volumes; pamphlets of recent law are not. But both the inserts and pamphlets generally include cumulative tables showing which sections of existing laws have been modified by recent acts, as well as a cumulative descriptive word index for these acts.

After the current applicable law has been located and read, the reporter should tackle the annotations of court decisions which interpret the various sections. These usually are arranged under the subject headings, but the headings often tend to be somewhat technical. Therefore, a few annotations under each heading must be scanned to avoid overlooking something important. Finally, an investigator should check the current insert and any published pamphlets of recent decisions interpreting the pertinent sections of law. Only after taking all these steps can a reporter be reasonably sure the key statute wasn't repealed in the last session of the legislature or ruled unconstitutional in recent months.

As we have noted, constitutions generally are included with codes or compilations of law. A reporter should be sure the index being used also cites pertinent sections of the constitution. Most state constitutions are much more detailed in what they permit or prohibit than the U.S. Constitution. For example, often they will specifically proscribe conflict of interest and require that anyone found guilty of such a conflict be removed from office.

Administrative regulations and local codes generally are not annotated with relevant court decisions. The best way to find important court decisions in these areas is to consult with the local city corporation counsel (city attorney) or state attorney general. Nor are administrative manuals and local codes kept as up to date as federal and state codes. Therefore, a reporter must quiz a well-informed administrative agency officer—not, we repeat, not the public relations man for the agency—to be sure he or she has located the last word on the subject. City and county clerks can provide the latest word on acts passed by city or county governments.

The results of a reporter's research in these areas should be checked with a lawyer who has some experience in the area being researched. (Patent attorneys should not be asked, for example, whether rezoning a relative's ranch is a conflict of interest, or if campaign contributions in return for specific performance legally constitutes bribery.) Talking with a sharp lawyer may reveal that the reporter has been outwitted by some perverse indexer. Or, a reporter may discover that a law doesn't mean what it seems to. It may be that law made by judges without reference to a particular statute (common law) has an important bearing on the issue —and the somewhat simplified research procedure outlined here will not lead a reporter to the relevant common law. If the above procedures were all there is to the study of law, anyone could pass the bar after a one-semester mail-order course. No responsible reporter would use anything unearthed in this way to pronounce someone guilty in a story. The reporter may, however, want to quote certain sections of the law in a story. For a detailed explanation of legal research, we recommend William R. Roalfe, ed., *How to Find the Law,* 6th ed. (St. Paul, Minn.: West Publishing Co., 1965).

A reporter who takes the time to become familiar with whatever laws apply to the particular subject under investigation will be able to conduct a much more intelligent and useful discussion with a selected legal expert or experts. Ask a city attorney if a city official can moonlight and you will probably get a vague, virtually useless, opinion. Ask the attorney if he or she interprets sec. 23, paragraph 4 to mean that a city assessor cannot be hired as a property tax consultant by a large company he assesses annually, and you will get a much more useful answer.

9
Election Fraud

Most elections held in this country are probably fair. Nevertheless, the possibility of stealing an election is a temptation not always resisted by the unscrupulous. The election system is complex enough to allow those who would profit by its misuse to churn out an endless stream of new methods aimed at blocking the exercise of the popular will.

Sometimes people who should not be on the ballot get their names on anyhow. They may have filed their nominating petitions past the deadline. They may not have obtained sufficient petition signatures. They may have had ineligible people sign their petitions—people who aren't registered voters or who live in a different district. They may have forged some or all of the signatures. They may have coerced people into signing or circulating their petitions. Sometimes, for no good reason, candidates manage to get their name at the top of the ballot, giving them a head start on the opposition. Paul Powell, the late Illinois secretary of state who left $400,000 in shoe boxes in a hotel closet when he died, made a habit of putting his friends at the top of the ballot. Even when other candidates spent the night in line to be the first to file for office, Powell's friends would mail in their petitions and Powell would simply open the mail before he opened the doors. Who could say otherwise?

Sometimes people are improperly barred from the ballot by election officials. The common practice is for the party in power to accept the nominating petitions of their colleagues without question but to go over the opposition's with a fine tooth comb. Even if they don't find technical violations, they sometimes just disqualify legitimate signatures and leave it up to the candidate to pursue a long and costly court fight. For example, one candidate was ruled off the ballot because the people who signed his petition didn't include the abbreviations "St." or "Ave." in their addresses.

In 1972, Mayor Daley changed his mind about who would be

the Democratic machine's candidate for county prosecutor just seven hours before the deadline for filing nominating petitions. Daley had originally reslated the incumbent, Edward V. Hanrahan, who had just been indicted for obstructing justice in the cover-up of the slaying of two Black Panther leaders by his own investigators. When other candidates on the Democratic machine ticket complained that the indictment was hurting their own campaigns, Daley finally decided to dump Hanrahan and replace him with Chicago's chief traffic court judge. To do so, he needed about 12,000 signatures in a hurry. But Daley had nothing if he didn't have the largest, most resolute army of loyal patronage workers in the country. By 10 A.M., the petition blanks were off the presses, and a thousand had been distributed by 11 A.M. Shortly after 3 P.M. the petitions, containing over 20,000 signatures, were filed.

What is even more remarkable is that some of the signatures were genuine. At least half were forgeries: the names on some of the petitions were signed in alphabetical order, on others, every fifth or sixth signature bore the same handwriting. Hundreds of names were misspelled, others listed with the wrong address, and one sheet was almost all in the same handwriting.

The next day, *Chicago Daily News* columnist Mike Royko, one of the nation's top investigators, explained how they did it. The freshly printed petitions had been taken over to city hall and "round-tabled." Five or six city employees—all of whom owed their jobs to the machine—sat around a table and passed petition blanks and voter registration lists in a circle. Each person copied every fifth or sixth name from the registration list. That way, the forgeries weren't so obvious.

The following day, the Board of Election Commissioner's office was jammed with reporters trying to catch up with Royko and with lawyers for other candidates trying to find someone to subpoena. The story was easily verified even though the city workers denied everything. Reporters simply looked up the names on the petitions in the phone book and called people who allegedly had signed the blanks. Some were amused, some angry, and, of course, some were frightened they would go to jail for "signing" something they hadn't signed.

The less sporting of the reporters tracked down the city workers whose names appeared as petition circulators and asked such rude questions as, "Tell me, how did you manage to get all those people to line up alphabetically?" It was all good, clean fun, of course, and nobody got in serious trouble because in Cook County, the mayor names the judicial candidates. But it made good reading and the mayor's candidate was defeated in the primary.

There is another very common, but rarely reported, type of election fraud that takes place long before the voters get into the polling place. That is using federal employees to circulate petitions, ring doorbells, and raise money. The law outlawing such activity—the Hatch Act—was written to prevent incumbent office holders from using the vast federal bureaucracy as a campaign staff. It also applies to employees of federally funded, locally administered programs. Put simply, the law prevents local politicians from using federal grant money to build patronage armies.

Catching federal employees, such as Model Cities employees, working elections is easier said than done. The 1972 Chicago petition forgery scandal we have just discussed led two Lerner Newspapers reporters to the largest Hatch Act violation scandal in the history of the U.S. Civil Service. One of the reporters had put together a list of the people who had done the forging and was in the process of trying to see if any of them felt pressured or intimidated to break the various election laws. The mayor had long maintained that his precinct captains and other election workers served out of loyalty to the cause. But every now and then a city worker would complain about the long hours of precinct election work required to keep a city job or get a promotion.

Precinct captains had never been interviewed on a large scale because the Democratic party closely guarded its lists of campaign workers and nobody thought to check the names of those who circulated the party's nominating petitions. One of the names on the list the reporter was about to begin calling was Saint Joseph Smith. At the next desk sat the paper's urban affairs reporter, Roger Flaherty, happily thumbing through the Model Cities interoffice phone directory that he had been trying to get for over a year.

The first reporter, a person deeply committed to trivialities, said, "It's quiz time, dummy. Who was St. Joseph Smith?" Flaherty, now a reporter at the *Chicago Sun-Times,* was about to look up with his usual pained expression when he noticed that a Saint Joseph Smith was listed as a Model Cities employee in the agency directory, a coincidence he gleefully announced. If the Smith in the Model Cities agency was the same Smith who circulated the nominating petition (and not the Joseph Smith who founded the

Church of Jesus Christ of the Latter Day Saints), he was in violation of the Hatch Act.

The reporters called Smith's home, and his wife gave them his
office number, the same one that was listed in the Model Cities
directory. Then the first reporter began reading names from his
list while Flaherty looked them up in the agency directory. Within
an hour, they turned up about 20 violators of the Hatch Act. Not
bad for a day's work: the *Chicago Tribune's* previous investigation
of the Model Cities program had unearthed only one Hatch Act
violator.

The next step was to compile the names of everybody who had
circulated petitions for candidates in the last two elections to find
out who the city's election workers were. Then, the reporters
needed to compare the list to more than just the telephone directory of one agency. They needed a list of all the employees of
federally funded, city administered programs—the city payroll. So
one of the reporters visited the city comptroller. He knew without
asking why the reporter wanted to see the federally funded payroll
and tried to discourage him by pointing out that there were over
12,000 names on the unalphabetized list. The reporter said he
wanted to look it over anyhow; that he had turned up a number
of relevant names by comparing the petitions to the Model Cities
directory, but he didn't want to accuse anyone who was innocent.

The comptroller consented, apparently certain that one reporter, in the two hours that remained before the office closed for
the day, couldn't find more than two or three names in such a
long, unalphabetized list. To this end, the comptroller refused to
sell the reporter a computer print-out of the payroll or permit him
to photocopy the print-out, saying that the city could not give out
such information. The reporter, however, could copy down by
hand whatever information he found. Rather than brawl over the
details and risk not seeing the list, the reporter said he had another
appointment to get to that afternoon and would be back in the
morning. The comptroller said he would be out of town the next
day, but since he had already committed himself, buzzed his
assistant into the room, introduced the reporter, and said, "Show
him any of the payroll he wants while I'm gone tomorrow, but no
xeroxes and don't sell him a print-out."

The reporter made small talk until the assistant left, noting
which way he went, then excused himself. He found the assistant
and said casually, "We'll be in about 8:30 in the morning. We'll

be glad to work out in the hall there so we won't get in your way if you can set us up with a couple of tables." The assistant comptroller, thinking his boss had okayed the plan, assented. The following morning, the two reporters and three typists showed up with five portable typewriters and eight reams of paper. Before the day was out they had copied the names and social security numbers of 7,000 of the 12,600 federally funded workers.

There was no longer any reason to keep secret what they were looking for. The reporters openly canvassed every political source they had for any lists of precinct captains and campaign workers who had happened not to circulate petitions. They got about 500 such names through "Operation Eagle Eye," a civic organization that had staffed a number of polling places during the previous election. Each poll watcher, it turned out, had noted the name of the Democratic precinct captain who worked each precinct the day of the election.

Next, the reporters took both lists, the workers and the employees, to the Better Government Association, another civic watchdog group, whose staff laboriously alphabetized one of the lists. Then, the reporters read names from one list to fifteen or twenty volunteers sitting around a large room, each with three or four pages of names from the other list in front of them. Every time a name was found on both lists, a volunteer yelled "Bingo." That raised the total to about 100 names. A story could then be written charging the city administration with using model cities funds to provide jobs for loyal campaign workers. The story noted that since neither the payroll nor the political list was complete, there were undoubtedly many more Hatch Act violators.

The local U.S. Attorney's office passed the story on to the Civil Service Department in Washington, and a few weeks later civil service began its own investigation. In a two-day weekend blitz, catching the workers at home and away from their supervisors, civil service agents from five other cities got about 75 of the payrollers to sign depositions admitting their guilt. Then the Civil Service subpoenaed the entire city payroll and ran the total of suspects up to over 200.

The week the Civil Service hearings were announced, the city comptroller was fired. (That same week, however, another reporter had bluffed him into admitting that Mayor Daley had ordered him to transfer the city airport insurance to the mayor's son.) The first batch of Hatch Act violators brought to trial were building inspectors. Two days after the trial began, one of the reporters' homes was visited by three city inspectors and he was hit with $3,800 worth of code violations. But that's another story.

The Chicago Hatch Act investigation was a success for a number of reasons, not the least of which was luck. But, had the reporters not understood the details of the Hatch Act, particularly that it applied to locally administered programs, the investigation would have never been started. There is no substitute for knowing the law.

This is the case with most unreported election frauds. They go unreported largely because so few reporters take the time to familiarize themselves with local election laws. The easiest way to learn election laws is to get a copy of the brochures published by the local election agency to educate its election judges. They are written in simple language and are amply illustrated. They should be read far enough in advance of the election so that a reporter can get explanations for anything that is not clear.

Also prior to an election, a reporter should get a copy of the local election board's voter canvass in precincts where fraud is suspected. It is a good idea to spot check the list by ringing doorbells to see that everyone ruled eligible is still alive and living in the precinct. Then the reporter can wait for election day and see how many of the dead-and-gone come back to vote. While it could be argued that a person should not be discriminated against just because he or she was unfortunate enough to expire the week before election, it is still against the law for a dead person to vote and any reappearance should be reported.

There are a number of irregularities to watch for in the polling place itself. Crippled, blind, or illiterate people can ask whoever they want to help them vote, be it their mothers, the precinct captain, or Donald Segretti. But if the voter is simply unsure how to mark the ballot or work the levers on a voting machine, then he or she must be accompanied into the booth by an election judge from each party. Sometimes, in elections involving long ballots, the precinct captains will get people to invite them into the booth on the pretext of illiteracy. That is also illegal. The impaired voters must sign cards attesting to their disability and even if they can't write they are to make their mark, usually an "X," on the card. That is where experienced reporters keep a sharp eye out to see that the signature matches the one in the registration binder and that the voter has adequate identification if challenged. Generally, the word of an election official who recognizes the person is considered adequate identification. To watch for ghost voting, the reporter must stand in a place where the signatures can be compared. If the ghosts are unable to spell the name of the person they are ghosting for, it's a safe assumption that something's up.

Election-scarred reporters watch closely for people who vote "early and often." They check the counters at the rear of the voting machines before voting begins to make sure some candidate isn't starting with a 100 vote edge. They also watch for bribes, particularly in poor precincts. Bribes are not so much given to get someone to vote a certain way (as most people believe), but to get loyalist troops out to vote. Campaign workers will generally not attempt to bribe people to vote a certain way for two reasons. First of all, that involves the risky proposition of offering bribes to people planning to vote for the opposition. Secondly, unless the polling place is really up for grabs, a precinct captain has no sure way of knowing who someone voted for.

The *Chicago Tribune* won a Pulitzer Prize in 1972 for a series on election fraud in which a reporter was secretly hired as a clerk at the Board of Election Commissioners. The paper also convinced a Republican party official to appoint a number of other *Tribune* reporters as election judges in precincts where votes were said to be regularly stolen. In one polling place, three of the journalists reported that voters were being given bags of groceries. When the three were questioned before a grand jury, however, each said another had actually seen the bribery. The moral here is to be sure you are seeing what you think you are seeing, and not what someone else says you are seeing. Incidentally, they kept the Pulitzer.

Another popular method of winning elections when paper ballots are used is chain balloting. Here a party worker gets a blank ballot, generally from someone who comes in early and asks for assistance. The ballot is filled out to the party worker's satisfaction, but instead of being deposited in the ballot box, it is given to the next friendly voter who comes in to vote. The second voter deposits the marked ballot and passes the blank one to the precinct captain, generally outside the polling place. Every time friendly voters come along, the process is repeated. This system guarantees that friendly voters vote the preferred way, especially on long and complicated ballots. It is a very difficult practice to catch. Sometimes a reporter can see the ballot passed, other times a careless voter will pocket the unmarked ballot in plain view. In all cases, however, the number of ballots cast at closing time will equal the number of voters, because the precinct captain will vote last and drop two ballots in the box.

Just seeing a voter take a ballot from the precinct captain, stick it in one pocket and pull another ballot out of another pocket doesn't make much of a story. What a reporter really needs are names, dates, instances, and confessions. Some reporters would advocate catching the voter outside, after he or she votes, and reciting the penalties for election fraud to persuade the voter to turn state's evidence on the spot and give up the blank ballot. That ought to produce an interesting reaction. Then, these reporters would advise taking the blank ballot over to the precinct captain and telling him that six people have told them what the precinct captain has been doing. They would ask him why he did it, what's in it for him, and if he says he's been forced to do it, ask by whom.

Sometimes elections are stolen because extra ballots are printed, marked, and substituted for legitimately cast ballots. This can be done any time from before the polls open until shortly before the results are turned in. One reporter we know found a bunch of blank ballots in the gutter outside a polling place. Nobody seemed to know where they came from and the reporter still gets a far-away look in his eye when he thinks about it. Obviously, something was going on, but neither he, nor we, know just what. But it must have been a good one.

The simplest way to steal elections is to miscount the votes. That is hard to catch, because if a newspaper reporter is leaning over shoulders while the votes are counted, they will be counted accurately. Voters could be polled, once the election is over, but many probably would not talk, some might lie, and there is no guarantee the lies would be self-cancelling. One solution, used by the *Chicago Tribune,* is to have reporters appointed as election judges.

One party is often able to steal votes in the presence of the other party's election judges because those judges often do not really belong to the other party. If they do, they are paid off. In a few cases, the dominant party's workers are able to outsmart or intimidate them. But in most cases they are wolves in sheep's clothing. This comes about because in many rural and suburban areas there are not enough Democrats to supply the requisite number of judges in each polling place; in many inner city areas there are not enough Republicans to go around.

In an inner city area, for example, the Democrats will give out a certain number of patronage jobs to Republicans. The grateful Republicans, hired as judges, "don't make waves" on election day. In other cases, the election judges are just not alert. It is difficult to find people who will miss a day's pay to work eighteen hours in a polling place for the pittance generally paid election judges. Consequently, many of the judges, particularly of a minority party, are the aged, the unemployable, the apathetic, or the inebriated. A hustling precinct captain can literally take over and run such polling places.

Journalists observing such polling places should watch out for themselves. Emotions run high and it is not unusual for reporters and photographers, especially photographers, to take a beating. Reporters may be challenged on many things they want to do in a polling place, particularly if something sneaky is going on. And in most jurisdictions, an election judge can have a reporter removed from the polling place or arrested, with or without cause. The experienced reporter tries to avoid disputes that end this way because that's exactly what crooked officials want. Our best advice is to sit back and work crossword puzzles, simple crossword puzzles. The idea is to look stupid or bored, and not to let a campaign worker catch the reporter focusing on anything unusual while it is happening. To be really convincing, the reporter might show up late smelling of liquor.

If the reporter successfully avoids attracting attention, however, he or she will be faced with a rather sticky ethical problem. There they are, stealing votes right and left. It may be possible to try to stop the stealing, but then the reporter is making news, not discovering it. So he or she might decide to let the corruption proceed and write a story about it, secure in the knowledge that the exposé will have a more salubrious long-range effect on election day honesty than the temporary reform of one precinct. But the problem with that approach is that the reporter, if appointed as an election judge, displaced someone who might have prevented the vote stealing. So silence makes that reporter an accessory.

Another aspect of election fraud is campaign fund raising. What fund-raising laws there are frequently do not require disclosure until after the election is over. So, even when fund-raising fraud is exposed, it is too late. Fund-raising laws vary, and as we said earlier, will be subject to considerable change in the next few years. They will undoubtedly get tighter and reporters are going to have to keep abreast of the changes. The best way to learn the latest rules is to talk to the chief fund raisers for both parties. They'll both be glad to tell a reporter what the other one can't do and how to catch the other's violations. (See *campaign records*, chapter 6.)

Campaign fund-raising methods include selling advertisements in magazines published by the party. The ads cost a fortune, nobody reads them, and the merchants who buy them know that nobody reads them. In some areas these "ward books" constitute a virtual shakedown of the local merchants. They are often used to build war chests in off-years, when there is no election, making it much harder for the reporter to find out how much money a candidate has spent. Another trick is to use official stationery, or stationery that looks official, for fund raising. A Lake County (Illinois) sheriff was caught sending out letters on sheriff's office stationery which promised voters that if they donated money to his cousin's campaign for coroner, they would get a deputy sheriff's badge and the right to carry a gun. A clever fellow, he even offered to give a reporter a gun permit. The offer was recounted in the reporter's story, of course.

Once a reporter investigating campaign finances has compiled a fairly complete list of campaign donors, fund raisers, and benefit party hosts, they will have to be identified. Are any of them on government payrolls? If they are businessmen, do their firms handle city contracts? What has happened with any land they own or owned? Anytime a local election is held in conjunction with a federal election, it becomes a violation of federal law to coerce government workers into making contributions or to make working in a campaign a condition of employment.

A large source of campaign contributions are the various lobbies and lobbyists. Lobbyists are so named, it is said, because they stand in the lobbies of state capitols handing out twenty-dollar bills to passing politicians. Many states require lobbyists to register and the registry book in some states includes a lobbyist's picture as well as background information. A good way of ascertaining how much money any particular pressure group donated during an election is to talk with those who didn't get any of the money and with opposing lobbyists. Lobbyists always seem to have copies of the opposition's mailings and fund solicitation documents. If a reporter wanted to find out how much the automakers gave congressmen during the last election, a good place to start would be with Ralph Nader's group.

The latest craze in election fraud is "dirty tricks." By this we do not mean the good-natured or obvious pranks of the sort played by Dick Tuck over the years, but the kind of tactics that portray a candidate as saying and doing things he didn't, or having friends and supporters he hasn't. The phrase "dirty tricks" is generally associated with the name Richard Nixon. Insofar as that juxtaposition may lead one to believe that Nixon and the Committee to Re-Elect the President have been the sole source of dirty tricks, it is inaccurate. For example, a wide assortment of dirty tricks, agents provocateurs, and planted hecklers and questioners were used against Illinois Governor Daniel Walker in the 1972 election. At least two members of his staff were on his opponent's payroll, and at a number of rallies, he was greeted by "spontaneous demonstrations" designed to convince Illinois' large Latino vote that he was their enemy.

Dirty tricks are also used at a suprapartisan level. Testimony in the Conspiracy Seven trial, following the 1968 Democratic National Convention, showed that much of the rock and bottle throwing was initiated by police agents who had "infiltrated" the demonstrations. While the convention riots were in progress, none of the hundreds of reporters there bothered to check on who was who among the demonstrators. The press blindly reported that the hippies threw things at the cops when, according to later testimony, it was often undercover agents throwing things at cops.

Not all dirty tricks are as obvious or dramatic as those used in the 1968 and 1972 presidential elections. In many cities, welfare recipients are threatened with loss of their benefits if they do not get out and vote a certain way. They are told that somehow or other the precinct captain will know how they voted. (We'll partially qualify our previous statement that there is no real way party workers can tell how a person has voted. It has been charged that a popular make of voting machine sometimes emits different noises depending on which straight ticket lever is pulled. It is said that a precinct captain with a good ear can listen to a few votes and distinguish among the various clicks. We have tried it ourselves, however, and have not been able to distinguish the sounds. It is possible, of course, to tell when a voter is splitting his ticket by the amount of time spent in the booth and by the shuffling of his feet, visible under the curtain.)

The threat that a person will lose his or her welfare benefits should not be confused with the political charge that if an antiwelfare candidate is elected, all welfare recipients may be hurt. The first is coercion, the second just politics. It is illegal to threaten individual voters with a cut in their benefits if they do not vote for a certain party or candidate. The best way to keep an eye on these tactics is to have some friends in the ghetto. Ringing doorbells the day after the precinct captain has been around will probably fail. It's foolish to expect people to risk their welfare checks by talking to reporters.

The phony heckler or the embarrassingly obnoxious sympathizer is probably the most sophisticated of the dirty tricksters and the hardest to catch. Generally, a reporter sent to cover a political rally is kept busy just recording the speeches and doesn't have time to find out whose side the various shouters and demonstrators are really on. But anytime someone is so severely heckling a speaker that the speaker is getting the audience's sympathy, a reporter should be suspicious. And anytime somebody particularly obnoxious makes a big show of supporting the speaker, it is a good idea to try to find out whose side he or she is really on. The same goes for campaign literature that smoothly backfires.

Whenever a politician is being hurt by supporters, or helped by opponents, a reporter is on to an exciting story. For example, if a candidate is known to support abortion and a number of supporters show up with placards reading, "Elect D. Encee—Legalize Euthanasia," there may be dirty tricks going on. After the rally, a reporter should follow some of the "supporters" to their cars and get their license numbers. If necessary, the reporter could follow them home or to party headquarters and persuade someone else to identify them. The next step is to call the opposition's party headquarters and ask for them. If the "supporters" appeared at a Democratic rally, and the next day the person who answers phones at the Republican headquarters knows who they are and takes a message for them, it could be the beginning of a very, very good story.

Some reporters would advocate other methods of discovering the true identities of the cast members of these political dramas. It is possible to ask them, have a cop bust them, get them to sign a petition, or have them photographed and then show the pictures around. It's even possible to take a picture into various party headquarters and try to find "the person who saved my child's life." Maybe it won't be possible to find out who the mysterious demonstrators are, or maybe they'll turn out to be just crazy people, but very little will be lost by trying.

Don't count on the Watergate scandal to end campaign fraud. It may just force the perpetrators of fraud to be more careful. Politicians learn from reporters' exposés; some learn what mistakes to avoid. Watergate was a third-rate burglary, so next time it will be a second-rate burglary. Next time the hired dirty tricksters won't know who hired them. Somebody is probably already planning to hire a dirty trickster who can then be exposed. The candidate will get voter sympathy and will charge that the hapless trickster was paid by his or her opponent.

Even Nixon wasn't cured of dirty tricks by Watergate. In April, 1974, four months before his resignation, crowd packing was used at a presidential appearance in upstate Michigan during a congressional campaign. There, the President's advance men gave out passwords to loyal supporters bussed in from other cities. That way, the more enthusiastic supporters were ushered to the front of the crowds to greet Nixon and make a good showing for the TV cameras. While most media were content to report that the President was wildly cheered by crowds of five and ten thousand in towns with only 500 residents, the *Detroit News* uncovered the password trick and presented a more accurate picture of the campaign.

Another election trick of growing popularity is to plant a phony story with a newspaper. Most reporters will listen to the phony tip and check it out. Finding it false, they will discard it and go on to the next story. But the fun thing to do is to go back to the source and ask a few very careful questions. Find out whose idea the phony story was, how it was dreamed up, and why it was done. Was it done in fear of losing? Was anyone convinced it was true? Will a public retraction of the story be forthcoming? Why not? If a reporter pursues this line of questioning, it will probably yield a far better story.

Part III

Techniques

10
Approaching and Interviewing Sources

Although many stories can be documented in their entirety without once leaving the record rooms of a governmental agency, most cannot. In addition to learning the paperwork, a good investigative reporter must learn to deal with people, all kinds of them. It's as necessary to decide which people should be interviewed first, as to decide which files should be explored first. The reporter who stops to reflect about a story before rushing off to interview the first person who comes to mind, may be able to mentally gather and arrange all the facts in a way that will make the missing details more readily apparent. It may be hard to explain to an editor why a reporter, on the verge of a major journalistic achievement, is sitting and staring blankly at the ceiling. But he or she should stare anyway. Fifteen minutes of reflection may save days of digging. If nothing else, forethought will make the finished investigative product more readable.

Some reporters begin by writing a preliminary draft of the story, leaving blanks in the appropriate places, to give them a clearer idea of the information they need and to prevent them from wasting time unearthing facts they may not use. This technique can backfire, however, by blinding a reporter to the need to kill or reinterpret the story later, in light of new or contradictory evidence. Underestimating the importance of unanticipated discoveries is another pitfall of an early draft that journalists must look out for.

Of course, some preliminary organization is crucial. Part of the plan should cover the order in which the reporter wants to gather evidence. In most cases, it's a good idea initially to verify that part of a story that is least likely to tip off the investigatee. And in most cases that means going to clips, other reporters, libraries, and file cabinets first. Even if the reporter talks to sources who aren't particularly close friends of the investigative subject, they might pass along word of the reporter's interest anyway, hoping the

subject may return the favor some day. The subject's worst enemies may present the investigator with other problems, such as
exaggerating the investigatee's sins.

Reporters find that in some investigations, they are unable to
determine which of their sources are sources and only sources, and
which are both sources and possible subjects of investigations
themselves. Journalists find they must return to each source several times, mixing the techniques of confronting the subject of an
investigation with the techniques of interviewing a source, in an
attempt to determine the truth about what each person is saying
about each of the others. As a result, their investigative process
sometimes resembles drawing and then tightening numerous con-
centric circles.

Some reporters find it more effective to confront their investigatees before they talk to his or her colleagues. That way, they're
more likely to catch the subject unaware and increase their
chances of extracting the full truth. They would then recommend
interviewing everyone else and gathering any other information
that will add to the scope of the story or make it more lively. A
tactful reporter can return to an investigative subject, interview
him or her a second time, and dig for additional details, once the
basic story has been drawn out at the first interview.

Obviously, different sources are best approached in different
ways. In most instances, one does not approach a businessman
who has had little press contact in the same way one would
approach an experienced politician who has dealt with reporters,
including investigative reporters, for decades. Nor does an experienced reporter use the same methods and techniques in interviewing friendly and unfriendly sources. Most of the time, however, a reporter doesn't know with any certainty just what side of
the controversy a potential source is likely to be on, or how much
experience that source has had with the media. So the reporter
broaches controversial topics circumspectly, and slowly, carefully
feels out the source's prejudices as well as the extent of the source's
knowledge and experience.

Nevertheless, some generalizations about classes of sources can
be made. Public officials, both elected and appointed, often consider press relations a sort of game complete with rules and a
scoring system. If they feel themselves falling behind, they will try
to score enough points to catch up. While some will take public
embarrassment or even political setbacks good-naturedly, many

more will not. The familiar motto of the Boston Irish politicians is "Don't get mad, get even."

As we've already mentioned, the Michigan state senate tried to get even in 1972 by voting to build a wood and glass cage for the legislative press corps. Reporters would be locked in it from fifteen minutes before a senate session began until fifteen minutes after it was gaveled to a close. The senators said the cage was needed to preserve decorum on the senate floor, and because a number of stories written by uncaged journalists had angered individual senators. (The cage was finally dismembered when the press corps refused to use it and sat in the public galleries instead.)

Businessmen, as opposed to politicians, are often deadly serious in their dealings with the press and are generally guarded by horrendously overpaid public relations advisors. Getting an appointment with a businessman can be as hard as conducting an entire interview with a public official. By the same token, businessmen generally read newspaper exposés less carefully than politicians and consequently are more likely to blurt out statements that would give the average politician heart failure. This is especially true in cases involving the payment of money to politicians and others. Businessmen are used to paying for goods and services and often ignore the ethical or political questions involved in such payments.

For example, *Detroit Free Press* reporter Dave Johnston was gathering information in 1974 for a story about a foundry constantly accused of severe violations of state pollution regulations. When he was informed by one of the foundry's neighbors that a certain state representative was very active in many forums defending the foundry, and was possibly on its payroll, Johnston decided to bluff a little. While touring the foundry with the plant manager, the reporter asked, "What are you paying him (the state representative) for?" The manager replied, "Well, we paid him to (very pregant pause), we paid him as a financial consultant." The upshot of this businessman's comment was that the "financial consultant" was censured by his colleagues in the Michigan state house and was trounced in the 1974 primary election.

Professional people, such as planners, accountants, and social workers, differ in many ways from both businessmen and politicians. They are often more loyal to their professions than to their superiors and thus are top-notch sources. A professional who feels that recommendations are being ignored or distorted for political reasons, or who feels that he or she is unfairly shouldering the blame for a bad decision, may well want to talk about it. But not all professionals, even those who feel betrayed by politicians, will talk to reporters. It's up to the reporter to find the ones who will.

Some reporters request interviews with professionals on the grounds that they need a quick but thorough education in that particular field. The reporters probably do need such grounding, even if getting it isn't a pressing concern. During the interview the reporters express no opinions until knowing what the source's opinions are. They portray themselves as friendly fellow professionals. They talk about how much they admire the good examples of work done in the interviewee's field and the comradeship they feel with people like the interviewee who struggle mightily against the awful forces of bureaucracy—struggles not unlike their own with the newsroom bureaucracy. They concentrate on what the interviewee is saying, picking up the nuances, understanding them, nodding sympathetically. They tell the person they almost entered the same field once, and sometimes wish now they had. Finally, they hint that it is too bad that the hallowed principles of the profession are so often compromised by expedient, greedy, or cowardly politicians.

If, after all this method acting, the source doesn't appear willing to talk, the wise reporter waits for a graceful interval and then leaves. Later he or she tries one of the individual's colleagues or someone else in the same professional field. In general, it is a good idea not to press the first potential source to the point where the journalist's interest will be reported to others.

If and when an inside source can be found who admits being some sort of good-government, anticorruption fanatic too, the reporter should guardedly lay out the cards, tell the source who or what is under investigation, and ask for help. If the source is on the reporter's side, the more he or she knows, the more help the reporter will get. If the source is afraid of being fired, the reporter may suggest that the subject of the investigation is in so much trouble, or soon will be, that he won't be able to demote a janitor. It might be wise to add that the newspaper (or TV station) is not without influence and, should the crunch come, that the reporter is friendly with public officials in other areas who would be only too happy to provide an honest hardworking person with an equal, perhaps even better, job. After all, if someone helps with an investigation and is fired or harassed because of it, there is no reason why the reporter shouldn't help the source find another job.

Some reporters pretend to be someone else when interviewing sources. Stories abound about the reporter who calls the scene of some tragedy and tells the voice at the other end, "This is Coroner O'Bannion. How many dead ones you got?" After a pause, according to the story, the voice replies, "No, *this* is Coroner O'Bannion. Who the hell are you?" Often reporters use their own names but imply they are someone else: "This is Jones calling from headquarters. Who'd you arrest out there?" The legendary Harry Romanoff, former city editor of the defunct *Chicago Daily American,* once managed to interview mass murderer Richard Speck's mother by pretending to be Speck's attorney. Some slightly more ethical reporters don't hesitate to pose as students during interviews to shield their purposes with the protective mantle of academia. These ruses are questionable and in some instances illegal.

Ethical questions aside, however, even a crooked reporter's self-interest might not be served by pretending to be someone else. Sources tend to tell fewer lies and exaggerate less when they're talking to journalists, who may print or broadcast what they say, than when they think they're just gabbing with a student or acquaintance. So the reporter who pretends to be someone else may not end up with the truth.

One newspaper reporter a few years ago began to investigate a tip that a mayor's aide in his city had been treated to an expensive gambler's junket to Las Vegas by a company doing substantial business with the city. Part of the investigation was on an ethical level with the Watergate break-in. The reporter enlisted the aid of a colleague and the two stayed late one night in the paper's city hall bureau. While one coaxed the night janitor into inebriation, the other entered the aide's office and rifled his desk, searching for airplane ticket receipts, thank-you letters, or anything that might have proven the company's financial sponsorship of the aide's junket. He found only telephone message slips indicating that a company official had called the aide both immediately before and immediately after the trip was taken. Further investigation was obviously necessary.

The reporter telephoned the manager of the hotel where the pair had reportedly stayed in Vegas. The reporter identified himself as a state policeman who wanted to know whether the men had stayed in the hotel and who had paid the bill. To the reporter's dismay, the hotel manager immediately announced that he was a recently retired trooper from the reporter's state. He began asking questions about the new kinds of handguns and a new organization plan in the works for the force. He also inquired about his former trooper colleagues. The reporter knew something about the force and was able to chat along for awhile, but in the end the manager would not reveal who had financed either the junket or the hotel stay, and the story was lost. *Caveat investigator.*

Another investigator might have pretended to be a police detective intent on arresting the two vacationers for passing bad checks. When told that two of his former guests had been fraudulent check artists, the manager would have summoned their payment record. No, he would tell the reporter, the check had not bounced. The reporter would sound puzzled and then ask which one of the two had written the check—the answer to this question being the sole object of the call—and the manager would name one of the two. The reporter would end the conversation by saying, "Oh, he writes legitimate checks, it's the other one who passes rubber money." And the reporter would know who had paid for the trip.

There are many other ways to worm information out of sources, some deriving from the mundane experiences of the average person's daily life, others from police interrogation manuals, Len Deighton novels, and Dale Carnegie courses. Some reporters time their calls to catch the source at a relaxed, unguarded moment, or at least at a less harassed, tension-filled time than during the nine-to-five business day. Sometimes they call in the evening after the source has had a cocktail and a chance to unwind; sometimes early in the morning before the source has had a chance to wake up.

Some investigators, knowing that many people see reporters as beaten-down subjects of tyrannical editors, attempt to elicit sympathy and information by explaining that they are subjecting a source to an interview only because "my editors forced me to come over here and bother you for no good reason." Or, they may beg for help: because they don't understand what's happening and are terribly frustrated by their own ignorance and incompetence; because they have wives or husbands and children to support and will be fired if they return without a story; or because they're new in town. (Considering the professional mobility of many newspaper reporters, this could be said with some truth every other year or so.)

If a reporter is unable to elicit sympathy from a potential source, it may be possible to inspire contempt, and the condescending carelessness that often accompanies contempt. If the source doesn't think the reporter will understand what is being said, he or she may be careless enough to answer all the reporter's questions merely to be done with it. Columbo, one of television's investigative wizards before he tripped on the Nielsen ratings, consistently employs this technique. The annoying, cross-eyed, confused look, which suggests he is paying more attention to his digestive system than to what his source is telling him, would probably have netted Peter Falk two or three investigative breaks a year had he switched from acting to reporting.

Playing dumb enabled one reporter to obtain some information probably unobtainable otherwise. The Cook County tax records showed only that a parcel of land under investigation was owned by someone using a trust number, a legal method of disclosing land ownership in Illinois. The reporter called the trustee-bank, identifying herself as the suspected land owner's secretary. Trying to sound distraught, she told the bank official that she had to finish typing a letter before her boss returned from lunch, but for the life of her she could not read the third digit in the number on the note her boss had left her. The bank official, talking to a woman he assumed was a lowly employee of one of the bank's more influential customers, gave her the third digit and then confirmed the rest of the number when she read that to him to "check the rest of the digits, too." Since the reporter had firmly identified herself as the suspected landowner's secretary, the fact that the number was read to her over the telephone in response to her "boss's" name confirmed her suspicions about who owned the land.

In this instance the telephone was a handy tool. But it can be a positive hindrance when a reporter is attempting to interview somebody who would rather not discuss what the reporter wants to talk about. Gestures, facial expressions, and body contact are important in establishing relationships; physical presence is important in discouraging the premature termination of a conversation. As one reporter told us, "I've been hung up on countless times, but no one's ever told me to get out of his house or office or has walked away from me at a bar." In addition, those little details of scene and personality which can lift a story up from the literary level of a laundry list can usually be gathered only in person.

One approach that often works well for some reporters is to simply and offhandedly ask for the information they want, as if it were the most routine request in the world. The implication is that only a scoundrel or crook would refuse the request. Should the request be refused, their answer is, "Really? You mean the state of Ohio is now refusing to let the public see its hiring records? How long has this been going on?" They whip out their notebooks and make the bureaucrat think his or her refusal will generate bigger headlines than Pearl Harbor. They make the potential embarrassment caused by the release of the information they seek pale by comparison. They paint a picture of a middle-level employee being mashed flat by a 400-foot tall printing press, and they keep a straight face while doing so. If that doesn't work, they go over the bureaucrat's head. Eventually, they will get to someone who depends on electoral popularity for his job and who will think twice before risking the anger of a television station or a large newspaper. If, for example, a patrolman won't honor a reasonable request, a reporter can keep going up the chain of command—to the mayor, if necessary.

Some newspapers pay for information. Many editors believe, however, that once word gets around that the paper is willing to pay, the flow of free information will dry up. Many papers, however, while refusing to pay directly for information, manage to have it both ways by dishing out small "stringer" fees to those who provide information in the guise of poorly written news stories. They also occasionally compensate people for providing information by putting them on a "stringer list." Other papers are occasionally willing to pay when the information they seek concerns illegal activities, in which cash traveling from hand to hand is the usual mode of exchange, or when the source provides information that can be verified, without paying, elsewhere. Especially in the underworld, however, an artificial market creates its own artificial suppliers, and if large sums are paid, people will begin "manufacturing" information to attract those sums. On some occasions, an intimation that money is available may work as effectively as an actual transfer of funds.

Many sources can be successfully approached and interviewed if they are told that the information they provide will be used either on an off-the-record or not-for-attribution basis. An off-the-record interview can provide valuable leads. Furthermore, it allows a reporter to ask other sources the same question on the record that was asked the first source off the record. The second time around, the questions will be more to the point because the reporter will already know a lot of the answers. And, armed with that information, the reporter is in a much stronger position to dig for other answers.

Experienced reporters don't always assume that when someone says something off the record that they should honor the request. In the same way that actors loudly stage whisper, sophisticated public officials sometimes talk off the record to add drama to their topic and thus generate more ink. In most instances, however, the source is serious about his or her name not being used. Often, a source will go on and off the record, back and forth, a dozen times in a brief conversation and it's hard for the reporter, let alone the source, to know what's mentionable and what's unmentionable. We've found that in most cases when a reporter wants to use something said off the record, it is possible later to persuade the source to agree.

On some rare occasions, off-the-record agreements are simply ignored. If a person walks up to a reporter and says, "May I tell you something off the record?" the reporter is in a fix. By saying "no," the journalist may miss a clue to a very significant story that could later be independently documented. If the reporter says "yes," the source may announce that he's just dumped a fifty-five-gallon drum of botulism into the water reservoir. By honoring the off-the-record agreement that reporter is just as responsible for the ensuing deaths as the source. On the one hand, investigative reporters have to strive to maintain their profession's trustworthiness, but on the other hand, they also must recognize their obligations to their readers and to the general population. Newspapers have occasionally printed stories containing criminal or semi-criminal off-the-record admissions, indicating, in the same paragraph in which the interview appears, that the conversation was conducted "off the record."

Often, when someone requests that certain remarks be considered "off the record," the reporter can suggest that if the source is just worried about remaining anonymous, he or she might wish to designate the remarks "not for attribution" instead. Many laymen confuse these two categories and ask for the more restrictive off-the-record treatment by mistake. This is unfortunate, since the not-for-attribution device is the more useful of the two. Attributing vital information to reliable, well-placed, but unnamed sources is an honored journalistic tradition. Some editors argue that if a source wants to criticize some other person or institution he should be "man enough" to stand up straight and tall and reveal his identity. But relying on unnamed sources is an investigative reporting technique of some merit, which Bob Woodward and Carl Bernstein of the *Washington Post* used to their considerable advantage.

One of the major sources of information for Woodward and Bernstein's Watergate investigation has been identified only as "Deep Throat." According to *All the President's Men,* "Deep Throat" was a friend of Woodward's who held an "extremely sensitive" executive branch job and who had access to information from the White House, the FBI, the Justice Department, and the Committee to Re-elect the President (CREEP). "Deep Throat" was so concerned with maintaining anonymity that he (or she) met with Woodward only in the wee hours of the morning, and then only in a parking garage or an obscure tavern. When there was some especially important information to impart, "Deep Throat" would move closer to Woodward in the semidarkness and whisper directly in the reporter's ear. Obviously, "Deep Throat" was completely convinced that Woodward would not reveal his identity either accidentally or on purpose. The problem of convincing sources that their confidentiality will be maintained can be handled in different ways.

Paul Branzburg, as a reporter for the *Louisville Courier-Journal,* wrote a number of drug peddling stories based on interviews with drug dealers whose identities he promised to conceal. Later, he was indicted for refusing to identify his sources and fled Kentucky to avoid prosecution and avoid naming his informants. He found sanctuary in Michigan where the governor refused to cooperate with Kentucky's extradition efforts. At the *Detroit Free Press,* Branzburg, whose appeals to the U.S. Supreme Court were denied in the Caldwell-Pappas-Branzburg decision, told his own story to a number of potential sources to convince them that he would go to great lengths to honor his commitments to them.

Telling a nervous source something like, "You will be astounded at the lengths I will go to to keep your name secret," or, "I haven't lost a source yet," or, "You won't even recognize yourself in the story," generally works well. The information a person may not tell a reporter outright can often be gleaned by asking, "Would it be inaccurate to print a story saying . . ." Then all the source has to say is yes or no, and for some reason many people feel more comfortable saying yes or no than uttering complete sentences.

In *All the President's Men,* Woodward and Bernstein reported using a subtle and convincing method of demonstrating their commitment to confidentiality when they began interviewing CREEP employees in the summer of 1972 to gather information for what turned out to be their Pulitzer Prize-winning exposé. In their late-night appearances at the homes of CREEP employees, they would say, "A friend at the committee [CREEP] told us you were disturbed by some of the things you saw going on there, that you would be a good person to talk to . . . that you were absolutely straight and honest, and didn't know quite what to do." When the person they were seeking to interview asked which fellow employee had given the reporters the lead, Woodward and Bernstein politely, but firmly, refused to reveal the name of their source. They explained that their refusal was based on a commitment to the protection of confidential sources, thus giving an implicit assurance that the person's identity would be similarly protected. The other reason for not naming names, of course, was that the reporters were operating from an employee list smuggled out of CREEP headquarters: their source at the committee was nonexistent. Nevertheless, it was a great door opener.

U.S. Supreme Court decisions allowing reporters to be jailed for refusing to reveal their sources have had little perceptible impact on those sources. Memory is short, and although several reporters were jailed shortly after these decisions were handed down, to the accompaniment of much hand wringing in the media, most sources were ignorant of the whole to-do even then. Since it is no longer front page news, even more have forgotten about the controversy.

If a source refuses to reveal information because of a fear that colleagues may consider it an impropriety, it is often convenient to obtain the information off the record, then return later and convince the source to allow the use of the information on a not-for-attribution basis. Perhaps newly discovered information, or newly found relationships among sources and principals in the investigation, may change what the source sees as his role in the matter.

Nothing prohibits a reporter trying to extract information from using several interview techniques at the same time, or from switching from one technique to another. Changing tactics is often the only course left open. When a reporter has exhausted all the tactics, however, or realizes that further attempts will only appear ridiculous, a good final approach is to ask who else knows about the matter. Unless the source snaps back, "I don't have the slightest idea," and terminates the interview, the reporter will either get the name of another source or have an excuse to continue the questioning, or both. By suggesting a potential source, the person being interviewed is left open to more questions: How does he know the other person knows about the matter? What is his relationship with the other source in the context of this investigation? These are questions the reporter could not logically have asked if the interview had continued to focus belligerently on the person's direct knowledge of the scandal.

A journalist can avoid the problems inherent in a one-to-one interview, of course, if the source can be heard in a non-interview context, such as a public meeting. Some of these public meetings are open to the public, other "public" meetings are closed. If a reporter is unsuccessful in getting in to an illicitly closed conference, it is standard procedure to begin a sort of ritualistic bobbing and weaving. The reporter may interview as many of the participants as possible, perhaps hint to one person that others have already given their versions of what went on (suggesting that a possibly distorted story will result unless this person gives a straight account), or the reporter may imply that others have already sketched an outline of the events in question and that only a few minor details are needed to fill in the gaps.

It is relatively rare that major scandals are revealed at closed-door "public" meetings, but as we have discussed earlier, tips are often spun off in great profusion by such closed discussions. And such pseudo-public meetings are often entered by determined reporters. Most states have public meeting statutes which require that certain types of meetings be open to the public, and many newspaper or broadcast lawyers can be convinced to threaten legal action against recalcitrant bureaucrats.

Some reporters attempt to find someone the source likes, make friends, and question the source through the friend. Suppose a reporter has heard a rumor that the grand jury has just voted to indict a local prosecutor, but that the convening judge quashed the vote and ordered the jury to hear more witnesses. Suppose the reporter knows that the judge and the prosecutor are members of the same political organization and are friends, but doesn't know any details, such as the charge or charges, who else may have been indicted, or even if the rumor is true.

The judge probably won't talk about it, nor will any of the special prosecutors, court reporters, or grand jurors. What the reporter needs is someone who can talk to somebody in a position to know what actually happened. A clever journalist will remember that many of the indicted prosecutor's assistants went to a certain city law school. The reporter then will call some personal acquaintances who attended that same law school, and ask if they know any of the assistant prosecutors. If they do, the reporter repeats the rumor and explains that he or she wants to find out for certain what happened. If the reporter is lucky, the prosecutor threw a tantrum on learning of the grand jury vote, and some of his assistants were aware of what happened and told their friends about it when they called. If the reporter is very lucky, the friends will have all the details—how the jury voted, what the charges were, who the others indicted were, and who was named as an unindicted co-conspirator.

11
Abbreviated Investigations

Not every investigative story is worth the time Woodward and Bernstein put into Watergate. This is doubly true if the story has already appeared somewhere else and an investigator is assigned to write a new and updated version of that investigation for his or her own publication. This chapter deals with investigations of this sort—recovery investigations—and with those original investigations which do not appear to be worth a substantial investment of time, which we call short-term investigations.

Short-Term Investigations

If a reporter feels that the human condition will improve only slightly as a result of a possible investigation, and that the time put into that story will drastically reduce the time available to pursue more worthwhile leads, there are three choices: drop the story; perform a major investigation; or, employ the techniques of the short-term investigation. What the editors think of a story, of course, will play a large role in helping a reporter choose among these possibilities. If a reporter and the editors disagree on the worth of a proposed investigative story—assuming the disagreement is purely journalistic and not based on management's desire to protect the person or institution proposed for investigation—there is little reason for that reporter to put a lot of effort into the story. It will surely be buried on page 58, substantially reducing whatever impact it otherwise may have had. Unless there is good reason to believe that the story might develop along the way into something the editors might appreciate, or unless there is some hope of free-lancing it to another publication, the reporter might as well go ahead with the quick once-over approach.

Out-of-town assignments—especially for a big-city reporter investigating a small town scandal—are often tailor-made for short-term investigations. The public records in a small town's archives are likely to be somewhat less complicated, and a lot fewer in number, than those a reporter would have to peruse doing the same investigation in a large city. (With luck, the town will also be the county seat, and the available public records will be centrally located.)

Once the reporter has sifted whatever information he or she can from the town's public records, it will be possible to use that information more quickly and effectively than in a larger jurisdiction in interviewing local officials and other prominent persons. Part of the reason for this is that small town officials are less bombarded by the media. They are also less likely to be the targets of the public service law firms, political groups, or aggressive neighborhood associations that bedevil public figures in larger cities. (Small town or not, however, some stories force their own pace. A story based on sources' memories will not be as solid as one buttressed by public documents, but under some circumstances, it will be a much quicker story to research. Some such stories require a reporter to interview people so closely linked with one another that they must be interviewed almost simultaneously, to prevent them from contacting each other and coordinating their versions of events. A long pause for research and contemplation between interviews could be disastrous in that situation.)

Short-term investigations are grounded on reliable informants, rapid-fire collection of information through interviews, and bluffing. A reporter should begin a short-term investigation by attempting to hypothesize the shape and structure of the completed story on the basis of what is already known, rather than attempting to draw a conclusion from gathered facts. This process is very similar to one used by scientists in attempting to explain various phenomena. First, they create a hypothesis that would explain the circumstance, then they draw a conclusion from that hypothesis that can be easily tested, then they test it.

This method was put to very good use by a U.S. Civil Service investigator, attorney Ben Joseph, while he was working on Chicago's Hatch Act scandal. Joseph correctly reasoned that since so many political appointees were employed by the Cook County Democratic machine, some mechanism must have existed to insure that people who hadn't actually worked precincts were not hired accidentally. When it came time for him to cross-examine various personnel department employees, Joseph stood so that he could see into the manila folders the witnesses brought with them to the stand. On the second day of questioning, his hand shot out like a snake's tongue and withdrew a patronage hiring authorization form signed by the mayor. Nobody had ever hinted to Joseph that these forms existed; he simply assumed they must to insure that the machine made maximum use of the approximately 40,000 payroll jobs at its disposal.

Joseph, incidentally, was an absolute master at luring sources and investigatees into believing that he was the least competent person they had ever met. He sported baggy suits and raincoats that he appeared to have slept in. He would ask people three or four questions that proved beyond all their doubts that he had absolutely no idea what he was talking about. Then, without changing mannerisms in the least, he would fumble his way through a question which would elicit an answer that would literally drop a judge's jaw open. A Philadelphia lawyer, Joseph penetrated further into the inner workings of the Cook County Democratic machine in the few weeks he was in Chicago than most Justice Department lawyers had penetrated in a lifetime.

Had the hiring authorization cards not been in those personnel files, Joseph would have lost nothing except perhaps the comfort of leaning against a court railing while questioning the witnesses. Although reporters are not afforded the luxury of compelling testimony in court, the same method works for them as well. What would the personnel man have said to a reporter who, in the midst of a rambling interview, asked to see the payroller's hiring authorization from the mayor's office? In nine out of ten tries, the official would have refused to show it. Perhaps he would have said something like, "Those forms are none of your business." The reporter would protest that they certainly were and there they would be, discussing the hiring forms. The reporter would know that such things existed just as surely as if he or she had seen one.

There's no reason why reporters on a short-term investigation shouldn't be influenced by their own journalistic assumptions, even if by assuming too much they risk losing the story. If the assumptions prove wrong, little is lost. And if the assumptions are correct, that bold hypothesis will have allowed a reporter to complete an investigation in a much shorter time.

By their nature, short-term investigations must rely heavily on the successful confrontation. So, it helps if the principal involved is someone who is not constantly in contact with reporters and thus is likely to tell the truth when interviewed. Public officials not used to dealing with the press sometimes fall into this category. For example, a Detroit reporter received a frantic telephone call one morning recently from the son of a dead Orthodox Jew. According to the son, the Wayne County medical examiner and his assistants, without excuse or explanation, had wrested his father's body from the hands of mourners who were in the midst of giving it a strict religious burial. Then, according to the son, the examiner performed an autopsy, although none was necessary, and did it on a Saturday, the Jewish sabbath. Both actions violated Jewish religious law. The son also charged that the examiner had removed his father's brain from the body without medical justification and had allowed the body to be buried without a head, in glaring violation of religious law and modern custom.

The reporter found these charges difficult to believe, since even the most bigoted medical examiner should have sense enough to avoid antireligious activities, at the very least in the interest of staying in office. So, only half-believing the charges, and not wanting to take the trouble to arrange all the interviews a major investigation would require, the reporter decided on the short-term approach: he'd simply confront the medical examiner and watch his reaction.

At the interview, the reporter was astonished to hear the examiner not only admit the son's charges, but then deliver a lecture on the problems caused by dead Jews. While the reporter took copious notes, the doctor complained that the only way the county could satisfy Jewish burial requests would be to "bury dead Jews immediately and then dig them up again. . . ." He went on to say that "Jewish people present a unique problem. First you have to talk to the brother, then the wife, then later the rabbi. . . . How long is the Talmud anyway?" According to the medical examiner, burial policies in Wayne County were "set up by Irish Roman Catholics" and "inflexible." He then admitted that there had been no real reason for performing an autopsy on the dead man, nor for removing his brain.

With these admissions, all the reporter then needed to do was to check the hospital's diagnosis of the deceased's lengthy illness with the surgeon who had operated on him, and confirm the son's interpretation of Jewish religious law with the area's chief rabbi. Since the medical examiner had already admitted the son's charges, the reporter didn't need to interview the mourners and the examiner's aides for corroborating accounts.

The Wayne County commissioners reacted furiously to the story. They summoned the medical examiner, interrogated him until they were satisfied the story was accurate, and forced him to resign. Four hours of work had resulted in the unseating of the official, and an end to some anti-Semitic burial practices.

The medical examiner's loquaciousness made him a particularly easy target for a short-term effort. But even laconic officials can be successfully unseated with something less than a lifetime's work. One Wayne County commissioner met such a fate in 1972. Although the commissioner, Ed Jones, represented a low-income district on Detroit's west side, he lived in a luxury high-rise apartment on the city's east side—at least that's what his political enemies charged as election day approached. The reporter they told knew election-time tips were generally untrustworthy, but it was a serious charge. If the rumors were true, Jones was violating a state law requiring county commissioners to live in the districts they represented. In addition, Detroiters were very conscious of residency at that moment; city police were fighting hard to invalidate a city ordinance requiring them to live within the city limits. So, although overloaded with other assignments, the reporter decided on a short-term investigation.

His first step was to interview a few of the people who lived near the slum apartment Jones claimed he occupied. They said they rarely saw the man. The reporter then telephoned Jones's secretary from a handy pay phone, implied that he had to reach the commissioner at home on a political matter of the utmost urgency, and was given Jones's true home telephone number. He then called the telephone company's public relations man, who told him that, based on the digits, the number couldn't possibly be located in the commissioner's district but might well be located in the east-side high rise. By calling the secretary of state's office, the reporter learned that Jones's driver's license bore his business address rather than the home address he claimed. That information didn't prove he lived in the high rise, but it didn't prove he lived where he was supposed to live either. Satisfied that his suspicions—although aroused by politically inspired rumors—were well-founded, the reporter visited Jones's high rise. When he knocked, Jones's door opened to reveal the beer-drinking politician wearing a bathrobe and talking to a scantily clad woman. The reporter turned on his heel and returned to his office to write the story. County Commissioner Jones lost his re-election bid in the fall, 1972, election. Total time on the story—two hours.

Reporters shouldn't let a few such short-term successes sour them on research, however. They may occasionally waste time on the rigorous and extensive background research that is part of a full-scale investigation only to find the principal in the story ready to tell all to the first person who asks a leading question. But research is never wasted. Even if the principal spills all before the reporter has had a chance to impress him with his voluminous knowledge, the reporter's research will enable him to understand his subject's admissions in depth. With this understanding, the reporter can recognize and pursue any new leads revealed during the interview. Research will also protect the reporter against the possibility that the subject will squirm away to relative safety with a partial admission that the reporter, with only partial knowledge, has no choice but to accept as the whole truth.

Recovery Investigations

Recovery investigations usually begin when a reporter staggers into the newsroom one morning, staggers over to the coffee machine, picks up the competition newspaper, and reads the headline: "MAYOR ADMITS TAKING $1.2 MILLION IN KICK-BACKS." The first thing the editor will want to know is where the reporter was when the mayor confessed. That question will be asked with a straight face. Then the editor will say, "We oughtta do something." That something is called a recovery.

Bad recoveries are easy: all the reporter does is rewrite the opposition's story, after making a call or two to see that they didn't make it up, and put a second-day lead on it. Bad recovery leads usually begin, "Authorities Tuesday are investigating charges that . . ." Good recoveries require considerably more effort and ingenuity. The reporter should set out either to add substantially to what the other paper has published or, finding their story false, knock it down. (A reporter shouldn't knock down a competing newspaper's story out of mere spite; any uncontrollable urge to do so should be treated by counseling.)

Almost every investigative story has holes in it and those holes are what a reporter builds the recovery on. There is almost certainly some aspect the other reporter overlooked, sources and officials who weren't interviewed, and even facts omitted because of a lack of space, news judgment, or nerve. A recovery reporter will generally have between six and eighteen hours—maybe a day, if the editor isn't hysterical—to gather those facts and reactions. The editor will probably assign the recovery to a reporter who already knows something about the topic or at least knows many of the public officials involved. If, however, there is no one on the staff with an obvious head start on the story, the reporter assigned to the recovery should count on skipping lunch.

First, of course, the recovery reporter should read the initial story very carefully. If the competition dug their story out of file cabinets, the reporter will have to get to those file cabinets right away, before some prosecutor or investigative agency subpoenas them or ties them up. It is a good idea to find out which bureaucrats helped the other journalist gather information and persuade them to reveal whatever they showed the first reporter, plus whatever they think may have been missed. The recovery reporter should do as much of the story as possible by telephone, since it's faster and will quickly uncover any errors the competition has made. (The person under investigation may be screaming foul very loudly by then.) Since the reporter will be under time pressure—perhaps trying to do in one day what another reporter took two months to do—there is good reason to politely, but frankly, cut people off if they begin to ramble.

Some reporters interviewing the subject of another investigation use the ruse that they think the allegations are untrue, and indicate that they are trying to clear the person's name. For example, they say that they heard the same rumors a long time ago and decided then that they were untrue; or they confide that they think the other newspaper or broadcast station took a cheap shot. Some subjects approached in this fashion will reveal more to the second reporter than they did to the first.

Frequently, however, the subject of the investigation will be unavailable, on the advice of an attorney. Or, if the recovery reporter does find the subject, the only comment may be, "I'm afraid I can't comment since this whole thing may end up in court." The reporter might ask what's going to happen in court and the subject will probably hint that he's considering suing the other newspaper (never that criminal charges may be filed against him), on the theory that the threat of suit will scare the recovery reporter away. Unless the recovery lead will be, "Dog Walk Mayor E. M. Bezzlement refused comment Thursday on charges that he accepted a $1.2 million stock option from Wing-and-

Prayer Airlines shortly after one of their 747's made a forced landing in the reactor core of the city's nuclear generating plant last November . . . ," the reporter should not settle for a "no comment."

Some reporters ask why there is no comment and if the person isn't afraid that a "no comment" will cause readers to believe the other paper's charges. If there is still no comment, they'll badger the lawyer and ask what the defense will be. If the attorney claims not to know, they'll ask why, then, he or she thinks the client is innocent. If the lawyer hangs up, they'll call back.

Some reporters will call the subject's friends and political associates to solicit their reactions. They'll ask those associates if they knew what was going on, and why not. They'll call the local investigating agencies even if none were mentioned in the original story. If those agencies are working on the case, they may have cooperated with the original reporter. There's no reason why they shouldn't share their information with the recovery reporters as well. If they balk, reporters ought to get tough and tell them official agencies shouldn't play favorites.

Some will even go so far as to call the original reporter, explain that they've been assigned the recovery, and congratulate their colleague on the story. It's sometimes wise to ask the original reporter for any recovery suggestions. Parts of the story, for example, may have been watered down and the investigator might wish to see those sections printed in full somewhere. After all, once the story is out, the recovery reporter might be regarded not so much as an enemy but as someone who can help expand the scope and impact of the original investigation. If, on the other hand, the recovery reporter is satisfied that the story is untrue—not just in minor details, but substantially untrue—he or she may wish to find out if the account was deliberately falsified and why.

A good recovery, then, accomplishes four things. It verifies or shows to be false the other media's account, up-dates it, adds to it, and puts it in perspective. It retains the good parts of the original and improves on its weak points. It performs a tremendously useful social function, almost as useful as the original, by reinforcing the good investigation and serving as media criticism for the bad.

Writing a recovery is also very useful for the recovery reporter who will make a lot of new contacts and learn as much in a day or two about a new subject as would be possible in weeks of work as the original investigator, and who may find whole new fields to cultivate in the process. Finally, writing a recovery may inspire the reporter to research and write initial investigative stories to such high standards that the opposition will be hard pressed to improve on them. While it is a goal rarely achieved, it gives an experienced journalist a warm glow to read a recovery in another paper that begins, "Authorities launched an investigation Tuesday into charges that . . .".

12
Confronting the Principal

Any reporter who spends more than two weeks on a story is likely to have accumulated a lot of seemingly disjointed information. It may be hard to tell whether the story involves three people or seventy-one, whether it's a corrupt-system story, a man's-inhumanity-to-man story, or something entirely unique to journalism. But somewhere along the line, preferably before the interviews, and definitely before beginning to write, the reporter will have to organize the story. If the story is complicated, as most good ones are, it will need to be outlined (at least a list of the high points made), and may even need a few charts and diagrams. Then, there is no substitute for sitting back and looking for connections, explanations, relationships, and causes and effects that may have been missed at first. Listing the various events in chronological order may help. Perhaps the reporter hadn't previously noticed that someone admitted knowing a certain parcel of land was for sale in May although the land was not publicly listed until July. That knowledge would certainly give the buyer an edge over others interested in that parcel, and the reporter would then want to find out who told the buyer it was available and how that person found out.

At the outlining stage of an investigation, a number of very important things must be accomplished. By completely and accurately analyzing all the information, the reporter should not only understand exactly what happened, but also understand the motives of everyone involved, and the details of what was done. Everything done on a certain date may have been done purposely on that date. Why? The amounts of money involved were not determined randomly. Why so high; why so low? Whose complicity was necessary? When the number of answers begin to approximate the number of questions or when the left-over questions begin boring everyone involved or when the editor says produce or move on to something else, the reporter will have to

quit asking questions of a mirror and prepare for the major interviews.

This heralds the confrontation. The reporter must approach the
subjects of an investigation, outline the story, and elicit their
reactions. It's only fair, after all, to hear and report their side of
the story. If the reporter handles a confrontation correctly, it's
possible not only to verify the information already in hand, but to
expand it and thus round out the story. Some methods for accom-
plishing one or both of these ends are the subject of this chapter.
In the ideal case, if the file cabinets and sources have been good
to the reporter, there will be but one question for the principal:
"What do you have to say for yourself?" It is more likely, however, that there will be a few missing details that only the subjects
of the investigation can supply and the reporter will have to work
to worm those details out.

First, a word about timing. Suppose a source tells a reporter
that the parks commissioner owns the company that sells swimming pool chlorine to the city at inflated rates. The reporter picks
up the phone, calls the commissioner, and screams, "I've got you,
buddy. I know all about the chlorine connection and I'm going to
set up a tent in your office and root throuugh your file cabinets
until I nail you. Why don't you just save me the trouble and
confess right now?" The commissioner is likely to say, "I have no
idea what you are talking about," and threaten to call a cop if the
reporter doesn't stop being a nuisance. It's possible that the commissioner will hang up calmly, dash to the files, rip up every
chlorine contract, and type new ones. Then they will be back
dated, signed, stamped, photocopied, and left on a sunny window-
sill for two days to age.

When the reporter calls back the next day the commissioner
will be out, as will everybody but the secretary, who will say it is
impossible to just open the files, no matter how vividly the reporter
describes the state's wonderful public records act. When the reporter finally does contact the commissioner a week later, they
will set up an appointment for the week after that. Finally, when
the request to go through the chlorine contracts is made, the
commissioner will lean back, look very businesslike, and say: "I'm
fully aware of the public records act and I'll be glad to show you
anything you'd like to see. However, I can't take the time to
supervise you as you go through the whole filing system and we
must protect the records since they belong to the taxpayers. Nor

can I put óne of the secretaries on it as they are all very busy trying to get the summer swim program going. If you have a specific document in mind, and can give me either the invoice date or record systems billing number, I'll be glad to comply with the law and show it to you. Oh, you don't have any dates or billing numbers in mind? Well, then, I'm afraid I can't help you." There now. The reporter must get a court order, spend a lot more time and money, or give up.

Instead, the reporter might have called the commissioner's chlorine company, told someone there that he or she wanted to . buy a summer's supply of chlorine for a pool the size of those in the park, and asked for a rough estimate of the cost. Suppose the answer was 25¢ a pound. Then, while the parks commissioner was out, the reporter could visit the commission office and tell the business manager about a "discovery" that a nearby town is pay-ing $5.00 a pound for chlorine. The reporter might say that the records of two other towns showed that they are paying 30¢ to 45¢ a pound, and that just one more set of records is needed to verify that the $5.00-a-pound park district is being wasteful. It might help—if the reporter is in a white, Republican town—to tell the commission business manager that the wasteful park district is in a black, Democratic town. Of course, if a reporter decides to employ such roundabout tactics, they must precede the confronta-tion to be effective.

In many ways, preparing to confront the subject of an investiga-tion is similar to what a trial lawyer does in preparing to cross-examine a witness. It is said that good lawyers never ask questions of a witness for which they don't already know the answers. While that is a luxury rarely afforded investigative reporters (or lawyers), a reporter should be sufficiently prepared so that no answer is completely bewildering. A list of questions and their possible an-swers, plus questions based on those answers, should be drawn up before the confrontation interview. The only way to avoid being stumped by an answer is to anticipate the situation and be thoroughly prepared.

For example, suppose the president of the local police benevo-lent association says, "Sure, we have cops out selling member-ships. But they only do it when they're off duty, so there's nothing wrong with it." Even if the answer comes as a surprise, the re-porter could respond that whether on or off duty, everybody knows that the men selling the tickets are cops, so it's still a shakedown. Armed with a copy of the department's rules of conduct, however, the reporter could quote verbatim: "Police officers are not permitted to solicit money or valuable considerations for any purpose, in any manner, whether on or off duty." Then the policeman might respond by saying either that it's a ridiculous regulation or that the department doesn't enforce the rule, equally intriguing answers for story purposes.

A good way for a reporter to prepare for a confrontation is to ask a friendly prosecutor to take a look at the material prior to the final interview. In many cases, a good attorney can point out laws violated by the subject of the investigation of which the reporter was ignorant. While it is good to prove that someone has acted unethically, it is better to prove that the person acted criminally. Moreover, it is always wise to avoid accusing someone of violating a repealed or otherwise inoperative law. Perhaps a court has recently declared the law unconstitutional or interpreted it so narrowly that it no longer applies. After talking to a lawyer, the reporter may end up with a story about how a company or union dove through a legal loophole to wallow in the public trough rather than a story about how so-and-so broke such-and-such a law.

In preparing for an interview, the reporter should learn as much as possible about the subject's background. Knowing a person's past not only makes for a more useful interview, but can make the story much more interesting: "Twelve years ago, I. Will Steele ran for county tax collector on the promise of cleaning up scandalous Sewerville. Now he's . . ." It's important to try to get some background from the subject himself, if possible, even during the confrontation. Everybody writes about *how* he did it. Rarely do reporters exert sufficient effort to find out *why* he did it. To this day, former President Nixon's conduct in the Watergate affair has been much better reported than his motives—whatever they were.

An experienced reporter reels off as many investigative findings as possible during a confrontation with the subject of the investigation. Not only is this fair, since it gives a chance for rebuttal, but it also allows the principal to correct whatever minor errors the reporter may have made that, if left in the story, are likely to detract from its credibility. For example, if the reporter writes that a politician was given one hundred shares of preferred stock as a bribe, the politician, when interviewed, may point out that it was common stock or that he was given a stock option instead of stock.

It is better to correct such mistakes before publication than after.

Sometimes investigative subjects will raise an argument or disclose some fact that effectively destroys the story, proving, for example, that nothing wrong was done, no laws were broken, and nobody was hurt. Or, more commonly, they will argue that something wrong was done, but they aren't to blame. They may argue that they had a right to do it; that the whole thing is a coincidence; that there is nothing illegal or immoral about it; that everybody does it. Perhaps they will say that their staff did it and that they didn't know about it until the reporter mentioned it; that their end justifies their means; that they will sue if it is ever mentioned; or, that the reporter will shortly discover that the story is untrue because the principal is a friend of the publisher.

Some of these arguments may be rational and effective. If any of them convince a reporter that the original concept of the story is wrong, then that concept should be revised. Going ahead with a story that has been robbed of its original justification will only make the reporter and the newspaper look silly. But the newspaper, the public, and the reporter should not lose a genuine story just because someone argues that everybody does it, all companies operate like that, and the whole world is corrupt anyway.

The argument that "everybody else is doing it" should carry as much weight with the investigative reporter as it carries with a traffic cop. The obvious response is that exposing one person or institution may discourage others from acting similarly, an argument that supports the nation's entire judicial system. After all, it is said of many successful investigative reporters that their very appearance in a government office means that thousands of dollars less will be stolen from the taxpayers that day. The "everything's relative" argument is harder to refute. One writer vividly portrayed the persuasiveness of this line of reasoning in a *Harper's* wraparound article entitled "Corruption: Now You See It, Now You Don't":

> He (the subject of your story) will fatigue you with questions of degree. He will advocate small elasticities—pushing a boundary, stretching a point, bending a truth, extending a justification. At any given moment he will assure you that outright transgression is at least three more fudges away. If you grow impatient, he will lecture you on the social machinery, arguing that it runs only because of the tolerance of slight accommodation. . . .

He will maneuver you off the ground of principle and onto the ice of rules. While you slide around, he will calmly explain why certain rules don't apply or don't mean what they seem to. If you haven't lost your balance by then, he will hand you the pencil and ask you to draw the line. When you do, he will erase it. He will counsel you to reasonableness and ask you to draw it again. Again he will erase it, challenging your fitness to live in a relativistic universe. . . .

When their conduct is challenged, even obliquely, most people will take whatever opportunity they are given to defend themselves as vigorously as possible. Very few people do something they think is wrong. It may be wrong, and they may call it wrong when someone else does it, but because they are the ones doing it, they persuade themselves that it is okay. And some reporters find it difficult to remain unswayed when they confront a fellow human being who, in effect, begs for mercy. On the other hand, some investigative subjects will feel that they did what they had to do to advance their own personal best interests, and would just as soon nobody else knew about it. Investigative subjects of this sort make a reporter's life easier by refusing to comment and allowing the findings to stand uncluttered by denials or rationalizations. More often than not, the reporter will face the subject of a story only briefly, perhaps for as long as it takes him to say "no comment" or to gloss over the charges and refuse to discuss it further. Occasionally, an investigative subject will threaten legal action if the story appears in the paper. Rather than flying off the handle, an experienced reporter will ask why the subject isn't as pleased as most people seem to be when told their names might soon appear in the paper. In other words, the reporter will use an attempt to end the interview as an excuse to prolong it.

A small percentage of journalists argue that investigators should not only confront their subjects but later show them the story written about them, or the institutions they represent, before it is printed. It has been counterargued, and we think effectively, that if a reporter with weak-kneed editors shows a story to the person who is featured in it, it will only cause trouble. The subject of the story is likely to call on the editors and the publisher. If they haven't closely followed the course of the investigation, its subject may be able to convince them that the reporter is all wet. Particularly if the principal and the publisher belong to the same country club, the reporter is better off letting the publisher read the story when it appears in the paper. Then the publisher will be defending a fait accompli when the subject of the story calls—as well as trying to stave off a libel suit—and will be more likely to take a hard line in the reporter's defense.

Different interviewing techniques must be used with different subjects, depending on how much they know the reporter knows (and on how much the reporter knows they know he knows) about their involvement in the matter under investigation. Some reporters find it helpful to scatter significant questions among a number of insignificant ones to mask the purpose of the interview and perhaps avoid a quick brush-off or panicky denial until the interview is well-advanced. (For different reasons, this same tactic is employed by the psychologists who make up personality tests. Sprinkled among such questions as, "What street do you live on?" and, "Where were you born?" are questions like, "Do you hate blacks?" and, "Should children be beaten?") Stories about intricate financial dealings are most adaptable to this scattered question technique. When financial dealings become very complicated and interlinked with applicable laws and regulations, it is relatively easy to conceal the trend of many of the questions—especially when a reporter seems to be an admiring financial writer doing a "success story."

A related distraction technique is to touch on issues that have emotional meaning but are unrelated to the investigation. An example might be the person's divorces or romantic attachments. By referring to these matters as if intending to write about them, the reporter can distract the principal while probing for answers to the important questions.

Sometimes camouflage questions will even turn up leads to new stories a reporter might never have discovered otherwise. Two *Detroit Free Press* reporters conducted a confrontation interview in late 1972 with a Michigan state representative who was campaigning for the elective post of Detroit Recorder's Court (criminal court) judge. The reporters were questioning the candidate about a story, already confirmed through documents and sources, that the representative had been seeking the early release from state prison of two mobsters even though he was not their attorney and had had no previous legitimate contact with them. The implication, of course, was that he owed the mobsters a favor for something illicit they had done for him in the past. The reporters scattered their questions concerning the mobster-related activities in among a number of other questions on what they thought were relatively non-controversial aspects of the judicial candidate's life. For instance, the candidate, who was divorced, was said to be friendly with a divorced woman. Hardly, one would have thought, a sensitive matter. But when the reporters asked the candidate about her, to divert attention from what they considered more important questions, he leaped to his feet and shouted, "Who I sleep with is none of your god-damned business!" ending the interview. (His outburst also ended—for several moments—all other conversation in the exclusive restaurant where the interview was being held.) When the reporters told their editors of the representative's reaction to a mention of his girl friend, a third reporter was assigned to look into the matter. The upshot was the exposé of the woman payroller who did nothing, discussed earlier.

Investigators should not be embarrassed about using such camouflage questions, no matter how transparent they may seem. After all, without knowing what the reporter is really after, the principal won't know which questions are serious and which are not. Even if an investigative subject begins to grasp what the reporter is doing, there's no need to stop. Perhaps the person fears exposure of a multitude of sins and will still have to guess which area is under scrutiny.

Pressure of a different sort can be brought to bear by having two reporters present at the confrontation interview. One reporter can pepper the principal with sharp, accusatory questions while a colleague, cautioning, "Take it easy, be objective," asks softer but still relevant questions. (The police frequently use this good guy-bad guy technique in extracting confessions.) If the principal is anything but a computer, he or she may blurt out honest or at least accommodating answers to the friendly questioner as a protection from the nasty one. The principal may even see cooperation as a way to influence the outcome of what seems to be a competition between the reporter who likes him and the reporter who is out to get him.

Some reporters even choose to augment this two-on-one technique by seating themselves far apart, forcing the principal to keep snapping his head back and forth. This will contribute to an impression of being alone and defenseless and greatly increases the chance that the truth will be blurted out. The state representative who reacted so violently when his girl friend's name was mentioned, incidentally, recognized this ploy immediately. When the two reporters initially sat down, almost facing each other, the representative motioned angrily straight ahead and told them they had better sit together—"So I can look at both of you boys at once"—or he would end the interview. Experienced investigators don't make it obvious.

If a reporter decides against taking another reporter to a confrontation interview, he or she may discover that the principal has not been so foolhardy and has asked one of his cohorts to sit in on the session. In this situation, the reporter is at a tremendous disadvantage. Not only must answers and comments from two people be dealt with and kept separate in the notes, but it is also likely that the reporter's preparation won't have been sufficient. Thinking up new questions while taking notes is an exhausting and usually unprofitable procedure. About all a reporter can do in this situation is to delay. By asking a few questions that will produce answers you already know or don't care about, it is possible to gain a little time to catch up on note taking or question preparation.

A reporter lucky enough to have a friend in a governmental investigative agency, who has cooperated on other stories, may be able to convince the G-man friend to come along on a confrontation interview and lend the implied weight of the agency to the questioning. If an organized crime investigator or an FBI or an IRS man is sitting next to a reporter during the interview, the principal may fall into the erroneous but tongue-loosening assumption that it is one of those agencies asking the questions, not a lone reporter.

Few government agents, however, are likely to agree to this procedure. But if a reporter is working in the same general field, or on the same specific investigation as a government agency, friendly agents might be willing to ask questions or obtain documents during their own interviews that are more relevant to the reporter's story than to their investigation and to pass the information on. Cooperation, however, works both ways. Journalists should beware of a government agent who wants information on someone they don't think is doing any wrong or who they think is performing some positive good. It is sometimes easy to feel pressured to turn over that information because the agent has helped out on a few confrontation interviews in the past.

Experienced investigators find that a friend also comes in handy when two people who should not be allowed to coordinate their answers must be interviewed. Sometimes a reporter is able to do this by telephone, if a call to the second person can beat the warning call from the first. It is possible to win this speed dialing competition with a push-button phone if the first person is still using a dial model or if the reporter dials the second person on another phone before hanging up on the first. But, as we discussed earlier, a reporter can't see the subject's reactions nor use physical presence to keep the interview going if they are linked only by a telephone wire. (Of course, that way the other person can't see the reporter's nervous tics either.)

The obvious solution to this dilemma, but one that is often ignored because reporters feel they must do all the work themselves, is to brief a colleague and then conduct the interviews simultaneously. Reporters not connected with the investigation can often be counted on to solicit better answers, anyway. For instance, if the subject of the investigation is at all well known, it is likely that another reporter once wrote a favorable article about him and could be persuaded to visit again and ask the nasty questions that need to be answered. The person will be more likely to respond to a reporter responsible for a puff piece than to a reporter who may be preparing something uncomplimentary.

Nothing, however, should prevent a reporter from being as kind as possible to the subject of an investigation. It is possible to indicate that there is nothing wrong, in the reporter's opinion, with what the subject did, although the story as eventually written may take the opposite point of view. For instance, if a reporter has just asked a politician about a secret interest in a business firm and the politician seems reluctant to respond, the reporter can interject, "You know, it doesn't matter to me. If people didn't invest in businesses nothing would ever be manufactured." Or, if the reporter has asked an official about taking a bribe, one approach might be, "Don't worry about it. If I did stories on all the people I know who have taken small gratuities, I'd have nothing but penny ante stories all the time. I'm after much bigger stuff, stuff you can help me with. . . ."

A reporter can attempt to mitigate the implied accusations of a confrontation interview by reserving the hard questions for that part of the person's conduct which is under investigation and praising other aspects of his or her work. This may sound a bit forced, but it is a rare confrontation interview at which the average reporter asks all the important questions. Generally, after studying the principal's answers, the reporter will think of more. By being pleasant and complimentary to the subject during the confrontation interview, the reporter may be able to call back, ask those additional questions, and have them answered. But if the reporter was insulting during the interview, it will be rough going to get the subject to answer any more questions. If an investigation is running as a series, the wise reporter will solicit all the needed answers before the first installment appears and alienates the subject forever.

Some reporters go so far as to tell the subject of a story that they believe his or her version of the events, and that the only reason they are doing the interview at all is to substantiate their belief in the person's honesty. Rone Tempest III, formerly an investigative reporter in Oklahoma City, used this technique to gain admission to the mansion belonging to the man responsible for the scandal-ridden Four Seasons nursing home empire. Tempest used the interview to gather colorful details about the mansion and its luxurious furnishings, which he used to good effect in his story. (See appendix, "The Four Seasons Saga.")

Another ploy reporters find useful is to tell the subject of a story that they think the person was wrong but suspect there were other forces at work, perhaps sinister people higher up or tragic circumstances, such as debts, alcoholism, or family problems. The reporters sympathize, list their own troubles, say they know what it means to protect a job and that is why they have gone through all the trouble to investigate—so that other people don't get so hassled. If it turns out the subject of an investigation was "just taking orders," so much the better. It means the possibility of an even deeper, more incisive story about who gave the orders.

If an investigator can manage to don a feature writer's smile, it is sometimes possible to get in the door. If, for instance, the subject violated all but 2 of the 805 articles of the city building code in constructing a housing project, a clever reporter may be able to imply that the subject of a Sunday supplement feature will be "one of the rare men who can profitably turn urban renewal rubble into gleaming new houses for the poor."

Other ruses are often difficult to pull off, but can vastly improve the quality of a story. Without knowing everything, a reporter can drop a couple of hints about the investigation and then tell the subject, "Well, I've got a job to do and have to go ahead with it. I'm sorry about it because I've always liked and admired you.

What I'm really interested in, though, is a sidebar to run along with the investigative piece which would tell our readers what you feel about being caught, your regrets perhaps." Approached in this way, the principal may cooperate, thinking the story will be told in any case. With luck, he will try to recoup as much ground as possible by "coming clean." A reporter may even say that all the investigative work on the story was done by another reporter and that he or she is there only to hear and record the principal's side.

During an interview, an experienced reporter does not always insist on directing the conversation. The more the principal talks without the reporter's direction, the more likely it is that important new topics will be uncovered. A Chicago reporter once began an interview simply by telling the general counsel for a large railroad company that he was about to write a story about how the railroad was selling land it wasn't legally allowed to sell. (The land had been granted by the state to the railroad for railroad purposes only.) The lawyer could hardly dismiss the reporter with a "no comment" for fear that would enrage certain politicians who would summarily snatch the land back. Instead, he set out to convince the reporter that the project was good for the city. Before he had finished, he had also admitted that neither the railroad nor those who were buying its land were paying property taxes. Had the reporter belligerently insisted on directing the conversation, the subject of taxes might never have been broached.

Despite the efficacy of these approaches, reporters need not always treat their investigative subjects with great deference or conceal their natural antagonism toward someone who may have been, for example, forcing low-paid city employees to finance an expensive re-election campaign. Arrogance is sometimes an effective technique. Some reporters advise telling the principal that a lot of the reporter's time will be saved by talking at this stage of the inquiry, implying that cooperation will make things easier on him. Some reporters say that others involved in the scandal have talked, and that they can't understand why he or she is the only one who isn't cooperating. Does the person have more to hide? Does the person want to be the only one mentioned in the story who refuses comment? If others have admitted their roles, it may be possible to convince the remaining holdout to cooperate by spelling out a few details from their statements.

Even more blatant techniques sometimes work, especially with less sophisticated investigative subjects. If someone has committed a possibly criminal offense, a reporter might want to drop very subtle hints that somehow the prosecutor is involved in the investigation. If the prosecutor is, so much the better. There's no law against talking to the prosecutor and detailing an investigation under way. It might help in producing follow-up stories, anyway, if the prosecutor launches a public investigation. Once a reporter becomes fairly well known as an investigator, it may be that people are very reluctant to talk no matter what approach is used. A reporter in this bind may want to ask another reporter to take over questioning the subject of a story.

It would be a mistake, incidentally, for a reporter to assume that questions must always be straightforward. Reporters should do what lawyers do: ask leading questions. A certain fact or relationship can often be confirmed by asking a question that presumes it is so. For example, suppose a reporter wants to find out if A knows B. A person-to-person call placed to B at A's number may provide the answer. Or, the reporter might call B, say that A's number doesn't answer, and ask for a confirmation that the number is correct. Of course, as investigative devices grow more and more complex, there is always the possibility that the subject of an investigation will see through one of these reportorial machinations. Some may have even read this chapter.

Any reporter, however, worried about looking foolish in pursuit of a story should remember the case of Illinois Secretary of State Paul Powell. Powell's every deed, and many of his words, conveyed the same message to the media: "Sure I'm a crook. Just try and catch me." No one ever did. And when Powell died, $400,000 in cash was found in his closet. It is too bad somebody wasn't a bit more curious about the secretary of state's office while Powell was still alive and running it.

13
Gadgets

Most reporters are familiar with the paraphernalia of the profession: pencils, note pads, typewriters, telephones, and coffee machines. Recently, reporters have also taken up the use of slide rules, pocket calculators, cassette tape recorders, polygraphs, and even various kinds of wiretaps and bugs. Even though the average investigative reporter would never need or want to use a surreptitious bugging device, some idea of the current state of the art is useful in reporting on another person or agency's use of such devices.

Although most reporters could never take a picture worthy of publication, cameras and pictures can also be a help. Roger Flaherty, a reporter for the *Chicago Sun-Times,* once used some incriminating eight-by-ten glossies, stacked on top of a pile of unrelated photos, to insure himself of a successful interview with a team of shoddy home repair racketeers. Even tiny Minox and Yashica cameras will photograph documents under a flashlight if a tripod is used or the camera is braced. It is important to use a very fine grain film, however, or the prints will be unreadable when enlarged. These cameras are useful because they can be concealed in a king-sized cigarette pack and because they have viewfinder adapters that disguise the direction in which the camera is being aimed.

Pictures can be taken surreptitiously even with a full-sized 35mm camera. Experienced photographers are able to set, aim, and shoot pictures with one hand while the camera hangs at their side. If they wish to take more than one picture, or not get caught taking the first picture, they simply cough, sneeze, or drop something on the ground to mask the sound of the shutter clicking.

Even though it is rare for a reporter to take pictures for a story, it is often the reporter's responsibility to insure that the accompanying photographer gets the necessary pictures. Most investigative stories are substantially improved by at least a head shot of the subject of the story. Often such pictures must be taken at the same session in which the investigator confronts the principal with the findings of the investigation. If the subject does not wish to be photographed, it obviously should be postponed until after the interview is concluded. On the other hand, if the subject is not yet aware that the newspaper is preparing an embarrassing story, a fact that may come out as the interview progresses, it is best to take the pictures at the beginning of the interview.

Many experienced photographers are tremendously competent at getting subjects to consent to being photographed. Sometimes, however, people simply refuse to have their picture taken and will not willingly get within 100 feet of an investigator's photographer. Such problems simply call for a little more creativity. When the subject is appearing in court (where pictures are not permitted), for example, many reporters will simply notify the person's lawyer that the news photographers will be waiting outside the front door. They then station their photographer at the rear door.

The use of tape recorders requires a bit more finesse. During the 1968 Democratic National Convention in Chicago, a local TV station was caught attempting some bugging. It is reliably reported that the *Chicago Sun-Times* managed to bug a session of the Illinois delegation at the same convention, although everyone involved in the *Sun-Times* caper has denied it. Perhaps those involved do not wish to discuss the incident because they feel some embarrassment, in retrospect. One journalism review editor, who sought in vain to gather enough information to write a story about the bugging incident, argues that a party caucus is not like a city council meeting, where the public business is being conducted and where the public's right to know is protected by law. The distinction, however, between a political meeting of politicians and a governmental meeting of politicians is quite fine and perhaps meaningless. Convention delegates are chosen, directly or indirectly, by the voters of the respective parties and those voters, it seems to us, have some right to know what their representatives are up to.

In a similar instance involving public officials, two Louisville, Kentucky, reporters were arrested in 1974 outside a room in which the Louisville police chief was meeting with officials of the local police union to discuss a very sensitive matter. The following day, Barry Bingham, Jr., publisher of both the *Louisville Courier-Journal* and the *Louisville Times,* issued a public statement on the

matter. Because the statement addresses many of the ethical problems confronting investigative reporters, it is reprinted here in its
entirety.

Since the two reporters arrested last night at a Fraternal Order
of Police meeting are facing a misdemeanor charge in the
courts, it would be improper and irresponsible to comment on
the facts of their case, as others have done, except to say that
Mr. Hicks and Mr. Fineman have entered a plea of innocent to
the charge of disorderly conduct and these newspapers stand
squarely with them in this plea.

However, there is a very important moral issue involved in the
incident, and it's one of which all of us here, as news men and
news women, are constantly aware. That is the question of
eavesdropping to get a story.

It is my feeling that eavesdropping is morally wrong. Period.
But I want to stress that this does not mean I place any blame
on Mr. Hicks and Mr. Fineman or any of their editors for the
attempt to cover the closed FOP meeting from an adjacent
room. To the contrary, the blame—if, indeed, "blame" is to be
assigned—rests with me.

As editor and publisher of *The Courier-Journal* and *Louisville
Times,* I am committed to a policy of aggressive investigative
reporting on issues that are of vital interest and concern to the
public. To be complacent or unconcerned about important
issues affecting the community would be an act of grave
irresponsibility. This is true for any newspaper but especially
true for us, since *The Courier-Journal* and *Louisville Times* are
the only metropolitan daily newspapers serving this community.
The reporters involved in last night's incident were exhibiting
the vigorous enterprise and competitive spirit that is not only
the unalterable policy of these newspapers, but also a standard
of excellence in journalism that we constantly strive to achieve
and for which these papers are nationally recognized.

Furthermore, it should be pointed out that the topic under
discussion at the FOP meeting—allegations of improper or
perhaps illegal "bugging" of police cars—is of vital interest and
concern to the public. It is an issue that has been brought
under public scrutiny in recent days despite the best efforts of
the FOP and others concerned to shroud it in secrecy. I think
everyone would agree that it is an issue that requires searching
public examination. Granted that the FOP has a right to a
private meeting, but that right is diluted somewhat when it
involves a confrontation with the Louisville Chief of Police on

critical issues of public interest that are already in the public
domain. Indeed, if the responsible officials involved had been
frank and open with the public from the outset, as they should
have been, last night's regrettable incident would never have
occurred.

In fact, what is involved here is almost a textbook clash
between the First Amendment right of a newspaper to collect
news and an individual's or organization's Fourth Amendment
right to privacy. The Fraternal Order of Police has forced the
question to the courts, and it will be decided there. But it is my
position that when public servants (police officers) meet with
their publicly appointed leader (Chief Nevin) to discuss the
question of electronic bugging devices paid for with public
funds and placed in a public vehicle, then the public's right to
information at least rivals the organization's right to privacy.

Finally, I understand that Sergeant Denton and the Fraternal
Order of Police have filed a formal complaint with the Federal
Bureau of Investigation concerning the reporters' actions at last
night's meeting. I urge Sergeant Denton and the organization to
expand that complaint to include other allegations of improper
surveillance—especially those discussed last night by the
Fraternal Order of Police so that all these issues may be
resolved before the public in a court of law.

Both reporters—Jerry D. Hicks of the *Times* and Howard D.
Fineman of the *Courier-Journal*—were found not guilty of
charges of disorderly conduct six months later. A federal grand
jury which heard evidence on the charges of electronic eavesdropping refused to indict the pair.

Obviously tape recorders can go places where a reporter can't,
such as to secret meetings. Some reporters have given recorders
to "friends" attending the meetings, because tapes are more accurate than recollections. A tape recorder can also be planted in a
room prior to a closed meeting, and attached to a simple appliance
timer ($10 to $15 for a quiet one) that turns it on. (It would be
unwise in this situation to use a recorder which beeps when a
cassette is completed.) Reporters have also been known to use
suction cup microphones, of the type used to record their own
phone conversations, placed against a window or thin wall to hear
what the naked ear cannot.

When taping a conversation in which the reporter does not have
the other person's permission—a practice which is legal in some
states—it may be a good idea to conceal the recording, even if the

reporter is acting within the law. There are a number of ways to do this. There is, for example, a long-playing tape recorder on the market that looks like an attaché case, and even has some room on top for papers. With the handle down, it records everything in the room. (Reporters who don't want to buy such an expensive case may be able to borrow one from a child guidance counselor; children have even less patience and understanding than Mafia dons.) Other cassette recorders can be concealed under a belt, in the small of the back, with the microphone hanging by its cord down the sleeve. With this arrangement, it's necessary to keep the cord taut so that the mike doesn't fall out of the sleeve.

There are other uses for a tape recorder, of course, beyond getting into a closed meeting or secretly getting a verbatim record of a conversation. A tape recorder permits the reporter the luxury of not taking notes. The principal's comments can be closely listened to and further questions can be jotted down as the interview proceeds. Indirectly, a tape recorder may even draw out a recalcitrant source. Suppose the conversation begins with the recorder on. After a few grave but meaningless questions, the reporter leans forward, dramatically turns the recorder off, and says something like, "Why does someone like your boss, who was already making a good buck, do something as risky as that?" The reporter doesn't say the conversation is either off the record or not for attribution, but the source may assume it has become so.

Aside from jail, there are several dangers to avoid when using recording or note-taking equipment. Some people are very flattered to be recorded, and in their zeal to be immortalized on tape will ramble on ad nauseam. Others are simply afraid to talk into a tape recorder, even though a reporter's notes will generally carry as much (or as little) weight as a taped conversation if the matter goes to court.

A frightened, defensive source or principal may balk when a reporter takes out a note pad. When conducting interviews during the summer of 1972 with numerous employees of the Committee to Re-Elect the President (CREEP), Woodward and Bernstein reported that once admitted to their houses, "notebooks were never used." Some interviewees, once they catch sight of a standard reporter's notebook, clam up or chase the interviewer out, and any note-taking alternative, no matter how transparent, is often preferable. For this reason, many reporters take notes on the edges of newspapers they just happen to be carrying, or even borrow a scrap or two of paper from the person they're interviewing. Some reporters put pencil to paper only when an interviewee is saying something he or she would like to see in print. Of course, the reporter is actually writing down whatever damaging admissions slipped out a few moments before. At the actual moment of slippage, the reporter writes nothing and maintains a poker face. Other reporters attempt to avoid taking any notes at all in the interviewee's presence. They develop bladder conditions and run to the bathroom a couple of times during each interview so they can scribble down everything in private. This cautionary advice presumes, of course, that the people being interviewed feel defensive. If they are proud of what they did, or think the reporter is, there isn't a gadget made that will scare them out of talking.

A person who has been under investigation for some time and knows it, will often have a recording device at the climactic interview, whether it's visible or not. For that reason, reporters must be very careful to say nothing during a confrontation interview that could be held against them in a libel suit. It is particularly important to avoid anything that could be used to bolster a contention that the reporter harbored some malice towards the principal or any of his associates, or that the reporter has anything but enormous respect for the truth of the facts being gathered. If both sides are using recorders, incidentally, it's convenient to start them simultaneously so that they can also be changed simultaneously. Finally, since some tapes are defective and won't record on one or both sides, every cassette should be tested before an interview.

Besides tape recorders and notebooks, several other gadgets are worthy of mention. A cheap device for detecting unsophisticated phone taps can be bought for about $10. It simply measures line resistance and lights up if there is a third party on the line. It will also light up if someone picks up an extension phone on either the reporter's end or the other party's end. The more sophisticated taps, however, do not materially affect resistance and cannot be detected this easily. (We are informed that some government agencies have taps so sophisticated that they need not puncture the insulation around a phone wire, either in the office being bugged or on the pole outside.)

Another device uses the phone line itself as a microphone. Rooms can be bugged, even long distance, by first dialing the number of the phone in that room and leaving the tape on after the bugee has hung up on a "wrong number." In these instances, the bugee can break the connection by dialing another number. Parabolic microphones can pick up quiet conversations from long distances much as telephoto lenses take close-up pictures. Running water and all those other counter-devices employed on TV don't work, incidentally, since the voices can still be heard when the sound of the running water is removed electronically from the tapes.

We would hesitate to proceed in this somewhat sleazy, cloak and dagger vein except for the uneasy feeling that eventually such devices will be readily and cheaply available and will become a very common part of politics and business. After all, how many reporters wouldn't use a good phone tap if they could buy one for $20? Or a $15 microphone that looks like a dead cockroach and could be surreptitiously dropped under a mayor's desk? Some reporters we know are already beginning to think in these terms. One fellow we know has been talking for years about buying or borrowing some cheap transmitters, hiding them in used TV sets, and hiring some slum-dwelling teenagers to ride around with the sets in the back seat of a car until they are stopped by the cops. Then the reporter plans to find out what the cops do with the confiscated "evidence." We also suspect that newspaper reporters are going to find themselves using computers more and more in the years to come, particularly if their newspaper owns one.

Sometimes a little science or even a friendly testing laboratory can help the average investigator, particularly on consumer affairs stories. During the height of the 1973 energy crisis, one enterprising but not very astute television reporter in Detroit lifted the lid on the underground storage tank of an abandoned service station, stuck a long pole in the hole, pulled it out, smelled it, and triumphantly announced the discovery of 60,000 gallons of hoarded gasoline. The next day, a newspaper reporter lowered a weighted pop bottle into the tank. He found eight feet of water with two inches of residual gasoline floating on top. The moral: gas floats on water.

Now that polygraph evidence is being admitted by some courts under special circumstances, reporters should make more use of the devices commonly called lie detectors. While the devices cannot prove a person to be telling the truth, beyond a shadow of a doubt, they can help a reporter avoid printing outright lies. A competent technician and device can be rented for between $100 and $150. Should a source refuse a lie detector test, it's wise to think twice before using the information. Sometimes even the suggestion of a polygraph test will flush out a liar.

14
Dropping the Investigation

Reporters who give up on difficult stories after checking two or three sources and finding nothing useful quit too soon to pierce the facade of anything well concealed. On the other hand, reporters who continue pursuing fruitless leads for weeks after it has become apparent that the story they are seeking doesn't exist, or is unprovable, waste time and discourage their editors from spending money in the future on investigative reporting.

Once a reporter has decided to embark on a particular investigation, he or she must be prepared for numerous discouragements. Many investigations will not result in stories: there are just too many rumors, jealousies, and fabrications in the world. And while the reporter is finding out whether a story is going to be one of the many failures or one of the few successes, colleagues and readers will ask questions like, "Do you still work for the paper?" or, "Say, are you an editor now?" or, "I haven't seen your name in the paper lately. Something wrong?" Many investigations move so slowly that an average of only one publishable, relevant fact may turn up per day, and that fact may be a very small piece of the puzzle. There will be many days when the reporter will find nothing or will discover that a trail leads nowhere.

One major psychological advantage that kept Woodward and Bernstein going on Watergate was that when they started their digging they already knew that several men, one of whom claimed to be a former government agent during a period of Republican rule, had been arrested while breaking into Democratic Party headquarters. Rather than coming from anonymous tipsters, this information surfaced in court. Woodward and Bernstein knew there was a story there somewhere. Their only worry—and it was a major worry—was developing the rest of the story. Also to their advantage was the freedom to write the story as it unfolded without resorting to a series format. The readers already knew that the break-in had occurred and presumably would be interested in more information as soon as it could be uncovered.

Obviously, an investigation should be dropped when a reporter becomes convinced that the original information was inaccurate; that the subject's actions are neither immoral, illegal, nor novel; or, that no matter how much effort is expended, the reporter will not be able to nail down the story. The difficulty comes in deciding when any of these is true. Far too many journalists decide which stories should or shouldn't see print or be broadcast on the grounds of "what's good for the public"—an indication of the amount of ego involved in journalism.

Unreliable information is part of a normal day's work for most investigators. Nine out of ten tips that apparently point toward investigative stories actually point nowhere except the wastebasket. An inspiration for much unreliable information are attorneys who charge outrageous fees explaining to their clients that someone had to be paid off. The lawyer then wins the case on either its merits or a legal technicality, but the client thinks it was won because the fix was in. Consider the case of a drunk driver who pays a lawyer $5,000 to bribe the judge. The lawyer has the case continued five times, telling the client the judge is holding out for an extra $3,000. Eventually the harried arresting officer doesn't show up and the case is dismissed. At first, the client is glad it took only $5,000 instead of $8,000, but a few months later he or she decides it's time to get even with the judge by calling an investigative reporter. After talking to two or three such persons the reporter may become convinced that the judges are on the take, even though they are not. What may have prompted the journalist to investigate was the sources' sincerity; after all, they were sure the judges were taking bribes.

On some occasions, a reporter will drop a story without knowing whether it is true or false. It may be that, even if the story is true, it is of such minor importance that it would not be worth the time required to do it. The reporter may have tried a preliminary confrontation with the principal and failed to elicit any encouraging information or admissions, or perhaps the relevant documents and witnesses are spread out over such a large geographical area that the story would cost more money to complete than it would be worth.

Sometimes reporters report their findings to officialdom rather than to their readers and then write a story about the beloved officials having corrected the situation. This can happen quite by accident if an investigation into some situation begging for reform comes to the attention of the responsible officials, who hurriedly make the necessary changes and then call a press conference to herald their good work before the reporter can write the story.

A reporter may ask a mayor why one of the staff was allowed to commit some awful deed, and a half hour later the mayor may fire the aide. This is probably not a bad happenstance as far as public policy is concerned, but a reporter should never take the results of an investigation to a public official with the understanding that if the official speedily rectifies the situation the story will not be printed. That makes the reporter an accomplice in whatever malfeasance was committed and deprives the public of knowing if the government is doing its job properly.

Some investigators drop stories when they learn a competing newspaper is on to the story and far ahead of them. A strong case can be made for that decision. If they are reasonably sure the competition is competent and will report the scandal as thoroughly as they could, they might as well work on another story. That way, at least two stories will be written instead of one. If, in a white heat to beat a rival to the punch, a hurriedly inadequate story is produced, the reporter does little but blunt the impact of the findings, and perhaps make it easier for the subject of the investigation to squirm out of danger. Of course, a reporter can take up an investigation where another reporter leaves off. There may be sources the first reporter doesn't know, or doesn't know well enough. A fresh approach can produce a recovery that is even better than the original story.

A reporter should never drop an investigation so completely that notes are discarded, sources are forgotten, and the whole idea is lost. One never knows when the information gathered during a partial investigation will suddenly become very useful. Weeks or months later, the roadblock which stymied earlier efforts may disappear. Or, perhaps some official agency will later investigate the same area and the reporter can use that partial information in writing an analysis or as background for a straight news story. When dropping an investigation, some reporters make it a habit to write up their notes and file them in the newspaper's library among the relevant clips so someone else will stumble across them in preparation for another investigation of the topic. (For example, Detroit's port is an on-again off-again subject of investigations because, like many other ports, it seems to be a magnet for racketeers. Over the years, the *Detroit Free Press* has done stories and investigations—some of which panned out and some of which didn't—on the port. As a result, its library has provided reporters with an ability to do thorough background pieces on major waterfront developments as they occur.)

Before filing away notes and putting the story on a back burner, a reporter should take one last look. Perhaps there is a good feature, analysis, or hard news story in what has been found. For years, Detroit reporters had heard and passed on rumors that the inner-city suburb of Highland Park, Michigan, was the most corrupt place on earth. Finally, in late 1974 and early 1975, two reporters spent three months checking the allegations, all of which proved to be vastly overblown or completely false. But their notes were so full of charges and countercharges by the time they decided their research was no longer worth pursuing, that they were able to turn the relatively minimal investigative findings into a readable account of political and economic incest in a small town.

Even if a reporter's material doesn't lend itself to this kind of treatment, he or she ought to look very closely at what has been discovered to see if it contains the germ of a story requiring investigation in a different direction. In any one of a number of American cities, for example, the belt of "bombed-out" urban renewal land may spark a journalist's curiosity, prompting a suspicion that the city officials owned that land and condemned it to get high prices for their own properties. An investigation may show this is not the case. But what may have been uncovered is the story of how racist officials—or officials representing racist constituents—discourage black families from moving into white areas by creating an urban renewal no-man's land between white and black neighborhoods.

Suppose a reporter hears that certain city contracts are being awarded without bids. By finding out which people are being awarded these contracts, and what their relationships are with the contract-awarding officials, the reporter may hope to find a brother-in-law or two in the pot. Instead, it may be that in some areas certain sorts of contracts—such as professional service contracts —are awarded quite legally without the submission of any bids. The reporter may end up with a story not about illegal contract awards nor about officials awarding contracts to their friends and relatives, but perhaps an even more significant story about lazy bureaucrats awarding contracts to the same old firms again and again, without searching out the best contractual bargains for taxpayers' funds.

Another example of how a search for one investigative story can lead to another is provided by Robert Enstad of the *Chicago Tribune*. When a source told him that driver's license examiners were taking bribes, Enstad took a driver's license test himself and purposely did very badly on the driving part. The examiner, instead of asking for a bribe, passed him without any illegal payment, in spite of the reporter's shoddy driving performance. So Enstad did a story on how he tried to fail the test and couldn't—not the story he had in mind, but a good story nevertheless.

Almost every investigator wonders at one time or another whether there's any story worth writing hidden in that pile of notes. When such doubts set in, it is often wise to try the story out on a neutral observer or two. Sometimes a reporter can become so enmeshed in the intricacies of a story, or one side's point of view, that it is hard to see what the facts will suggest to the reader who hasn't been immersed in researching the story. When a reporter is delving into a technical field, where a generalist's knowledge alone does not suffice, there may come a point in the investigation when both sides seem to make equal sense, especially if the story involves a lot of numbers. Or, after spending so much time talking to those who seemed to be the perpetrators of a scandal, and finding them to be pleasant, likable people, the reporter may begin to wonder who's really who. Many reporters give up at this point. It's easy to do. All the reporter has to do is to tell the editors that if continued, the investigation will yield only a confusing, somnambulatory article detailing charges and countercharges—that the investigation isn't going anywhere.

Rather than abandon the story, however, and waste all that effort, a reporter's best course is to enlist the aid of a third party, preferably a knowledgeable neutral. A situation ripe for this approach occurred a couple of years ago in Detroit when some citizens began to complain that the new houses going up on vacant lots in among their own houses were rickety "cracker boxes" that would bring local property values down. The reporter assigned to the story talked to one of the neighbors, an old-time construction man, who denounced what he called scandalous inadequacies in the construction of the new houses. The reporter then consulted a city housing inspector, who admitted that the houses weren't well-built, but insisted that most modern construction was equally shoddy. At this point, the reporter should have consulted with experienced people from other construction firms (not firms in direct competition with the company putting up the cracker boxes), housing inspectors from nearby cities, or architects to obtain an informed, neutral assessment of the work in progress. But he didn't, and the houses were built, for good or for ill.

Another story susceptible to this approach dealt with a refusal by federal officials in 1972 to approve an allegedly less costly redesign for Detroit's new federal building. The report implied that officials rejected the proposed new design because they were being pressured by Senator Robert Griffin, who was running for re-election, to stage a ground-breaking ceremony prior to the election. And a ground-breaking ceremony could not be held unless building plans had been approved. The report dealt sensitively with what appeared to be evenly balanced arguments on both sides. The federal officials argued plausibly that with inflation, the time spent on writing the new design into the construction plans would offset whatever savings were inherent in the plan itself. The story also pointed out that proponents of the redesign included contractors who would profit from its adoption. Although politics was obviously a factor in the rejection of the new plan, what the article badly needed was the testimony of a neutral, out-of-town architect to provide the paper's readers with a nonpolitical view of the merits of the competing arguments.

If outside, neutral testimony will not help a story and dropping it becomes the foremost thought, the reporter should take a minute to consider what dropping it will do to relationships with sources and potential sources. If a reporter drops a story out of laziness, and it is rumored that it was because of political pressure or other professionally dubious reasons, the flow of tips may come to a complete halt.

The best thing to do with a good investigation that is temporarily in bad straits is not to drop it, but to think more about it and work harder on it. Call more people, read more documents, talk to more sources, discuss the story with fellow reporters, get more ideas on how to keep it alive, and keep the faith.

15
Writing Investigative Stories

Writing styles for investigative exposés range from the quasi-legalistic to the new journalistic. Further, some of the articles are so short that readers are given the impression the topic is of only marginal importance while others are so long-winded that they are read in their entirety only by the paper's copy editors. Between these extremes there is some very good, clear, lively writing. For a variety of reasons, however, the stories that derive from investigative reporting are usually not as well written as most other newspaper and magazine articles.

Perhaps investigators become so totally absorbed in their projects and find them so fascinating that they believe the reader will share their interest and hang on every word, ill-chosen or not. Sometimes investigators put so much of their mental energy into the investigation itself that none is left over for the typewriter. Often, we fear, they are so relieved of tension when the threads of their yarn are finally knit together that they merely go through the motions of writing, in the belief that somehow the story has already written itself.

Some of the quasi-legal briefs that pass for investigative stories are probably written by reporters anxious to impress their colleagues, or anyone else possessing a high boredom threshold, with technical jargon and legalspeak. The new journalism pieces are too often attempts to dazzle with footwork: "Look ma, at all the uncovered facts!" What it all comes down to, we think, is that there are too many reporters willing to spend 400 hours investigating something who then write up their findings in four hours so they can get on to their next exposé. All too often, the stories are practically incomprehensible to readers who are not already experts in the areas covered by the investigation.

It may be difficult to accept, but most readers cannot name their two U.S. Senators, have no idea who their state representatives are, and think zoning is something that happens on football fields.

Some Chicago reporters refer to their hometown as "no-shit city" in the belief that newspaper readers see a scandal on page one, read the first paragraph, say "no shit," and turn to the advice columns or the sports page. Journalists say that readers display this attitude because there have been so many scandals for so many years that the stories have become repetitive. What is unexplained by this theory is that the advice columns and sport pages are equally repetitive. Perhaps the reason so few people bother to read many investigations is that they are so poorly presented.

In this spirit, we suggest some fairly simple rules for investigative writing. First, it is important to write to the length warranted by the importance of the material and likely reader interest in it. Sometimes editors will want a river of verbiage stretching on for days or weeks to justify the amount of time invested in digging up the story. Or, perhaps the editor wants to keep the story short because it is scheduled for publication the same week a comely suburban heiress goes on trial for the axe murder of her milkman boyfriend. In this case, the reporter should certainly ask to have the piece delayed until she is acquitted or elopes with the bailiff.

Experienced reporters do not overestimate their readers' education or knowledge about an esoteric field. They explain in clear, simple language why a particular example of conflict of interest is against the law, how property taxes are determined, what effect a future land use plan has, or the rationale for spot zoning. On the other hand, it is important not to underestimate the reader's intelligence either. The average IQ in this country is a little over 100, among newspaper readers it's probably around 110, and among those likely to read investigative stories it's probably even higher. You need not insult readers by informing them, for example, that a lot of people like money.

When possible, a story should be related to its effects on the readers. Comparisons and analogies are particularly useful to illustrate just how the wrongdoing is costing them tax money, or how it relates to the destruction of their neighborhoods. If, for example, the city designated 30 acres of some hapless neighborhood as an urban renewal area and then delayed rebuilding it, point out that the loss in property taxes, building permit fees, and payroll taxes would have hired 10 more cops and 20 more school teachers. Or, explain that if the local judges worked a 40-hour week like everyone else, the county prosecutor could have tried another 1,000 felony cases instead of plea bargaining, which would have had the effect of getting perhaps another 300 muggers, burglars, and rapists off the streets. (See appendix, "The Patronage System.") Not every story, of course, need be linked so concretely with the reader's life. Stories dealing with sex, glamour, or immense wealth are gobbled up voraciously by newspaper readers even if their lives are not affected at all.

Writing an investigative story is not like preaching a sermon. There is no reason to assume that the audience is on your side, or even that it wants to be in its better moments. Every allegation should be supported with as many facts as possible; every instance in which the subject of the investigation has violated either the law or accepted practice should be pointed out. Even when this is done, reporters will find that many readers display a surprisingly high level of tolerance for corruption. It's a reporter's job to show why and how the corruption that's been exposed is bad for them, for a significant number of other people, or for an individual they can relate to.

Reporters who have spent week after frustrating week trying to corner the subjects of their stories for confrontation interviews, or locate public documents hidden on purpose by obstructionist bureaucrats, are often angry at the principal of their investigation even if the investigation uncovered little. But in most cases, readers are not interested in the trouble and frustrations a reporter suffered. They're interested in the story itself. Unsupported allegations or gratuitous insults directed at the subject of an investigation will always work against the reporter. Readers will not be interested in those opinions unless the reporter is overwhelmingly famous or respected. They're interested in the facts the reporter has uncovered, and insults thrown at the subject of the story will only get in the readers' way.

There is no need to cram every single fact uncovered into the story. The journalist is writing a newspaper story, not a legal brief. If a lawyer were to describe the nature of proof generally accepted by newspapers and broadcast stations, the "preponderance of evidence" cliche would probably be cited. Not necessarily enough to convict anyone of anything, but enough to reveal the substantial truth to the mass of readers or listeners. So unless every bit of evidence gathered is independently sexy, or necessary to the story, the reporter should be discriminating.

Excluding extraneous information from an investigative story is important because most investigative stories are too long. No one reads many of them except specialists in the field, the close friends or bitter enemies of the subject of the story, and the subject himself. For example, in 1971, *Newsday*'s famous investigative team produced a fascinating series on Nixon pal Bebe Rebozo's finances and land dealings that was at least thirty newspaper pages long. The number of Long Island newspaper subscribers who were willing to read thirty pages about Bebe Rebozo's bank accounts while their children ran through the living room and their television sets broadcast prime time football could have danced on the head of an editor. In any case, the massive investigation didn't seem to hurt Rebozo any. Perhaps its length reduced its impact.

It is possible, however, to write at great length and still interest many readers. New journalists like Norman Mailer and Tom Wolfe have shown one way. Wolfe's magazine articles read like novels. He tells us what the subject of the piece was thinking when he did such and such, and what he was wearing while alone in his study. Some of this information can be deduced from what is generally known about the person, the rest comes from asking him. Investigative journalists would be wise to try the same approach. Even the dreariest financial scandals are perpetrated by real people, often by colorful, charismatic spellbinders. Their personalities are as much a part of their corrupt schemes as the stocks in their portfolios. People like to read about people, and the more human a reporter can make the subjects of an investigation, the more reader interest that investigation will generate.

So, let's assume a reporter has packed the story with colorful details, supported every assertion with enough but not too many facts, eliminated egregious criticisms, and crossed out the sermons. The article may still be ruined by poor layout and display. Nothing is as discouraging to the average newspaper reader as a mass of gray type. Yet many newspapers give their best investigative stories this kind of deadly play. Simple common sense would surely dictate spending 10 hours to lighten an investigative story with art, or cleverly lay it out, or break it into readable parts so it can be run as a series, when 200 hours were spent researching and writing it in the first place.

One of the reasons news magazines have attained such immense popularity over the years is their coupling of good writing with charts, graphs, and photographs in an attractive layout. Newspapers often say they can't match such graphic achievement because of the pressure of daily deadlines. Yet even when daily deadlines are not a factor, effective graphics are often ignored. One exception was a *Philadelphia Inquirer* story by Tony Lame revealing that a member of the board of directors of the Philadelphia 1976 Bicentennial Corporation apparently had voted to purchase land in which he had a direct financial interest. The story's readability was aided by an aerial photograph of the general area on which was superimposed a mug shot of the board member with lines leading from his photo to his holdings.

Television has demonstrated its own creativity in presenting investigative and analytical reports that may jog some newspaper editors out of their ruts. In a recent story on housing projects and their use as tax shelters by the rich and powerful, one television network portrayed the participants in one such project as a group of people sitting around a card table. They played a simple game with stacks of play money and toy apartment buildings to illustrate each step in the complex process of drawing a tax profit from each housing project.

The device made use of television's obvious strength: its ability to broadcast moving pictures to its viewers. But even investigative reports printed on flat, smudged news pages can be made more attractive. Printing an investigative report in series form breaks up its bulk, allows the use of more creative page make-up, leaves room for more imaginative art, and allows multiple repetition of the main themes of the story. Not the least of the advantages of a series is that it allows the use of such end-of-installment questions as, "What happened to the pay-off money?" and "Did the blonde disappear with the dough?" Corny? Yes, but useful. When the various parts of a series are given unequal play by the news desk on different days, however, the readers may miss a crucial point if installment four is buried on page 63. Also, the longer a series runs, the more likely it is that a major breaking news event will come along and drive the story deeper inside.

Readers who might not tackle a massive, one-shot investigation may well be tempted to by the creative use of sidebars. These might detail past scandals the individuals were involved in, similar scandals elsewhere, other scandals involving the same project or institution, or possible legal remedies for what has taken place, all spiced up with their own graphics. The *New York Times* performed an amazing feat of sidebarism when the story broke that one of Mayor Lindsay's top aides, James L. Marcus, a city commissioner, had taken a $10,000 kickback to award a reservoir refurbishing contract to a certain firm on orders from a Mafia figure, Tony "Ducks" Corallo. ("Ducks" got his nickname because he had avoided jail so often.) The *Times* ran sidebars which described the investigation in detail, traced Marcus' rise in the city bureaucracy, profiled the FBI man who supervised the official investigation, detailed the refurbishing work on the reservoir, and explained why the feds were prosecuting rather than the state. Perhaps stretching the point, the paper also included a sidebar on the infamous Tweed Ring and a reprint of the famous Thomas Nast cartoon, "Who Stole the People's Money?"

Since most newspapers are committed primarily to daily news coverage, rather than long-range investigative coverage, an investigative reporter can almost never lose by taking advantage of some current event as a news peg for an investigative story. Some investigative reporters have been lucky enough to dream up an idea for a story, work long and hard at it, and then have it ready just as some disaster made the story topical. They are then able to impress their colleagues by producing, "overnight," a major investigative report related to an occurrence everyone else learned about just the day before. A Detroit reporter was lucky enough to have finished an investigative story on the misuse of city-owned art works on the same day that a vandal in Cambridge, England, defaced Rubens's "The Adoration of the Magi." The reporter's paper may have been the only one in the world that day to run an investigative story on possible damage to local art works concurrently with the story about the damage to the Rubens.

Some investigators argue that making investigative stories too appealing tends to cheapen them, and that a story should be aimed exclusively at those expert enough to understand the issues involved and influential enough to end the illicit practices the story reveals. But the powerful are more likely to do something about a scandal if they are convinced that the masses are about to storm the palace. If the stories are dull, readers will ignore them and so will experts and responsible officials.

16
Objectivity

In squabbling over whether a story is "fair" or "objective" too many journalists have lost sight of the more important criteria—accuracy. Does the story mirror the events? Does the reader come away with the same information he would have if he had covered the event at the reporter's side? In researching the story has the reporter asked the same or even more pointed questions than the reader would have asked had he been there? Has the reporter taken every precaution to insure that the event was reported the way it actually occurred?

Mature, allegedly experienced journalists go round after round debating whether a story is objective, whether the language is suitably neutral, and whether it is fair to the subjects of the story. Such debates are most entertaining when everybody involved is using a different definition of "objective." To the great distress of journalists, and to the even greater confusion of readers, the definition of objectivity varies widely from newspaper to newspaper and from city to city. What is considered fair at the *Manchester* (N. H.) *Union Leader* is not necessarily considered fair at the *Boston Globe.*

At any rate, nobody who has thought about it for more than ten or twenty seconds believes that perfect objectivity is attainable. It is not expected on the sports, society, real estate, or fashion pages. It is not attained by scientists or IQ tests, and it should not be expected from investigative reporters. We do not mean to suggest, of course, that on second reference the person under investigation be called "the crook" or "that snake." Relevant, clearly stated, and well-ordered facts can speak for themselves with very little help.

The very nature of an exposé presumes a subjective, not objective, viewpoint, i.e. that whatever is exposed is wrong, either morally or legally. It also presumes that whatever is exposed is important enough to be exposed. Not everyone will agree, for example, that all corruption is bad. Many political theorists, and even muckraker Lincoln Steffens in his later years, have argued that a certain amount of bribery, backscratching, and thievery is necessary to oil the machine of society. Exposés of such activities imply that there is something wrong, that the activity should cease.

Objectivity, nonetheless, is not without its uses. The reporter who goes into an investigation with rigid preconceptions about what will be discovered is not only likely to fulfill those preconceptions (even if they are false), but is also liable to overlook evidence of other activities that may be even more reprehensible. Objectivity builds credibility, making it easier to get investigations past nervous editors and to attract more (and more accurate) sources. Furthermore, any biases a reporter may have will be apparent to the readers. If a reporter investigates only liberal politicians or institutions, for example, or if the stories are written much more dramatically than the findings justify, a knowledgeable reader will realize it and the reporter's work will accomplish very little beyond impressing his or her relatives.

Striking a balance between listing seemingly unrelated facts and writing a story that reads like propaganda is one of the most difficult things an investigator tries to do. The closer a reporter is to a story and the longer it is researched, the more difficult that feat becomes. Rarely will a reporter uncover a story so clear that its undisputed facts can be simply stated without background, interpretation, or analysis. Most investigative stories are too complicated for the average reader to understand unless they are written in precise, simple language that details what happened, what it means, why it happened, what effects it has on the readers, and whether or not any laws were broken.

Take the classic example of the politician who rezones land he secretly owns (or which is owned by people who give heavily to his campaigns). Most readers will be able to understand that the politician used his office to make himself or his friends a lot of money. But many will not connect these zoning practices with the fact that most cities and suburbs are very poorly planned: factories adjoin once peaceful residential neighborhoods, busy shopping centers are located across the street from grade schools, and the main thoroughfares of most suburbs have become ugly neon forests. A reporter who goes too far, however, in tone or choice of language will lose everything—including, possibly, a libel suit. Underground newspapers, for example, often publish exposés in very important areas, some of which are accurate and some of which are not. But they employ loaded language, shrill tones, and draw conclusions in such a way that the careful reader is led to believe that the conclusion came first and supporting facts were found later. Consequently, the underground press in this country has been effective in exposing abuses only to the extent that its leads are picked up, verified, and amplified by the more established press.

Investigative reporters also have to be careful to maintain their objectivity when under pressure to reach a certain conclusion. Perhaps the source is a personal friend, or perhaps the newspaper's management has indicated in advance what conclusions it would like to read. This is sometimes referred to as the "hired gun mentality." Some publishers send their investigators out to do hatchet jobs on their enemies. Typically, the reporter is casually told, "I think So-and-so is a crook. Why don't you take a few weeks and look into it?" The hired gun then goes out and comes back with a story that says So-and-so is a nefarious crook, philanderer, and child molester. The publisher pats him on the head, gives him a three day weekend, and maybe a small raise.

In other cases, reporters find themselves under pressure to conclude that "both sides are wrong." For example, if a story is being prepared showing that one candidate is a crook, editors will often ask for a similar story on the opponent. Then some small indiscretion committed twenty years ago is dragged out and given equal play with the first story. Often such pressure is so subtle that a reporter doesn't even notice it. It is a good idea, therefore, to develop a reflex habit of pulling back from a story every so often to see just what the facts are and if they warrant major, clear-a-space-on-the-trophy-shelf, treatment. Once an objective and thorough investigation, however, has led a reporter to conclude that a major political or social change is necessary, there is no need to become overwrought if the story reads like it is advocating that change. If a reporter writes a story about slum kids being eaten alive by rats because landlords only have to pay a $25 fine for each death, anyone reading the story will conclude that the fine should be increased.

To advocate dispassionate investigating and writing is, obviously, easier than to actually do it. After a reporter has been on a certain story more than a few days, some conclusions about the direction in which the story is going are inevitable, and sometimes are either inaccurate or an oversimplification of the actual situation. In these situations, some reporters find it very helpful to talk over what they are doing with outside experts or ask a friend to play devil's advocate with them. They then attempt to close the loopholes, double check the facts, and perhaps quiz additional sources. If too many holes have been punched in the story, it should be either changed or dropped.

A factually accurate story, however, should never be killed simply because it is "unfair" in the sense that contrary assertions are not published along with the damaging facts. The stories published about the space program, for example, were true even though they didn't contain rebuttals from the Flat Earth Society. Conversely, a sloppily researched story is not made more thorough and accurate simply because it "tells both sides." Nothing makes a story look sillier than an obvious and unnecessary attempt to do so:

> DOG WALK, IOWA—*Nov. 5*—A Wing-and-Prayer Airlines 747 crashed into a nuclear generating plant near here Tuesday killing 348 passengers and seven crew members, while 12 other Wing-and-Prayer flights landed successfully at their destinations.

The public relations people at Wing-and-Prayer may love it, but then none of them live in Dog Walk.

17
Getting the Story Published

It is only a slight exaggeration to say that in all but a handful of newspapers in this country persuading the editors to print an investigative story is often more draining and time consuming than reporting and writing the story. Yet there are few newspapers where management and ownership have an explicit policy against investigative reporting. Most newspapers pride themselves on their "hard hitting" investigations. But what they often mean is that they will joyously investigate Mafia capos, dope dealers, cops on the beat, minor politicians, and anyone else without great power who is not one of their advertisers. The crunch comes when reporters investigate corruption involving large corporations, powerful local politicians, police administrators, charities, churches, and other newspapers or broadcast stations.

It is rare for an editor to tell a newspaper reporter that his or her story will not be published because it will offend an advertiser or bring more heat than the newspaper is willing to handle, although we do know of a few such cases. Generally, the story will be attacked on its merits or because of judgments implicit in it.

For example, Lerner Newspapers in Chicago once had a story in hand about two aldermen who voted to sell two alleys to a real estate speculator for about a tenth of their market value the same month they came into a large number of shares of stock in a bank run by the speculator. The aldermen paid about half what the stock was worth. A conflict of interest, you say? Not so, said the editor. He argued that since the alleys were sold to the banker, not the bank, the case was not solid enough to warrant a story. Two years later, when both the reporter and editor were working for other newspapers, the editor mentioned that he knew all along that it was a bona fide story, but the publisher had chanced across it in the back shop and ordered it killed. The editor told the reporter he had questioned the merits of the story rather than admit the real reason for dropping it and risk the reporter's quitting the paper.

Management may have many different reasons for killing good stories. In the previous case, the newspaper stood to derive substantial revenues from the city government in the form of legal notice advertising and the aldermen involved had sufficient clout to curtail that advertising had the story been published. In other cases, editors will not publish a story for fear of losing a libel suit. Others, even those who believe a story is not libelous, will still spike it to escape incurring the cost of defending themselves against even the most futile of libel claims. Journalism reviews are full of accounts of stories killed for reasons of political kinship or personal friendship between the subject of the story and management. These abuses occur most frequently in smaller cities, particularly those with a single newspaper.

But the reason most stories are killed, we think, is that editors and publishers are simply unwilling to take the heat a controversial story generates: charges and countercharges, enemies, outraged readers, anger among advertisers, denials, explanations, perhaps even lawsuits. The editor who publishes a controversial story knows that it will have to be defended on its merits to his superiors, some of whom may not share his sense of moral outrage. To ask an editor to run a story he thinks may precipitate a confrontation between himself and the publisher means, in too many cases, asking him to jeopardize his chances for further advancement.

Attitudes towards publishing controversial stories vary widely from newspaper to newspaper and from reign to reign within each newspaper. A lot can hinge on the reaction to the paper's last foray into investigative reporting, and even on such things as the level of tension between editors and reporters due to labor-management negotiations or union organizing drives. Consequently, there is no single best way to handle such confrontations. What would be a convincing argument at one newspaper or broadcast station would be considered nonsense at others.

In most cases, however, we think the best way to persuade management to publish a controversial story is to act as if it is as innocuous as the most routine obituary. The least bit of apprehension will certainly be transmitted to others handling the story. The reporter should simply slop the story on the editor's desk and wander off to the coffee machine. The same advice applies to asking for the time necessary to do a difficult investigation. The reporter should simply tell the editor what the tip is, what the preliminary research shows, and that a few days will be needed to work on it. The reporter should leave it to the editor to explain why it's more important to do a cute feature story.

Suppose the editor reads the piece, ponders it two-tenths of a second, and screams, "What! Are you crazy? We're not about to print a story attacking every bank in the city, just because they won't make home loans in certain neighborhoods. They're all advertisers. Their friends are advertisers. They pay our salaries." Or, more likely, suppose the story is set aside and two days later the reporter learns it has been spiked. That should not be the end of it. After conniving, digging in files, making endless phone calls, and having showdowns with heavyset security guards, one more such encounter should not discourage an investigator. What probably happened is that a bunch of editors discussed the story and one faction either convinced the other that the story shouldn't run, or one of the higher-ups overruled one of the lower-downs. That's why it took two days. The problem with letting the decision stand is that whoever was arguing in favor of publication obviously doesn't know as much about the story as the reporter does and probably didn't argue for the story as well as the reporter could have. The reporter should find out who wanted the story killed and then talk to that person.

In order to get the story published, the reporter must permit some face saving. Consequently, it is wise to stay calm and relaxed, and discuss the story rationally. The first step is for the reporter to say that it's a good story—not that it's good because it will prevent communism or halt creeping socialism or because the readers will like it, or the publisher will like it—just that it's good. The reporter should let the editor supply a definition of "good" and argue that it doesn't measure up. That way the reporter will get an inkling of what the editor doesn't like about it, or about its likely effects, and will be better able to find a way to get the story published. Perhaps the editor will say the story needs more work—more research or another rewriting. The reporter should ask for suggestions and, politely but carefully, find out just what facts the editor wants or what the lead should say. It is important to be alert to any suggestion of a new lead or some particular wording. By using the editor's key phrases, the reporter may still be able to keep the story intact. If the editor isn't pinned down closely, however, he can say later on, "Something is still missing. Maybe we ought to let it sit awhile." Then the story is dead.

Often investigative stories are the result of many compromises between reporter and editor, reporter and libel attorney, and even between editors. How far a reporter should go in compromising a story, of course, is a matter of judgment and circumstances. In some instances, the journalist will be doing a greater public service by getting at least part of a story in the paper or on the air where it may be picked up by other investigators. In other cases, the proposed solution may either distort the facts of the story or compromise the reporter's integrity. If no compromise seems acceptable, the reporter could remind the editor that dozens of people have been interviewed and that by now everyone in the statehouse undoubtedly knows that he or she is working on the story. By killing it, the paper or station may seriously jeopardize its credibility and its reputation in important circles. Furthermore, one of those hundreds of people may tip off a competitor. Perhaps some government agency may begin looking into the charges or some citizens' group will file suit. If the essence of the story is going to come out in any case, the newspaper or station that has the story already might as well be the first to let it be known. The idea is not to let editors think they can abrogate the public's right to know.

In convincing the editor, a reporter may also find it handy to be conversant in libel law. The landmark *New York Times* vs. Sullivan libel decision by the U.S. Supreme Court is continually undergoing modification and reporters should keep up with these cases. In general, a plaintiff cannot win a libel suit if he is a public figure, even if some of what was printed about him was inaccurate, unless he can show the reporter deliberately falsified facts or acted in reckless disregard of the facts. Since virtually every story a reporter does will involve either a public figure or a public issue, in most cases, the reporter need worry only about the facts of the story.

Furthermore, those who are truly criminal tend not to sue for libel. That's because if they sue, the newspaper or broadcast station involved will have a right to what is commonly called "discovery": access to many private records. For example, if the subject of the story has been caught rezoning his own land in one part of town, and he secretly owns and has rezoned land in another neighborhood, the reporter will have a good chance of discovering that also during the suit. In most cases, the subject of the story would rather not risk broadening the charges or giving the local prosecutor something extra to hand a grand jury by suing for libel.

If management absolutely refuses to run a story for fear of a libel suit, and the reporter involved absolutely refuses to have it kept secret from the public, some perfectly ethical alternatives exist. A reporter can ask about selling the story to another publication. The question may incite an editor to genteel riot, but it will also make him think again about the story and his treatment of it. If a reporter is told it can't be sold, he or she is being misled. The story cannot be sold as written for the newspaper or station, but the information can be used to write another article: no media outlet has sole control over any set of facts. The reporter's superiors can put him on the night police beat or even fire him, if the guild has a weak contract, but they'll lose any lawsuits which claim they are the sole legal outlet for stories about, say, corruption in their circulation area.

While discussing whether or not an investigative story should be published, the reporter must decide how important his or her job is and how difficult it would be to get a comparable job elsewhere. We would suggest that quitting is not a very good solution. It doesn't result in the publication or broadcast of the story, it won't change a newspaper's or station's attitude toward controversial stories, and it won't aid in informing the citizenry. A wiser course for the journalist would be to persuade someone else—a prosecutor, a public service law firm, the local Ralph Nader organization—to make the charges. Then a straight news story reporting on the charges can follow. Extreme measures are rarely necessary. Knowing that most editors have retained at least a soft spot for journalism, a smart reporter avoids fireworks and probes calmly until that spot can be found.

18
Keeping the Heat On

Perhaps the rudest awakening for the novice investigator is catching a person or institution doing something outlandish in secret, writing about it in phrases that will live forever, then watching in dismay when nothing happens. Pulpits do not ring with scorn at the water commissioner's nakedness nor is he spat upon in the streets. In fact, he will be at his desk drawing a salary. By midafternoon, the reporter may have the distinct feeling that if anyone gets tarred and feathered it will be him. To get a reaction—someone being fired, disbarred, indicted, or officially investigated—the reporter will have to write follow-up stories. On many occasions, nobody in an official position will take a reporter's charges seriously until they read them in the paper the third or fourth time. The masses will not rise up after the publication of a single story. In fact, a lot of them will not have read it. They were on vacation, new in town, watching television, trying to earn a buck, fighting with their spouses, bowling, reading *Scientific American,* or blind drunk the day the story ran.

As is the case with any other newspaper article, a follow-up story has to have a reason for being. It is not enough to write "Yesterday this newspaper exposed the water commissioner. For all you folks who missed it, here is that story reprinted." The reporter will have to find a "newspeg" for the story, generally a reaction to it by some prominent person. The most immediate reaction is likely to come from the people most embarrassed by the story. They will say any of a number of things, usually:

"The charges are false. My lawyers are preparing. . . ."

"The charges are false. It is a plot by. . . ."

"The charges are false. I stand on my record of. . . ."

"The charges are false. The reporter who wrote the story is a. . . ."

"The charges are false. You can't believe everything you read in the. . . ."

"The charges are false. I broke no law and besides everybody does. . . ."

Rarely will the principals admit the charges. If they do, they'll often claim the charges are insignificant. Sometimes corrupt politicians are even revered as heroes. Former Cook County Assessor P. J. (Parky) Cullerton won re-election by a handsome margin months after he was charged with giving mammoth property tax breaks to his campaign supporters. (It has been estimated that the scandal cost Assessor Cullerton only 50,000 to 100,000 votes—the margin by which he ran behind other winning Democrats on the ticket.) Cornelius Gallagher, a former New Jersey congressman, was treated to a get-out-of-jail party attended by more than 2,000 of his constituents after he had served seventeen months for income tax evasion. One-time Jersey City boss Frank Hague managed to blunt a number of investigations aimed at him by depicting the charges as aimed at all the residents of Hudson County. Hague's successor, John Kenny, won re-election to a second term after he admitted lying to a waterfront commission during an investigation of racketeering. Edward Hanrahan won the Democratic primary for Cook County prosecutor while under indictment for conspiring to conceal evidence unearthed in the investigation of the slaying of two black militants by his office's investigators.

Public officials charged with doing something unethical may defend themselves by saying they did nothing illegal. Those charged with breaking a law may say they are innocent until proven guilty. Those found guilty may say the case is under appeal. Many people, incidentally, still think that Richard Nixon either did nothing wrong, or at least that he did no more than other presidents had done before, and therefore was unfairly castigated by the press.

The most savvy politicians, businessmen, or other public figures embarrassed by an exposé will go after an investigative reporter with all the tenacity and skill with which the reporter went after them or their agencies. They will hire very competent and articulate lawyers. They will attempt to convince editors and publishers that the story was nonsense; that the reporter made it up, was duped by their political enemies, or simply didn't understand certain processes of law. This is another reason for a reporter to develop an extensive background on the subject under investigation. If the reporter is unaware of any single, related fact, whether it is relevant to the charge or not, a sophisticated lawyer can use that lack of knowledge to convince a publisher or an editor that the reporter can't even spell his client's name correctly, much less write an accurate story.

If this technique doesn't work, it is not unusual to use threats, withdraw advertising, or even file a libel suit. We heard of one public official, Assessor Cullerton, who implied to a *Chicago Daily News* reporter that the tax assessments on a warehouse owned by the *News*'s publisher would be raised. This is the second rudest awakening an investigative reporter often comes to: learning just how rough professionals play the game.

Counterattacks can be flamboyantly newsworthy, sometimes even more so than the original story. For example, the rather harmless report that valuable art objects lent out by the Detroit city museum were being misused by various officials prompted Mayor Coleman Young to publicly denounce the reporter who wrote the story and bar him from the mayor's office without an escort. (The mayor was particularly piqued by a photograph of a valued statue sitting on a filing cabinet in a mayor's office hallway surrounded by telephone books and empty coffee cups. Weeks later, on a TV talk show, the mayor said the reporter was not barred from his offices to prevent such photographs, but because, the mayor said, the reporter set the coffee cups there himself and that on another occasion a secretary had caught him reading the mail of a mayoral aide. The mayoral aide, however, knew nothing about it when asked and the reporter denied reading anybody's mail.) A slightly more subdued response is exemplified by Chicago Mayor Daley's reaction to the charge that he transferred the city's insurance business to one of his sons. Daley told a press conference, "Any father that wouldn't help his children in a legitimate, legal way isn't much of a father."

Obviously, a reporter needs to write more than one story to make the charges stick. One way of doing so is to make maximum use of the glorious democratic system of government which has kept America strong and free, its sons and daughters virtuous and high-minded, and which always makes it possible for a lazy reporter to dig up one politician willing to denounce another. Almost anyone a reporter writes about—especially an elected public official—has an enemy somewhere, who will be only too willing to call for an investigation as a result of the story. Such a follow-up, based on a relatively uninformed denunciation, is, frankly, a cheap shot. But if a reporter believes in the findings of an investigation it is important to keep the story alive so the findings will have some effect.

Even if no denunciation is forthcoming, the same democratic system that enables a reporter to write a story about an elected official and then seek a denunciation without fear, enables a reporter to sit back and wait for voter reaction at the polls. Numerous officials justly pilloried by investigators have been defeated in subsequent elections. This has led some newspapers to delay publication of some stories, investigative or not, until election eve in order to inflict maximum damage on their targets. This practice is not only unfair to the candidate but may actually backfire because many voters will also think it unfair.

If, however, there is no newsworthy reaction to a reporter's story and the subject of the investigation is an appointed official, the reporter should not hesitate to ask the people responsible for the appointment what they plan to do about it. They may denounce their own man or take the more cautious, official approach and order an investigation of the charges. When calling for the investigation they may find themselves pressed to say why they think an investigation is necessary, thereby providing quotes for a follow-up lead.

The announcement of an investigation, however, should not be welcomed with unmitigated glee. In fact, an official investigation is often an easy way for a politician to get rid of some messy allegations—for the time being or forever. In many cases, an official will be glad to announce an investigation, bask briefly in the resulting favorable publicity, and then retire to a smoke-filled room while both the public and, unfortunately, the press forget the whole affair. Reporters have perhaps shorter attention spans than others, even in these situations. Someone once compared the average reporter to the family pet who plays with the rubber duck for a while, then drops it and charges into the living room to chase the plastic mouse.

The alert reporter, realizing that the announcement of an investigation is different from its consummation and from disclosure of its findings, should prepare several fall back positions in case the matter is quietly forgotten. The reporter could point out that the investigation announced with so much fanfare six months ago never got underway, was just a smokescreen to begin with, or never resulted in official findings. If the official investigation was stalled by pressure from the original subject of the journalistic investigation, it is almost imperative to do a second investigative piece. A diligent search should be made for any conflict-of-interest connections or collusionary links between the original subject and those people directing the official investigation.

This article could be coupled with, or written as, an analysis of the reasons the official investigation was stalled. Often, the same editors who demanded "facts and facts only" in the publication of a reporter's original investigative piece, will allow the reporter to use the news analysis form—with its greater latitude for editorializing—after the reporter's original investigative piece has stood a short test of time. Columnist Murray Kempton once wrote that "Editorial writers are people who ride down out of the hills after the battle and shoot the wounded." Nevertheless, it is no disgrace for a reporter to ask for an editorial in support of an investigation.

If an investigation has pointed out enough possible illegalities, any member of a grand jury may read the story in the paper and take up the cause without alerting the reporter involved. The reporter may get an inkling of what's going on only when the county prosecutor calls to ask for help in locating a witness to appear before a grand jury. If warrants are sought and the principals in a reporter's stories are arrested, charged, and tried, the follow-up opportunities are obvious.

Prosecutors and grand juries, however, are not always in constant action and sometimes even an editorial and a news offensive causes no forward movement. Nevertheless, the determined investigative reporter doesn't give up easily. If the statute of limitations will allow a pause until after the next election, a whole new set of officials may then be in office, men who have no stake in the conditions that led to the original investigation and who have something to gain from painting the previous officials as incompetent or crooked. If the reporter is truly lucky, the new officials will be the same politicians who denounced the old guard when the stories were first published and are now eager for immediate, favorable press coverage. For example, "Only two weeks after taking office, Prosecutor Smith moved today to investigate the assessment scandal which his predecessor in the prosecutor's office refused to touch. . . ."

Even if such favorable electoral circumstances do not develop, and the situation originally uncovered continues to exist, nothing prevents a reporter from waiting six months and then writing another story on the original theme. The story might say that the original subject of the investigation is still being permitted to do business as usual despite antics brought to the attention of the appropriate officials many months ago. If the malfeasance described peaks at certain definite periods—tax sales, court hearings, etc.—the reporter has natural newspegs on which to hang other similar stories. Stories detailing election fraud fall easily into this category. If no action has been taken on a scandal revealed during the previous election, the reporter is free to write such leads as "On election day next week, those 600 dead bodies who voted in last year's municipal race will have a chance to vote once again. They're still registered. . . ."

Other possibilities remain if all else fails. Perhaps the original stories will attract new sources with new information. Maybe something unfortunate will occur as a result of the unchecked continuance of the scandal that will bring the story to a head. Or perhaps the original subject of the investigation will do something else both evil and newsworthy, and the reporter will be off and running once again.

Appendix

Investigative Examples

The Four Seasons Saga

Unlike most investigative stories, Rone Tempest's Four Seasons saga, published in the *Oklahoma Journal* February 28–March 10, 1972 and reprinted here with permission, is concerned primarily with business wrongdoing rather than political wrongdoing, or a combination of the two. Several public bodies—the state of Ohio, the American Stock Exchange, and the U.S. Congress—were involved in the story, but only peripherally. The major part of the fraudulent scheme was the work of private individuals.

Tempest's story illustrates both the problems and the advantages of a series format. It allowed Tempest as many opportunities as there are parts in the series—eleven in this case—to use jazzy, seductive leads and stinging, thoughtful kickers. However, the series format also led to excess verbiage: the series is simply too long and too repetitious. One could argue, as Tempest does, that a great many people in Oklahoma City were willing to read and read and read about Four Seasons because they had invested in it or knew people who had, but the same argument could be used to justify a relatively long one-shot approach.

Tempest's writing is uniformly superior to the writing that makes up most business stories and most investigative stories. He made an obvious effort to interest readers in the subject of his investigation, a rare phenomenon among investigative reporters, who often seem to feel that facts will speak for themselves without any assistance.

There's no denying the appeal of the Four Seasons story even to those Oklahomans who had nothing invested in the nursing home chain. That appeal centered around Jack L. Clark, Four Seasons founder and president, who followed the classic American path of rags-to-riches and back again in the pages of Tempest's saga.

"Clark was a big dumb salesman who in such a short time went from nothing to something huge in a way peculiar to the Southwest," the Nevada-born Tempest said in a recent interview. "He wasn't an effete Easterner born into wealth and cynically dubious of the consumers' intelligence. There's an element of innocence in his conduct, as illustrated by the Walston Memorandum. Only someone somewhat innocent would author something as incriminating as that, would actually put something like that down on paper." (Tempest's surprise aside, we have argued throughout this book that the most startling admissions are often recorded—on paper, on tape, or in the verifiable memories of others—and often sit waiting for the right investigative reporter to come along and ferret them out. Who would have thought that Nixon's incriminating conversations were preserved on tape?)

Clark's appeal is summed up by Tempest as the appeal of "the country mouse who goes to the big city. The city folks sneer at his accent and his manners but in the end they get screwed. Everyone likes to see entrenched power duped."

Tempest said the main inspiration behind the writing of the series was his own desire for understanding. Assigned to cover the federal government by the *Oklahoma Journal,* he wrote one daily story after another about the ongoing Four Seasons bankruptcy proceedings, but the stories were fragmented and unclear. "One day I got furious with myself for not comprehending things and decided to go through everything until I did," Tempest said. "It was less a matter of recognizing a good story than outrage at not understanding how things work. That's why I wanted to get into the newspaper business in the first place, because I realized I didn't understand the government, which ruled so much of my daily life."

After he decided to understand Four Seasons, Tempest began checking all the files related to the case and talking to as many of the principals as he could contact or corner. He came upon the key to the story—the Walston Memorandum—when he noticed that two Securities and Exchange Commission investigators were taking copious notes on a particular Four Seasons file. The file included a letter referring to the incriminating memorandum.

Tempest's search for the memorandum itself led him to an Oklahoma City warehouse where all of the Four Seasons records were stored. Attorneys on both sides of the many suits filed against Four Seasons were going over the voluminous records. Tempest eased his way into the warehouse simply by stating that he wanted to see the records. He let the warehouse administrators assume he was an attorney connected with one of the suits.

Tempest's story was not based entirely on documents or court files. One of his principal sources was an officer of Four Seasons, whose name Tempest still refuses to reveal. This man was, in Tempest's words, "so scared for his own skin he was willing to incriminate others." Another source was an interior decorator who used to be the Four Seasons supply manager. One source, Tempest said, seemed to harbor a physical desire for the 25-year-old, mustachioed journalist. "We met in a restaurant," Tempest said, "and he insisted I sit beside him rather than on the other side of the table. He sat right next to me rubbing his body next to mine. He did everything but handle me right in the restaurant. But I got a lot of information from him."

Tempest's investigating was tedious only while he literally didn't know what he was doing, what the general outline of the Four Seasons saga was going to be, or, indeed, if there was enough for a story on the nursing home chain. Tempest said he understood the essence of the story, and knew he could write a series about the chain, when he finally read and understood the Federal Securities Act of 1933, understood what "not-at-arms-length" meant, and realized that the secret of Four Seasons was that the firm was selling nursing homes to itself. From then on, as the saying goes, he was home free.

Finding time to write the story was not exactly a piece of cake, however. Tempest covered the school board for the *Journal* in addition to his federal beat. "I was doing one to three stories a day on the federal government and was going to the school board meetings and writing a school board story every week," Tempest said. His usual shift, since the *Journal* was a morning paper, was from 2 P.M. to 11 P.M. "In the mornings," Tempest said, "instead of sleeping in, I would go through the files and interview Four Seasons sources and write at night after I had finished my normal assignments." At that rate, Tempest's investigation took six months.

The high point of both Tempest's research and the series itself was Tempest's interview with Jack Clark at Clark's home. No other reporters had been able to interview Clark since the scandal broke, according to Tempest. Tempest reasoned that Clark, "a total egocentric, who before the Four Seasons bankruptcy had spent his time flying around the country delivering declamatory speeches to approving crowds, had been holed up in his home, out of contact with the public, for several months, and might be willing to talk" if approached properly.

"So I called Clark," Tempest said, "and came on as a country bumpkin. I said I worked for the *Journal* but that I hadn't been a reporter that long, and didn't think Clark's real story had been told. I said that although Clark and Four Seasons had built all those nursing homes no one had given them the proper credit. 'Gee,' I said, 'I wish I could come out and talk to you and find out what actually happened.' "

Tempest brought a tape recorder along and Clark, Tempest said, was leery of the machine. As it turned out, however, Clark's attitude toward the machine didn't matter. Tempest had mistakenly brought only demonstration tapes, which shut off automatically after five minutes. So the reporter relied on taking notes, to which Clark had no apparent objections. But Tempest took no chances: whenever Clark launched into a self-congratulatory tirade, Tempest scribbled away. What he was writing down, of course, was as much as he could remember of Clark's remarks about the problems he and Four Seasons faced. At one point, Tempest excused himself to go to the bathroom and once there wrote down as much as he could remember of his conversation with Clark.

Tempest believed that it would help the Four Seasons story come alive if the appointments of Clark's luxurious mansion—which could only come from Clark himself—could be included in the saga. So, in the reporter's words, "I took a bumpkin view of the house. 'Gee whiz,' I said, 'you're just like Hemingway,' when I saw his trophy room. And he immediately told me the names of all the trophies and how he had bagged them." Tempest used that information to good effect in his story.

Tempest said that Clark was drinking heavily during the interview. Although Tempest was served liquor he says he sipped it and attempted to remain sober. But considering what the reporter recalls as his state of mind, that wasn't a very difficult task: "I knew the house was a big part of the story," Tempest said. "No one else had ever been in there, so I was like a sponge. I disciplined my mind to record as much as possible of what I saw."

Tempest admits that his interview with Clark "was not a confrontation interview by any stretch of the imagination." But, he said, "the story demanded lifestyle elements. You knew people would read that story—the part of the series devoted to Clark's house—even if they didn't read the other stories." The result of Tempest's interview with Clark was the well-written tenth part of the reporter's Four Seasons saga: "This is the House That Jack Built."

Tempest worried for a while about getting the story published. *Journal* Publisher William Atkinson had long been deeply involved in land development, Tempest said. So before Tempest did serious research on the Four Seasons stories, he made a point of telling the *Journal*'s Managing Editor what he was getting into. The M.E. said he'd check the idea with the publisher. Tempest held his breath until the M.E. returned from his conference with Atkinson. "As it happened," Tempest said, "the publisher didn't like Four Seasons' corporate officers; Clark had once asked him for a lot of money or something." With the publisher neutralized, Tempest found it easy to sell the story to the M.E. "I kept feeding him anecdotes about the sex parties the Four Seasons officers were alleged to have had. He began to live vicariously off the big-money exploits of those guys."

Only one hurdle remained: the paper's attorneys. "As with most newspapers," Tempest said, "we were just one of many clients our attorneys had. They weren't even too familiar with libel law. I had to go before these guys with the story as if they were judges." The attorneys, labeling Tempest's condemnation of Four Seasons too "apocalyptic," suggested he add to the series what became the final part: "Four Seasons Surviving Its Problems; Modest Profits Expected for Reorganized Firm." In 1975, long after the story appeared, Tempest said he believed that the series went on too long and that the saga of Four Seasons could have been explained in fewer words. "But that was my first major piece," he said. "Ever since then I've been waiting for something to intrigue me as much as that story did."

THE SAGA OF FOUR SEASONS

Courageous men facing impossible odds or wide-eyed princes kidnaped by pirates are the stuff of adventure stories.

This is only the story of an American corporation—Oklahoma-born Four Seasons Nursing Centers of America.

But the story is complete with its own outrageous odds and swashbucklers. It is an adventure story.

In June, 1966, Four Seasons Nursing Centers of America did not exist.

By June 30, 1967, Four Seasons was worth a modest $1.6 million.

By June 30, 1968, the company had assets worth $7.2 million and had built 24 nursing homes.

By June 30, 1969, Four Seasons had assets of $37.7 million, had constructed 35 nursing homes, was in the process of building 30 nursing homes and had plans for 33 nursing homes, nine hospitals and six child care centers.

In the last few months of 1969 the company had raised through stock sales and financing somewhere in the neighborhood of $100 million.

But by June 30, 1970, Four Seasons Nursing Centers of America, scarcely three years old, had filed for reorganization under Chapter X of the Federal Bankruptcy Act.

What happened in those three years from June, 1967, to June, 1970, is a story that has never been told.

The story is that "from the plains of Oklahoma," as one leading business magazine quaintly put it, a company grew in three years from practically nothing to the national pacesetter in the booming nursing home industry. And in an even shorter period of time, it fell.

When Four Seasons was flying high, mammoth operations like American Hospital Supply Co. of Chicago with over $450 million in assets, reportedly asked for merger.

The Four Seasons dream seemed boundless.

Jack L. Clark, Four Seasons founder and president, unabashedly talked of building one of the largest corporations in the world.

The company's stock was the first nursing home paper ever dealt on a major exchange—the American Stock Exchange.

Investor groups waited in line to get their hands on the stock as it soared from $11 per share to over $100, before splitting 2–1 and then rising again.

American institutional investors heavy into the company stock included Investors Diversified Services, Enterprise Fund, Gibraltar Growth Fund, Marine Midland Grace Pension, Manhattan Fund, U.S. Realty, Summit Management Research and Winfield Growth Fund.

The company and its debenture bonds ($15 million worth) were favorites with Bernard Cornfeld and the ill-fated International Overseas Services (IOS).

Foreign dabblers in its wares included such reputable banking houses as: Banque Rothschild; Creditbank Luxembourgeoise; Credit Commerciel de France, and the foreign divisions of U.S. firms with well-known names like American Express Securities S.A.; Bache and Co.; Burnham and Co. and Merrill Lynch LTD.

No single investor received as much recognition for its investment as the sovereign state of Ohio. It loaned Four Seasons $4 million while it was dealing out big sums to other doomed enterprises like Colorado's King Resources. Before the scandal over the first loan broke, Ohio had obligated another $18 million to Four Seasons.

In fact, the Ohio "statehouse loan scandal" is credited with removing the entire Republican Party from power in that state, starting with the governor.

As David Hopcraft, Columbus bureau chief for the *Cleveland Plain Dealer* tells it:

"These loans changed everything. Those who had power lost it. Those who did not have power got it."

Even the American Stock Exchange came in for some pillar shaking.

The American dropped Four Seasons like a hot potato when the Ohio loan scandal surfaced and Four Seasons' earnings didn't come near meeting projections.

One of the exchange's "specialists" assigned to the stock later drew a suspension and fine for his relationship with Four Seasons.

Two of the top executives with Four Seasons' underwriting firm, Walston and Co., were recently suspended from trading in the exchange and fined for their participation in the Four Seasons debacle.

Walston and Co. itself was fined $75,000.

Even Dun and Bradstreet came in for some sharp criticism.

The Wall Street Journal reported in its August 13, 1970, issue in a page one article:

"Second guessing investment advisers is an old game. But questioning the reliability of Dun and Bradstreet is something new . . . Short-term notes of Four Seasons Nursing Centers of America Inc., which filed a bankruptcy petition a week after Penn Central did, were also rated prime by Dun and Bradstreet . . . the Securities Exchange Commission is investigating the rating of the Four Seasons notes."

Following a two-year SEC investigation, attorneys are preparing evidence to present to a grand jury in the Southern Federal District of New York in New York City.

U.S. Attorney Gary Naftalis has been assigned to the case by the Department of Justice and he said in a recent interview: "This could be one of the biggest securities fraud cases in the country in many years."

Naftalis said he plans to present the case to a federal grand jury in "two or three months." Each defendant, and the names being considered include many prominent city executives, could face up to five years in prison and $10,000 on each count.

A separate count could be filed under federal rules for each share of stock alleged to be fraudulently sold. Theoretically there could be a million count indictment.

Big-name attorneys have already been retained by several persons involved in the case.

Former Secretary of Defense Clark Clifford has been hired as counsel by a prominent city businessman.

Former U.S. Sen. George Smathers of Florida and the famous Wall Street firm Breed, Abbott and Morgan have been retained by Walston and Co.

Four Seasons president Jack L. Clark has hired a Washington firm containing the former chairman of the Securities Exchange Commission Manny Cohen and former SEC chief prosecutor Arthur Mathews.

How did it happen?

How did an Oklahoma City construction firm grow to the point where it shook national political and financial institutions?

The growth of the company has been attributed to many things —a bull stock market, the wizardry of the underwriters Walston and Co., the emergence of Medicare and Medicaid programs thought to be endless fountains of money, the national need for good nursing homes and beds, the brilliance of Jack Clark, and pure dumb luck.

Clark himself said it was all because of the "Lord putting his hand on my shoulder."

Clark, the son of an Oklahoma oilfield worker, was for one short period of his life known as "the best damn fistfighter at Classen High School."

Later, he was a good milkman and then a great salesman. When he finally became president of Four Seasons he was considered by at least one top national investor to be "the most impressive corporate head I've ever met."

The personalities of Clark and his late partner and company vice president, Amos D. "Bud" Bouse, were colorful enough to give the young corporation a flamboyant life-lived-to-the-hilt image.

Both men liked gambling, frequent trips in the company jet, whisky and out-West business talk.

Clark, friend and foe alike agree, is a "supersalesman."

"Bud" Bouse "died with his boots on" in an Oct. 21, 1971 plane crash. He had just come from Dallas and baseballer Mickey Mantle's birthday party.

There are stories of fabulous wealth, $30,000 poker hands, Rolls-Royces, million-dollar jets and $2 million homes.

Clark himself is estimated to have cashed in $10 million in Four Seasons stock while it was still a "high flyer." Bouse collected an estimated $6 million and Clark's half-brother Tom Gray sold $4 million worth.

But the vast amounts of money only add to the myth.

Never did so much money change hands so quickly and vanish so fast as in the story of Four Seasons.

It will be years before the courts settle all the litigation filed after Four Seasons toppled.

A $60 million suit was filed, and later dropped without prejudice by Four Seasons trustee Norman Hirschfield against former company officials and insiders.

A $50 million suit originated in New York charging company officers and its Wall Street insiders with defrauding stockbrokers, issuing false financial statements and overly optimistic reports of projected earnings and developments.

There are dozens of other lawsuits alleging basically the same things.

But by far the most damaging and well-documented suit was filed by a Tennessee stockbroker named Frank Sher and his Birmingham, Ala., attorneys J. Vernon Patrick and Marvin Cherner.

It was the "Sher suit" that first revealed what has become

known as the "Walston Memorandum."

Allegedly dictated sometime before the company's first offering in the spring of 1968, it is attributed to Four Seasons insiders.

It was found openly filed in the company records after bankruptcy.

Included in the startlingly candid statement in the memo are the following:

"Let's get Walston's opinion as to when we could sell a sizeable portion of our stock, while the stock is at a good price, to guard against having to sell after the public realizes that nursing homes will not meet expectations."

And:

"Let's get a definite program established with them as to the earliest and subsequent dates when we can dispose of our stock to insure our personal wealth."

Another document, entitled the "McDonnell Memorandum," is in the hands of the U.S. attorney in New York. It reportedly makes similar statements.

But it was the Walston Memorandum that prompted U.S. District Judge Luther Bohanon to make some of the most direct accusations ever issued from an American bench.

These comments came at the end of a hearing Nov. 2, 1971:

"What happened, in my judgment," the judge said, "has done more to destroy the faith of the American people in the New York Stock Exchange and in the American Stock Exchange than any other thing that can happen. There are others too, but this case within the past two years is the rankest.

"I had no idea until the hearing started yesterday of the depth of the evil that was perpetrated upon the American people . . . It's shameful. It's disgraceful and shameless."

The judge ruled that all Four Seasons Equity stock purchasers were defrauded and entitled to a portion of the new stock to be issued by the company.

WHO'S TO BLAME IN FIRM'S FALL?

U.S. Attorney Gary Naftalis of New York City calls it "One of the biggest securities fraud trials in this country in many years."

Principals involved in the case are lining up nationally-known attorneys—former Secretary of Defense Clark Clifford for one;

former Florida Sen. George Smathers for another; a third is none other than Manny Cohen, former chairman of the Securities Exchange Commission (SEC). Arthur Mathews, former chief prosecutor for the SEC, is a fourth.

The stage is nearly set for the predicted securities showdown with former officers and associates of Four Seasons Nursing Centers of America.

The Four Seasons case has been approved for grand jury action by the Department of Justice after almost two years of investigation by agents of the SEC, the FBI and the U.S. Postal Service.

Subpoenas Have Been Issued   The case has been assigned to Naftalis, a young Columbia University law honors graduate who specializes in securities with the Department of Justice in New York.

Naftalis says it may be "three or four months" before the case is presented to a federal grand jury for possible indictments but that subpoenas already have been issued from his office to gather more evidence.

And the big-name attorneys have been calling his office.

"It makes you wonder," Naftalis said recently with a sigh of relief after finding his caller was not another attorney.

The list of possible defendants has been narrowed down to approximately eight names, authoritative sources have revealed.

Prosecution is expected to come on three fronts: mail fraud, "wire" fraud, and "securities fraud" under the strongly-worded Section 17 of the Securities Act of 1933.

Three areas of Four Seasons' operations are expected to come under scrutiny: accounting, done by the national firm Arthur Anderson and Co.; underwriting, performed by Walston and Co. of New York and Chicago; and internal management, featuring such familiar names as Jack L. Clark, the company's founder, president and chairman of the board, Tom J. Gray and others.

Stock Exchange Fines Officials   Arthur Anderson could be in trouble for certain accounting practices allegedly used by Four Seasons—such as declaring construction profits on partially-completed nursing homes; declaring franchise fees as profits before a single building had been constructed, and doing the accounting for both Four Seasons Nursing Homes of America and its controversial sister firm, Four Seasons Equity.

Walston and Co., the genius behind the company's public entry and creator of Equity, already has been severely penalized by the American Stock Exchange for its dealings in Four Seasons.

Walston President William D. Fleming and top executive Glen R. Miller both have been suspended from the exchange and fined $10,000 each. Walston and Co. itself was censured by the exchange and handed a $75,000 fine, the largest fine ever levied by the American.

In addition, the exchange, which has refused to release its report on the Four Seasons matter, gave the controversial specialist assigned to the company, Francis Santangelo, a minor censure, suspension and fine.

Civil Suits Assigned To City   Santangelo, who was supposed to have been an objective adviser from the exchange to Four Seasons, was called by Four Seasons President Jack L. Clark a "social" friend, and was involved in some big money stock transactions with former Four Seasons executives.

The name of Jack L. Clark is sure to head any list of indictments if criminal prosecution develops. Other names mentioned by government sources include a banker who helped in the development of Equity; and Tom J. Gray, the man whose small-town nursing home in a converted motel in Henrietta, Tex., started the ball rolling.

Two local attorneys who worked with the company also are being considered as well as the former head of the franchise division for the company.

Cohen and Mathews, formerly chairman and chief prosecutor for the SEC, respectively, have been retained as counsel for Clark.

Former U.S. Sen. Smathers has been hired by Walston and Co. along with the famous Wall Street firm of Breed, Abbott and Morgan.

An original organizer of Equity and one of its officers has hired the firm headed by former Defense Secretary Clark Clifford.

In the midst of all speculation surrounding the subjects of possible criminal charges, civil suits have been assigned to Oklahoma City by the U.S. Multi-District Judicial Panel and Maryland U.S. District Judge Rozel C. Thomsen has been assigned to handle the cases.

Both major civil suits, a $50 million class action by a group of New York stockholders, and a $100 million class action on behalf of a Tennessee stockholder, alleged basically that Four Seasons and Four Seasons Equity stock was sold on the basis of false and misleading earnings reports and public statements by company officers.

The chief question, key to both civil and criminal action, seems to be whether or not Four Seasons was guilty of selling nursing homes "to itself" or an appendage of itself in order to boost revenues and in turn, stimulate investment.

There are two prevalent theories.

The first is that Four Seasons from its inception was an "evil scheme" to defraud the public and "ensure the personal wealth" of a select few individuals.

This theory is based on the infamous "Walston Memorandum" apparently dictated some time before the first public offering in 1968, and found in the company files.

Among the more revealing statements in the "Walston Memorandum" are the following:

"Question: Let's get Walston's opinion as to when we could sell a sizable portion of our stock, while the stock is at a good price, to guard against having to sell after the public realizes that nursing homes will not meet expectations on earnings."

And:

"Question: Let's get a definite program established with them as to the earliest and subsequent dates when we can dispose of our stock and ensure our personal wealth."

It was this document that prompted U.S. District Judge Luther Bohanon to make his unequivocal remarks in the Nov. 2, 1971, Four Seasons hearing:

"The court now has before it," the judge said, "the problem of whether or not Equity (Four Seasons Equity) and Four Seasons were in effect one and the same. They worked together, a joint adventure (sic), helping one another, and helping Jack Clark and his robbers, and that is what they were—nothing short of robbed the American people.

"What happened, in my judgment, has done more to destroy the faith of the American people in the New York Stock Exchange and the American Stock Exchange than any other thing that can happen. There are others, too, but this case within the past two years is the rankest. I had no idea until the hearing started yesterday of the depth of the evil that was perpetrated upon the American people. . . . It's shameful. It's disgraceful and shameless.

"This equity company was founded and the court holds and finds, for no other purpose than to augment the income of the America (Four Seasons Nursing Centers of America) and so that those on the inside would make a killing and that's just what they did."

Another potent argument supporting the "evil scheme" idea centers around the details of the second stock offering.

In the first public offering of Four Seasons (May 9, 1968) 300,000 shares of stock were sold by the company, adding somewhere in the neighborhood of $3 million for the company coffers.

Also in the first offering, Four Seasons President Clark sold 60,000 shares at a personal gain of $600,000.

The ratio of gain—$3 million for the company and $600,000 for Clark as the selling stockholder—has been deemed acceptable by prevailing standards. It was this first offering that allegedly was the basis of the comments in the "Walston Memorandum":

"Question: Are our earnings important on a primary offering— in other words, can we take $500,000 out of the present year's earnings."

But in the second offering, Nov. 26, 1968, the tables were reversed. This time the company sold only 100,000 shares for company proceeds of $5.5 million while "selling stockholders," primarily. Clark, Four Seasons officers Amos Bouse and Tom J. Gray, and Montgomery Co. (wholly controlled by Walston) sold 497,000 shares for a personal gain of $27,379,000.

As it set out clearly in the prospectus for the second offering:

"The company will receive no part from the sale of the 497,800 shares being sold for the account of the selling stockholders."

Clark himself made over $10 million on the second offering; Bouse, $6 million; Gray, $4 million, and Walston (Montgomery) over $4 million.

With $27 million going into the company officers' hands, the sincerity of any long-range plans for the future of the nursing home industry by officers and other insiders comes up for question. It almost gives credence to the Walston Memorandum statement:

". . . to guard against having to sell after the public realizes that nursing homes will not meet expectations on earnings."

"Oh what a miserable scheme was put upon the American people," the judge said. "But the court need not look at this instrument (Walston Memorandum) except to look at what happened. Mr. Clark, Mr. Bouse, Mr. Tom Gray and some others simply made a killing."

If the first "evil scheme" theory is to be taken seriously—it would have to be in the context of this second offering.

This first theory could be called the "bad means—bad end" theory; that is, that Four Seasons officers and insiders seeking an end of "personal wealth" used "fraudulent means" to achieve it.

The second theory could be called the "bad means—good end" theory. It is based on the idea that Four Seasons directors sincerely wanted to build a strong company and be a permanent fixture in the nursing home industry but used dubious means to achieve this good end, and along the way made a considerable amount of money for themselves.

The advocates of this theory would assert that such entities as Four Seasons Equity and Four Seasons Franchise were not created solely to declare inflated earnings on construction, but were simply vehicles to be used for quickly building the company.

Under this theory you would be asked to assume that the fantastic projections issued by Jack L. Clark (100,000 nursing home beds in six years and 40 hospitals) were sincerely delivered.

This idea is partially supported by the fact that Four Seasons did produce a well-made and needed product. The nursing homes themselves were praised for outstanding design and the patients were more than adequately treated.

"To my knowledge we have never found a bed sore on any of our patients," said Jack L. Clark recently.

And the company seems to have been founded on a solid platform. It has done "well" in the words of the present bankruptcy trustee since it filed for reorganization and has compared favorably with similar firms across the country.

So we come down to the basic question: Who was at fault in the Four Seasons story? Was it a failed dream or a get-rich scheme? Was it created by a genius or a small-town personality in big-city pants?

Jack L. Clark says: "I would have to be a genius to do what the judge said I did."

He adds that he knew little about the market and "did not want to go public in the first place—I was fine where I was in the construction business.

"Walston waved that money in front of my eyes until I finally gave in."

To hear super-salesman Jack Clark talk you would easily believe that he was the author of the Walston Memorandum and still
not be guilty of participating in an evil scheme.

Others very close to the source agree with Clark's statements.

"Jack Clark is more of a fool than a thief," reports one former
executive. "He's a great salesman but not smart enough to come
up with the scheme like the judge said he did."

This same man points the finger at Walston and Co.:

"It's like a good movie with a good star and Walston was the
producer. Clark gloried in it. Walston pumped him up until he
thought he could do no wrong and then when he started getting
out of hand—they treated him like a star who went bad."

It's true that Walston and Co. officers turned sour on Clark, the
man whose career they were largely responsible for, just before the
company went bankrupt.

In depositions taken by the American Exchange and the SEC,
Walston's Glen R. Miller, a man behind Jack Clark's rise to
business stardom, made the following irreverent comments:

Question: (by officer Cecil Mathis of the Securities Exchange
Commission):

"Prior to May, or March, whenever the memo came through,
had anyone employed by Walston notified you that there might
be some question as to Clark's credibility when he made statements to the public?"

Miller: "Well, I think, as I indicated, at various times I cautioned him not to over-reach himself.

"This is a faculty that salesmen often have, so I cautioned him
about that.

"At times he tried, I think he really tried in a sense to—there
were times in there when he was toning down estimates along in
the second half of calendar 1969, along in that period. He would
say something and then kind of tone it down.

"I had the feeling that this was a natural attempt to rectify a
little overstatement, a little puffiness, that he just normally, naturally inclined to make so he was trying to get himself on base, so
to speak, so that he wasn't overstating the situation."

Arthur Anderson officials also started cutting down on certain
previous accounting practices and blaming Clark for them shortly
before bankruptcy was obvious.

Everyone was looking for a way out.

And for good reason.

According to SEC officer Mathis, any person who is convicted of securities fraud faces five years in prison and-or $10,000 fine for each count.

A separate count could be issued for each separate share of stock and million count indictments are theoretically possible.

"Who was really to blame for Four Seasons?" is a question for the court.

NURSING HOME EMPIRE BEGAN IN TEXAS MOTEL

Low-Profit Image Quickly Changes

It is somehow fitting that Four Seasons Nursing Centers of America, like so many of this country's newborns, should have been first conceived in a motel.

A man named Tom J. Gray started the Four Seasons saga in 1958 when he converted his Hillside Motel in Henrietta, Tex., into Gray's Nursing Home.

Prior to that, Gray had been known around Henrietta chiefly as the owner of the St. Elmo Coffee Shop. His background didn't prevent him from ten years later holding the title "director of operations" for the mammoth Four Seasons empire.

While Gray was busy managing the coffee shop and his new nursing home in 1958, the two other founders of Four Seasons were building their own careers.

Amos D. "Bud" Bouse was a pilot with the Air Force until 1958 when he resurfaced in his hometown Oklahoma City as a homebuilder and land developer.

He first worked with his father in the construction company Amos K. Bouse and Sons, and then became sole proprietor of his own Amos Bouse Home Builder Co. and Glennel Inc.

Jack L. Clark, the man whose personality was to shape the company more than anyone else's, started in the oil-fields, worked as a milkman for Meadowgold Dairies in 1950, sold building materials for U.S. Gypsum Co. from 1954–1958 and golfcarts for Fairway King Inc., before opening his own successful company, Fashion Built Homes Inc.

From 1958–1963, Tom Gray operated Gray's Nursing Home in Henrietta.

Toward the end of these five years he began to turn a reasonable profit.

It was about this time when, in Jack L. Clark's words, Gray saw the "great need for skilled nursing care in this country."

Gray is Clark's half-brother and had spent some of his early years in Oklahoma. He knew Jack was a construction man so it was only natural that he should approach him with the idea of building more nursing homes.

Bouse was brought in as a partner and the three men sat down one evening and designed their first home, which was completed in Odessa, Tex., in 1964.

At first they found it difficult to finance the construction of nursing homes.

The nursing home industry had a reputation at that time as a low-profit, mom-and-pop type field. The homes were usually, and many remain today, converted large houses that had seen better days with broken bannisters and balustrades.

The hallways smelled faintly like a sour combination of urine and Lysol.

Towns and cities were filled with such homes, and in the late fifties, they were the "nursing home industry."

But in 1964 and 1965, things were beginning to happen in the nursing homes. It was a time of frantic development in all the industry with new economic vistas to be conquered and wealth to be made.

Clark, Bouse and Gray soon found it easier to finance their homes—in fact, some banks were eager to finance the whole bundle, at rates the founding trio never dreamed of.

Some of the first homes were built for Gray, who would choose the location and eventually furnish and manage them. Clark and Bouse were pure construction partners.

Other homes were built for construction profits alone on contract with other individuals.

In the early days, one of the big sales advantages the three men offered was a unique design. The form of the home structure was actually four separate wings that met in a central hub.

This "X" design allowed nurses who were stationed at the center on the fulcrum point, to have eyesight contact with all the rooms.

"Within this circular hub," Jack Clark explained in the first Four Seasons Annual Report, "are two nurse stations. All controls and signal systems are located there. From this one vantage point the nurses can supervise all personnel. They have visual control over every portion of the nursing center.

"This design, coupled with our management program, allows Four Seasons to provide more than adequate care on a 100-bed facility with 36–44 employes. Facilities of similar size seldom operate efficiently with less than 65. The difference is about $7,000 a month in payroll."

Clark said the idea of the novel design came while he, Bouse and Gray were studying a stack of drawings in the early morning hours at his home.

"It became the envy of every nursing center in the world," he said in a recent interview.

Another insider in the company, however, claims the design was actually conceived by a local doctor and its first blueprint was a paper napkin in a small cafe.

Four Seasons was officially incorporated in Delaware in 1967 when it issued 300,000 shares of common stock for capital stock in 12 companies including: Bouse and Clark Construction Co.; Bouark Construction Co.; B. and C. Construction Co.; Tom Gray Inc. and corporations founded around nursing homes constructed in Liberal, Kan.; El Dorado, Kan.; Midwest City, Oklahoma City, Odessa, Tex.; Fort Collins and Colorado Springs, Colo.

Once incorporated, the company began its incredible boom.

The meteoric rise of Four Seasons was caused largely by two magic words—"Medicare" and its state-assisted brother, "Medicaid."

In January, 1967, the second phase of Medicare, the part with nursing home provisions, became available for persons 65 and older.

Under this phase the government would pay the full cost of care for the first 20 days and all but $5 a day for the next 80 days. And persons who needed to stay longer might qualify under title 19 for the "medically indigent."

Also there was "Medicaid," the part-federal and part-state aid program that was coordinated in most states through the welfare programs and usually paid all costs.

Later "Medicare-Medicaid" and the capriciousness of Congress in its allocations to the programs would prove to be a contribution to the fall of Four Seasons.

But in 1967 and 1968 it was billed a "bonanza."

Nobody believed you could lose money in any of the businesses that Medicare or Medicaid touched.

"We thought we were free and clear as long as Medicare kept paying the bills without blinking an eye," says a former nursing home investor.

At the height of the Four Seasons story, Jack Clark addressed the New York Society of Security Analysts Inc., where he outlined the foolproof welfare-Medicare argument:

"In 1962 when we decided to build a nursing center, our approach was based on the question: what was the worst we could do. If we developed a program that developed a high level of care in a facility that was aesthetically appealing, then it was reasonable to assume that we could fill it with welfare patients.

"We then needed to determine the possibility of making a profit with all welfare patients . . . we decided that a profit could be made."

Imagine an entire nursing home with public-supported patients that could still make a profit; there really seemed no way to lose money in nursing homes like these.

"A mis-estimation of the profits to be made from Medicare and Medicaid was responsible for the rise of Four Seasons," reports a former top official in a closely related company.

"Everybody played it up like a bonanza and it turned out to be a nightmare instead."

Another factor that contributed to the initial rise of Four Seasons was that nursing homes gave all indications of being in the middle of a fantastic growth area.

Jack Clark wowed prospective buyers of homes (in the early years they were usually doctors in medium-sized towns) with tales of the projected national need for nursing homes.

In the address before the security analysts he said:

"There is presently a shortage in this country of approximately 500,000 skilled beds. The industry is building at the rate of about 70,000 beds a year. The over-65 population in America is increasing at the rate of 350,000 per year."

The unique design, the benefits of Medicare-Medicaid, and the growth projections of the industry all made an excellent sales vehicle.

All the company needed was a salesman.

And Jack L. Clark is an excellent salesman.

GLAMOR STOCK SOARED ON DREAMS

For almost two years Four Seasons Nursing Centers of America was recognized as "glamor stock" and was a special favorite of investors of the American Stock Exchange.

When Four Seasons staged its first public offering in May of 1968, it was greeted like an emerging movie star.

In four months the stock soared to $42 and established itself as lead plane in a "high-flying market."

Medicare and Medicaid had arrived on the scene and were considered the keys to a nursing care bonanza.

The entire nursing care industry enjoyed a universal appeal.

For example, in the same period of time that Four Seasons stock swelled from $11 to $42, the paper of a nursing home concern called American Medicorp Care Centers jumped from $20 to $42.

Extendicare, one of the industry's leading firms, jumped in stock value from $8 to $34 over a five-month period.

The most often quoted example of the nursing home boom is the case of Lilli Ann Corporation.

Lilli Ann was first listed on the American Exchange in 1965 as a ladies garment manufacturer featuring fur-trimmed coats and suits.

In four years, Lilli Ann maintained a comfortable listing on the exchange somewhere in the neighborhood of $18 per share.

Then in January, 1969, Lilli Ann's directors announced plans to enter the "convalescent-care" field. Lilli Ann stock jumped 20 points within a month.

With the first offering, Four Seasons started its rocket-like climb that would eventually see its stock valued at over $100 and ready to split 2–1 all in the incredible period of 18 months.

Vital to the climb was the brilliant stroke of creating a partner corporation known as Four Seasons Equity.

Equity was a vehicle that allowed Four Seasons Nursing Centers of America to declare construction profits. It evolved from the time when the company sold "doctor packages."

After Four Seasons Nursing Centers was incorporated in September, 1967, the standard "modus operandi" used by the management to sell homes was to go into medium-sized Southwestern cities, collect a group of local doctors and physicians and offer a strong financing package with a certain amount of guaranteed equity.

Since they supposedly were selling the centers to an independent group of buyers, they could declare 100 percent of their construction profits as earnings. And construction profits always were the backbone of Four Seasons.

Liberal, Kan.; Santa Fe, N.M.; Midwest City and Guthrie were among those cities visited by sales representatives. In the early days, Four Seasons President Jack L. Clark visited the cities himself and offered a well-rehearsed sales package.

"Clark would go into a town, say like Liberal, where he had a friend that he'd known someplace," recalls a top official with a Four Seasons subsidiary. "He'd say he had a plan where the company could provide the doctors' group with the best design and build it for them at the lowest price.

"And he would say to show you my good faith in the deal my company will contribute 30 percent of the equity."

What this meant, for example, in terms of a $400,000 nursing home, was the following:

In the late '60s in order to secure $400,000 financing, you had to come up with 25 percent equity or $100,000.

Now if Four Seasons, as Clark might promise, would contribute 30 percent of the needed equity, or $30,000, all the doctors' group would need to come up with would be $70,000, or in a group of ten, $7,000 each.

In addition, the doctors would assume a "limited partnership" in the deal.

Four Seasons as the "general partner" would be responsible for managing the center and presumably would be liable for all the debts.

If the center failed, as some of them did, then the individual doctor or businessman would be out only that amount of money he invested—and to doctors with fat incomes, this would simply be a handy tax writeoff.

The advantages of dealing with the doctors' group were many:

—Doctors and local physicians usually have a high status in the community and ample resources to help in the financing.

—With limited obligations in the purchase and management, and a steady independent source of revenue, they were not likely to question construction costs or meddle in the management.

—Doctors would refer their own patients to the nursing home in which they owned an interest.

Nevertheless, despite these advantages, it became apparent in the fall of 1968 that the local doctor method was too cumbersome to continue at the rate the company was growing.

For one thing, the doctors did not prove as easy to deal with as was expected.

"To top it off," remembers a company executive, "most of those investor groups were doctors, who always wanted to tell you everything anyway. They would telephone and say: "Here I am, I am a doctor.""

It was decided that Four Seasons needed another vehicle to satisfy the tremendous public demand for nursing centers and at the same time reap the construction profits that comprised the bulk of their earnings.

That vehicle was Four Seasons Equity Corporation.

In November, 1968, executives of Walston and Company, the Four Seasons investment bankers, came up with the idea of Four Seasons Equity and proceeded to seek financing.

Equity basically replaced the doctors' groups. Its responsibilities were to choose building locations and buy the homes from Four Seasons of America.

Its agents would go out into different areas of the country and conduct what they called "feasibility studies" to determine if a home was needed in a specific area.

Walston and Company financed Equity with great success. They originally went after $15 million but came up with $19.5 million from ten major Midwestern insurance companies.

In order to show their confidence in the Equity idea, the three founders of Four Seasons, Clark, Amos D. Bouse and Tom J. Gray, contributed an additional $3 million which boosted the Equity package to $22.5 million.

Equity's only function was to purchase homes from Four Seasons America and to pay Four Seasons to manage the centers. Equity's only reward was 70 percent of the operating profits.

As Walston and Co. executive W.W. Geary was to write at a later date in the company memorandum: "Without certified construction profits Equity's only reason for existence ends."

The strange relationship between Four Seasons Nursing Centers of America and Four Seasons Equity, was administered by an entity known as FSN.

John W. "Jack" Johnston, the Quail Creek developer who was the first president of Equity, explained the role of FSN in a deposition taken for a lawsuit surrounding Four Season's dealings with a local corporation known as Mayfair Manor.

"Well, from the beginning," Johnston testified, "the investor group, the group of ten insurance companies who made the $19.5 million commitment, wanted to structure it in a way that they felt like the two companies would be separate, at arms-length as they could possibly be, although they were still going to be partners in the development of these centers, and so they structured a method of handling this long-term, loan commitment through a trustee of Continental, Illinois, I believe, of Chicago, in which the profits they participated would be put into another corporation which was called FSN and was owned 30 percent by Four Seasons and 70 percent by Equity. We had a very good set of books and contracts and everything related to these products to maintain our arms-length status."

It was very important that Equity remain separate.

Although it was a company conceived by Four Seasons investment bankers, constructed for the sole function of serving Four Seasons and had a staff handpicked by Four Seasons and Walston and Company, it was supposed to give the impression that it was independent.

Only if Equity was independent could Four Seasons declare construction profits. If it actually controlled Equity it would be like selling nursing centers to itself and it would be absurd to declare a profit against its own expenditure.

In addition, the Securities Exchange Commission (SEC) has set a limit on a seller's participation in a buyer's firm at 30 percent.

The "arms-length" distance of Four Seasons and Four Seasons Equity has proved to be the crucial issue in civil and criminal lawsuits against the company's former officers and Walston officials.

When it was at high tide, Four Seasons gave all indications of becoming a major American corporation.

Company officers, especially Jack Clark, issued fantastic growth projections at every opportunity, bolstering the investment community opinion that Four Seasons was a company on its way to the top.

"Good news was steadily forthcoming from former president Jack L. Clark, a great salesman who stepped down last May," a

Forbes magazine article reported in July, 1970.

Clark had announced ambitious plans for the construction of 100 child care centers and 40 hospitals in addition to hundreds of nursing homes spread across the country.

In a speech before the prestigious New York Society of Security Analysts on July 11, 1969, Clark predicted that Four Seasons would develop:

—7,000 nursing home beds (the equivalent of 70 100-bed nursing homes) by the end of 1969.

—By the end of fiscal year ending June 30, 1970, "we expect to have 13,000 to 14,000 beds in operation."

—"We will have in excess of 24,000 beds at the end of fiscal 1971."

—"It is our plan to franchise from 8–12 states under this concept which will reflect a total need of between 70,000 and 100,000 beds . . . we think that within six years, it is possible to develop 100,000 beds under our new franchise program."

Six years and 100,000 beds!

That's truly an American dream—the equivalent of 1,000 100-bed nursing homes or 1,000 100-room motels, all in the matter of six years.

If that happened, Four Seasons would become a household word. The pure physical assets of the company in nursing homes alone would be in the neighborhood of one-half billion dollars.

This would be quite a jump in ten years from the construction of the first modest nursing home in Odessa, Tex., in 1964.

But the seasons began to change on Four Seasons.

Perhaps the first indication, the first tremor of the earthquake that was eventually to shake Four Seasons, came in the second offering of the company.

The $27.5 million sale by principals in the company itself indicated at least to some investors that there was some misplaced faith in the company's future buried in the heart of the company itself.

Another factor which led to the decline was the general condition of the market itself in the fall of 1969. Also, construction costs were rising and digging into the company's major source of revenue—construction profits.

The market was tight.

Construction costs had almost doubled since the birth of the company.

A tight market is usually where the smart money sits back and rides out the storm. But Four Seasons, led by Clark like a cowboy on a bucking horse, spurred on.

It developed a labyrinth of subsidiaries and partner groups bearing names like Four Seasons Overseas, National Medical Supply Co., Embassy Construction and Four Seasons United.

Clark and other executives were zooming around the country at a fantastic rate in a $1.5 million Falcon Fanjet.

The fast pace, quick money and fantastic projections were later to create a credibility gap between management and the public.

"I don't believe in some kinds of research the way I used to," reported David Ehlers, who was president of the Florida-based Gibraltar Growth Fund that was responsible for millions of dollars in Four Seasons investment, "especially face-to-face meetings. In fact, now if a guy says, 'Sure, Dave, come right out;' and spends an entire morning with me, I wonder how much time does he spend with his company."

EMPIRE PROFITS BY SELLING TO ITSELF

The failure of Medicare to live up to public expectations was the swan song for Four Seasons Nursing Centers of America.

Other factors, like accounting problems and competition, contributed, but it was the failures of Medicare and state-assisted Medicaid to live up to bonanza projections that marked the end of the Four Seasons dream.

The nursing home industry is largely dependent on public money. Some 60 percent of all patients are paid for by a combination of Medicaid and state welfare and another 15 percent are financed by Medicare alone.

At first, Medicare-Medicaid paid all the bills the homes submitted.

But then the bureaucracy settled in and Congress began playing pull-and-tug with its funds.

The Social Security Administration in 1969 promised to eliminate franchise fees and all other non-medical payments to nursing homes. At the same time, Congress threatened to cut the Medicaid budget by $235 million.

Individual states, already out of money, threatened to cut off their matching support funds for Medicaid if Congress made the cut.

Investors began to realize about this time that Medicare-Medicaid was not the perpetual fountain of money they had thought. Its future would always be uncertain, subject to the whims and wishes of a capricious Congress.

Besides that, on the nursing home level itself, the two programs were a huge bureaucratic morass and a headache to operators.

The favorite example is the terminal cancer patient whose doctor sends him to a nursing home where he dies only five days later. His Medicare claim was submitted, but denied, because he did not require "extended nursing care."

Competition also was beginning to bloom in the nursing home industry and contributed to the decline of Four Seasons.

No fewer than 50 companies in the field had either joined the market or had announced registration by February, 1969.

The biggest of these (American Institutional Developers, Beverly Enterprises, Extendicare, Four Seasons, Hillhaven Medicenters and Ramada Inns) all were growing at a phenomenal pace and couldn't help but encroach on one another's market area.

There also was the problem in Four Seasons over accounting practices.

From the very beginning, the company had established the policy of declaring construction profits for partially completed nursing centers.

This practice allowed Four Seasons to declare earnings far in advance of the center completion and also to boost quarterly reports.

Amos "Bud" Bouse, one of the founders of Four Seasons and its vice president, explained this accounting practice in a deposition taken before his death last October.

"Arthur Anderson would always supply men who had construction background and we also would take licensed AIA architects along, and usually one person from Four Seasons Construction would go along with them. All of them would get together and estimate what they thought percentage was of completion," Bouse testified.

When the Security Exchange Commission and the American Exchange started putting pressure on the company in the fall of

1969, Arthur Anderson revised the percentage-completion construction process.

Another accounting practice that had to be dropped concerned the Four Seasons Franchise division exclusively.

Four Seasons attorney John W. Mee discussed the problem with Arthur Anderson's Kenneth Wahrman in the summer of 1969. Following are excerpts from a memorandum he wrote on that meeting:

"We advised Mr. Wahrman of the general plan now being used with regard to some statewide franchises whereby we would furnish 100 percent of the necessary financing pending a public offering by the state franchisee corporation. We advised Mr. Wahrman that immediately after such public offering, the state franchisee would "take out" 25 percent of such financing.

"Wahrman stated that the SEC looked unfavorably upon any situation where construction profits are derived from construction 100 percent financed by the seller . . . Mr. Wahrman further advised us that where the seller owned less than 30 percent of the purchasing entity, but provided the financing for the purchase, recognition of construction profits for SEC accounting purposes would be permitted only where the purchasing entity was of sufficient financial strength so that the risk of success or failure of the venture is not on the seller-lender."

This "take-out" practice is one particularly abhorred by the SEC. The SEC position is only logical—if you loan someone all of the money they need to buy your product and they buy the product, you are really selling the product to yourself.

The same accounting problem with the franchise division came over handling franchise fees. This was outlined in a note from Mee to franchise President James P. Linn:

"Apparently Arthur Anderson and Company has raised some question as to whether the guaranteed financing is in effect returning the franchise fee to the franchisee."

Mee suggested: "As an alternative, the provisions for financing could be arranged so that they appear elsewhere in the contract and are worded so that there is clearly no tie in between the initial franchise fee and the guarantee of financing."

Mee wrote this note to Linn in late June, 1969. Up to that point, and for a good amount of time after that, Four Seasons declared franchise fees as earnings in its financial reports.

This problem occurred in much the same context with Four

Seasons Equity, the partner corporation that purchased homes from Four Seasons America and paid them to operate the centers.

"It would have been all right," said a man involved in one of the lawsuits that followed the fall of Four Seasons, "if someone like H. L. Hunt or Ross Perot had come in and said to Four Seasons: 'We like your product and we want to purchase some of your homes.' Only they would have insisted that the homes be built at a slower pace and that they not be billed for the product before it was completed.

"Four Seasons was simply a construction company selling its product to itself and declaring fantastic construction earnings which made the company look like it was going great guns."

The point is that anybody can make money on construction if they have a guaranteed market that doesn't question their prices.

As long as Four Seasons had itself for a market through the guise of Equity or Franchise, they could make money as long as financing was available to feed the "buyer firms."

But it was a temporary boom for Four Seasons.

With the increasing complexity of Medicare systems, it was becoming more and more obvious that nursing homes were not going to reap the fantastic earnings from operations alone.

"It's a nickel-dime business," explains current Four Seasons trustee James R. Tolbert.

Sooner or later the financing packages that allowed the construction that boosted the earnings would have to run out, and the company would have to depend on operations—and then people would know the real strength of the company.

And the financing ran out in the tight money period of the fall of 1969. The boom and the company were doomed.

FIRM WHEELED AND DEALED

The last months of Four Seasons Nursing Centers of America before bankruptcy were marked by a feverish series of stock transfers and money-making deals.

Two local examples are the Northwest Oklahoma City Nursing Home matter and the Mayfair Manor deal. Another example is the case of the Falcon Fanjet.

The Northwest Nursing Center, 5301 N. Brookline, where Four Seasons President Jack L. Clark's father now resides, was incorporated in the standard fashion.

A group of local doctors and businessmen purchased the home from Four Seasons and issued 162,900 shares of stock in a corporation surrounding the center. They were approached by Four Seasons representatives and offered 4,943 shares of Four Seasons Nursing Centers of America stock, just beginning its decline, in exchange for all of their own stock and control of the center.

There was a delay in getting the Four Seasons stock and it shortly became almost worthless—leaving the company with the center and the doctors with nothing.

A similar situation came in a deal with Mayfair Manor Development Corporation of Oklahoma City. Mayfair Manor, a corporation owned by several persons, had as its sole asset a valuable piece of land called the "Old Branding Iron Clubhouse" property, located between Grand Ave. and Portland Ave. west of Baptist Hospital.

The land was valued at $2 million and Mayfair Manor, whose officers or directors included Four Seasons Equity President John W. "Jack" Johnston and Bill Jennings, executive vice-president of Fidelity Bank and secretary of Four Seasons Equity, voted to exchange the land for 22,356 shares of Four Seasons America stock.

This was pictured as a "good deal" for Mayfair Manor since Four Seasons stock was cresting at $80-per-share and because Mayfair Manor owners could easily liquidate their land assets.

Jennings abstained from voting on the stock exchange.

But the majority prevailed and on Dec. 5, 1969, the contract with Four Seasons was completed.

Jack L. Clark said he wanted to build a hospital on the land— and, in fact, foundations were set for the structure and remain there today, skeletons of the past.

It took eight weeks for the stock transfer to take place and in that period, Four Seasons stock fell from $80 to slightly over $30-a-share, cutting the Mayfair Manor value by almost two-thirds.

Both Mayfair Manor and the Northwest nursing center groups were later to file suit claiming that false and misleading information had been supplied by Four Seasons officials regarding the value of the stock—which is now worth 45-cents.

Another well-publicized deal surfaced in December 1969 surrounding the sale by a corporation established by Clark and Bouse of a $1.5-million Falcon Fanjet to Four Seasons Corporation.

Clark and Bouse had personally purchased the jet several months before through the use of a corporation they called Charter Jet Inc.

Bouse explained the Charter Jet Inc. arrangement in a hearing before Special Master Charles R. Jones Sept. 10, 1970. The direct examination of Bouse was conducted by Four Seasons trusteeship attorney Robert Pittman:

Pittman: "What is Charter Jet, Incorporated?"

Bouse: "That's a corporation. Jack Clark and I are the officers and directors."

And later:

Pittman: "What type of plane was this, or is it?"

Bouse: "It's a Falcon Fanjet."

Pittman: "A one seater or how many passengers?"

Bouse: "Twelve passengers."

Pittman: "Twelve passenger. I believe the record would indicate that company was incorporated with $500 paid in capital, and that Jack L. Clark owned $251 of stock and you owned $249 worth of stock; would that be correct?"

Bouse: "That's correct."

And later:

Pittman: "It is my understanding that that airplane has now been sold to Four Seasons of America Inc. When did this take place if you know?"

Bouse: "It was about, probably December of 1969, in that area, first of the year."

Pittman: "What was the price paid by Four Seasons?"

Bouse: "$1,500,000"

Pittman: "Who made the decision to sell this airplane, or Charter Jet Inc., whichever way the transaction was handled, to Four Seasons of America, Inc.?"

Bouse: "Clark and myself did."

Pittman: "And who made the decision to buy it as far as Four Seasons of America, Inc., was concerned?"

Bouse: "The directors of Four Seasons."

Pittman: "And were you and Clark both directors of Four Seasons at that time?"

Bouse: "Right."

Clark and Bouse bought the souped-up Falcon Fanjet in Nov. 1968 for $1.5-million. And in Dec. 1969 they sold it to the company on a decision of the board of directors, of which they comprised two out of five members, for $1.5-million.

In the interim period, before they sold the plane to the company, they leased it to the company according to the number of hours of use.

The number of hours of use was reported by the Four Seasons pilot Karl V. Keller.

Keller's other title with the company was "assistant to the president"—Jack L. Clark.

Clark was to say later that the decision to buy the jet in the first place and to sell it at such a crucial time in the company's history, when it was really out of money, came from Walston and Co.

Walston and Co. was allegedly afraid that the American Exchange would look unfavorably toward directors operating a company which leased a plane to a corporation of which they were also directors.

Clark said recently in a Journal interview that the airplane deal had been exaggerated and put out of proportion.

"I didn't make a goddamn dime off that airplane," he said.

The jet airplane is the central issue of a civil suit filed last month by Four Seasons trustee James R. Tolbert III.

The suit calls for a judgment of $814,734 from Jack Clark; Tom J. Gray, co-founder and former Four Seasons director of operations; Gordon H. McCollum and John C. Andrews, both former directors of the company; and William A. Collins Jr. and Maurine Bouse, co-administrators of the estate of Amos Bouse.

The suit claims that after the plane was bought for an original purchase price of $1,532,000 by the Charter Jet entity, Four Seasons Nursing Centers of America was charged $37,035 for its use and Four Seasons Franchise Centers was charged $139,250.

The interesting fact is that the franchise division was charged more than the parent company although franchise president James P. Linn has said his division did not use the plane nearly that much.

The Tolbert suit claims that the charges were "more than the reasonable value of the use of said plane. That said payments directly inured to the benefit of defendant Jack L. Clark, and the said Amos D. Bouse, deceased."

The pilot of an identical plane hangared in Oklahoma City estimated the average cost for the plane's use somewhere in the neighborhood of $1,000 per hour.

Tolbert claims in his suit that "the amounts charged Four Seasons Nursing Centers Inc. by Charter Jet Inc., ostensibly for business purposes of Four Seasons Nursing Centers Inc. were arbitrarily and capriciously determined without regard to any actual use of said plane by any of the plaintiff estates."

The suit also claims that "improper and false reports and charges were submitted" for the use of the plane.

As a result, the Tolbert suit claims that the company was ultimately damaged the full amount it paid Charter Jet, or $176,285.

In addition it claims that the $1.5 million paid Clark and Bouse was in "excess of the then market value of said plane" and that the sale-back came at a time that was "contrary to the best interests of Four Seasons Nursing Centers of America Inc. and was improvident, as each of the defendants named in this count knew or in the exercise of reasonable diligence should have known."

The trustee noted that the reorganized company was only able to get $861,551 for the plane when they were forced to sell it in November of 1970.

Using the trustee's figures, the company lost more than $600,-000 through the deal in only a few months time.

The end result of the frantic deals and wheeling dealing that went on in the last days of the original Four Seasons was that the corporate believability of the firm suffered even more.

It was obvious to most observers now that Four Seasons was on its way down, the miracle was over.

From now on, it was every man for himself.

EXCHANGE HOLDS CONFERENCE WITH CLARK

'Confidential' Memorandum Revealed

The first indication that Four Seasons was in hot water with the American Stock Exchange came in early November of 1969.

Four Seasons President Jack L. Clark was called in for a conference at the exchange's offices in New York City.

Information of the events of that conference has been discovered in a memorandum dictated by Four Seasons attorney John W. Mee Jr. and marked "CONFIDENTIAL."

The conference was held November 3.

It started with an initial interview with Ralph Southey Saul, former president of the American Exchange. Saul made it clear that there was to be no monkey business in the American Exchange.

He expressed in no uncertain terms that what he wanted for the American Exchange was "disclosure of all material facts to the public" and a "fair and orderly market."

Present at the conference other than Saul were Norm Poser, Bernie Maas, Phillip Guldeman, Fred Zucker and Murray Finebaum—all of the exchange. Saul, Poser and Zucker were all formerly associated with the Securities Exchange Commission.

Jack Clark and John W. Mee were there from Four Seasons.

Glen R. Miller and George Cabell of Walston and Co. were also present.

The questions that were asked by the exchange and recorded by Mee indicate clearly the areas of strain.

First, the exchange wanted to know exactly what comprised the $90 million in long-term financing Clark had revealed in a taped interview which had been picked up by the *Wall Street Journal* and Reuters.

When pressed to explain how much of the $90 million had already been accomplished, Mee reported Clark as citing the $15 million Eurodollar transaction, a $15 million private placement and $4 million in sale-leaseback agreements with franchises—a total of $34 million.

Clark also added that another $6 million in sale-leasebacks on the franchise system and $12 million in mortgages were being negotiated, bringing the total up to $52 million.

Maas and Poser complained that a $90 million announcement might be unclear to investors considering how much had actually been raised.

Mee reported he explained that financing conditions changed almost daily and were impossible to chart exactly. He said Clark "made it clear that it is not his intent to make such general statements in the future, as a matter of policy."

Another problem was also surfacing. The exchange asked how Four Seasons could declare 100 percent construction profits on nursing centers in which it had 30 percent interest. (Four Seasons owned 30 percent of all homes it constructed for Four Seasons Equity.)

The exchange attorneys requested that Four Seasons include a more detailed chart of its business associates in its next annual report.

Other questions that Mee reported included:—Had a "finders fee" been paid to secure the $15 million Eurodollar transaction? Clark responded that $150,000 had been paid to Argus Research Associates.

—Was Four Seasons going to meet the December 31, 1969, projection by Clark of 7,000 skilled nursing home beds? Clark responded that the goal was possible, plus or minus 31 days. The exchange made it obvious that any failure to meet such projections should be immediately reported to the public.

—What was the amount of stock Walston and Co. had loaned to third parties? Clark said he didn't know.

—How much of Four Seasons stock was held by institutions? Clark said that there were 1.9 million shares outstanding and estimated that 700,000 shares were held by institutions. Maas of the exchange hinted it might be more healthy if more of the stock was in the hands of the public.

—What was Clark's contact with Francis Santangelo, one of the exchange "specialists" assigned to handle the stock? Clark responded his relationship with Santangelo was primarily social and the market was only discussed in general terms.

Local sources indicate that Santangelo was a "very social animal" who liked to play golf and party.

The exchange asked Clark if such things as orders on his book, price, shares or limit orders were ever discussed between the two men. Clark responded that no such detailed matters were discussed.

This made the exchange balk slightly because the role of a "specialist" is to discuss those very "detailed" matters. It appeared there might be dust in Mr. Saul's "orderly" house.

Later it has been discovered Clark and Amos D. "Bud" Bouse, Four Seasons vice president, and Karl V. Keller, the company's pilot and assistant to the president, did in fact enjoy more than a social relationship with Santangelo.

Checks have been discovered from Clark and Bouse in the amount of $75,000 each, and Keller for $15,000, to Santangelo in exchange for shares of an over-the-counter stock called White Shield Corp. at $30-a-share.

The White Shield Stock, after a 2–1 split, now lists for $7-a-share.

One interesting feature of the stock transaction between the men and their exchange specialist is that both Clark's and Bouse's checks were dated June 28, 1969.

A letter from Santangelo to all three men setting out the terms "of my verbal agreement" is dated July 16. Keller's check to Santangelo was dated Sept. 10, 1969.

In any event, Santangelo apparently enjoyed a strange relationship for a specialist with his assigned company.

Sources reveal that he was fined and suspended from the exchange for a short period of time for his activities with Four Seasons.

In the conference, the exchange representatives made it clear, according to Mee's notes, that Four Seasons should work toward "obtaining outside directors." The board of directors at that time was composed entirely of insiders with the company itself—Clark was chairman; Bouse and Gray, the two other founders of the company, were board members; Gordon McCollum, of Walston and Co., and John Andrews, a Four Seasons attorney, were also on the five-man board.

"It was my impression," Mee reported, "that they would expect our board expanded by three or four persons not later than Dec. 31, 1969."

The expansion did not take place until one month before the company filed bankruptcy in June 1970.

The subjects discussed and the questions raised in the Nov. 3 conference between Clark and the exchange indicated the American Exchange had become wary of Four Seasons and would be watching the company closely.

"Jack Clark infuriated those people," said a former top official in the franchise division.

It was in November the public began indicating its own doubts about the company's strength. The stock value began to fall at a steady rate.

It would never rally again. But Clark remained indefatigable in the company's defense, always promising greater earnings.

"Four Seasons Nursing Centers of America continued its losing way yesterday," a Nov. 30, 1969, article in the *Wall Street Journal* reported, "dropping two-and-three-quarters to 67 on a turnover of 99,000 shares. The stock has plummeted nearly 15 points in the past week and a half, largely on rumors that its earnings in the second fiscal quarter, ending today, would be below expectations.

"Jack Clark, Four Seasons president, said he expects to report second quarter net earnings more than tripled the year's earlier figures. He adds, though, that net might have been even higher had it not been for a company decision to decelerate somewhat expansion of nursing centers and accelerate the entry into combined hospitals, plus child care centers.

"Asked whether he was still holding to a statement made in July that Wall Street estimates for the current fiscal year of more than $2.50 a share in earnings on $75 million in revenue were 'very reasonable figures,' Mr. Clark said: "It's still our intent to come up with earnings of between $2 and $2.50 a share, depending on the number of hospitals and nursing centers that will be started."

Jack L. Clark was determined to ride out the storm defiantly at the helm of a sinking ship.

EMBATTLED EMPIRE'S DREAMS TURN TO DUST

Four Seasons Nursing Centers of America at the turn of the new year in 1969–1970 was a sinking ship.

Jack L. Clark's hopes to build the "largest corporation in the world" were quickly turning to dust.

The dream was dead.

The projected 100,000 nursing home beds would never be built.

The child care centers never got a chance. The hospitals were left on the drawing boards.

From then on the company was on the defensive. It was a matter of retreating and digging in, retreating and digging in.

It all came down to a matter of financing.

Walston and Company executive W.W. Geary explained the financing problem in a note written to other company executives dated March 30, 1970. The note specifically referred to Four Seasons Equity, the partner firm to Four Seasons Nursing Centers of America, and was entitled, "Why is Equity Out of Money?"

"Why is Equity out of money?" Geary wrote. "The gross value of nursing homes and child care centers in operation or under construction by Equity was $42,016,874 according to the December 31, 1969, balance sheet. Equity must supply 70 percent of 25 percent of the total cost of nursing homes in equity money to the various partnerships and corporations in which Equity has a 70 percent interest.

"On this basis, $7.4 million of Equity's book value was committed on December 31, 1969. If we deduct from the reported equity base of $11,483,623 the 20 percent interest in Franchise Centers and other soft assets which amounted to $4,255,527, we are left with $822,000. Therefore, only $800,000 was available in equity money for future expansion on December 31, 1969."

So Four Seasons Equity, which was formed only a year before with $22.5 million, now had only $800,000 left—roughly enough to purchase two more nursing homes.

As Walston and Co.'s Glen R. Miller was to tell Security Exchange Commission agent Cecil Mathis in a deposition taken on March 3, 1971:

"Four Seasons Equity was way over-committed on the purchase of nursing homes. Nursing homes under construction had been started and, as best we could determine, billings had been made to Four Seasons Equity for nursing homes that hadn't been committed for, at least formally. I think the documentation was very lax.

"Supposedly, Four Seasons was to run the business for Equity to purchase nursing homes that could be financed by Equity and no more.

"I was astounded to find that even instead of writing letters back and forth they were using inter-office memos between the two companies. I mean it was this informal."

The point is that if Equity was out of money, then Four Seasons was prevented from buying any new homes. If it was prevented from building new homes then it could no longer reap the fantastic earnings claimed from construction profits. If earnings went down —so did the stock and the investments.

And so did the company.

Walston and Co. frantically tried to put the pieces together. In a memorandum written in the waning days of the company before bankruptcy, Walston's Geary discussed ways to "cut overhead" and considered the idea of merging Four Seasons and its supposedly "arms-length" brother, Four Seasons Equity.

Even the possibility of merging both companies into a larger company was discussed but vetoed, because in Geary's words:

"If the two companies cannot continue, then we should consider the merger. However, we should not merge unless we are forced to because we have raised $70 million for the two companies and have thousands of investors and employes committed to the idea of two separate companies. . . . We came to a fork in the road when we created Equity. To cross over to the other road now would be very difficult."

Geary states the problem point-blank later in the memo:

"Without certified construction profits Equity's only reason for existence ends."

Equity was the monster created by Walston. Now the monster was turning on the master. It was created as a "vehicle" for Four Seasons Nursing Centers of America to declare construction profits.

Although technically, according to the weird labyrinth of laws that govern securities, the two companies might have been considered "arms length"; in the cold light of reality, they were the same.

And that is how Four Seasons sold nursing homes to itself.

Geary wrote that the time had come for "Four Seasons Nursing Centers to convert its assets into cash. Specifically it should: (a) sell all excess land, (b) collect on its demand notes receivable and on past due notes receivable, (c) sell all aircraft, and (d) sell the yacht."

It was about this time that Walston and Co. informed Four Seasons officers that they "should find another investment banker"—Walston and Co. was bailing out.

Meanwhile, the American Stock Exchange, increasingly dubious of the company and the way it declared its earnings, got word of a certain scandal that was bubbling in the state of Ohio.

The Ohio Legislature in 1967 passed a series of bills which authorized the state to invest up to $50 million from general funds in commercial paper.

In March of 1970, Ohio loaned money from the state treasurer's office and the Ohio School Employes Retirement System (SERS) to Four Seasons, which unknown to Ohio was already floundering.

In addition, another $18 million was promised before the "statehouse loan scandal" broke into black headlines all over the state.

The first part of the loan scandal came because notes Ohio arranged with Four Seasons and other companies, including the ill-fated King Resources of Denver, were for a longer period than allowed by law.

Then it was discovered that Four Seasons arranged the loans by paying $160,000 in "finders fees" to Dee Gee Co. of Columbus.

It was later alleged that $800,000 of the Ohio loan money was "reloaned" to Financial Data Relations Co. of Beverly Hills and a man named Ronald Howard of Los Angeles.

What really blew the top off the Ohio statehouse was that one of the major "finders" for the loans, including the one to Four Seasons, was another Columbus Company called Crofters Inc.

One of the directors of Crofters was a young Republican politician with connections in all the right places, Gerald A. Donahue.

Donahue had been a former state tax commissioner and deputy Ohio attorney general. He also served as a chief aide to Ohio Republican U.S. Sen. William B. Saxbe.

Furthermore, it was learned that Crofters had made campaign contributions to Republican Gov. James Allen Rhodes; state treasurer John D. Herbert, a central figure in the loan scandal; Attorney General Paul Brown, and State Auditor Roger Cloud.

Conveniently, it also was an election year when the story broke and Herbert was the Republican candidate for attorney general; Cloud for governor, and Rhodes for the U.S. Senate.

"We had a front page story every day for at least three months," reports *Cleveland Plain Dealer* Columbus Bureau Chief David Hopcraft.

"I think we know more about Four Seasons up here than you do down in Oklahoma," he added.

The Democrats frolicked in the election and the controlling Republicans were wrested from power. The whole face of the statehouse was changed.

The American Stock Exchange, already keeping a close eye on the operations of Four Seasons, blew its top when the Ohio story started breaking.

On April 30, 1970, the American Exchange dropped Four Seasons from the market.

On May 1, Jack Clark announced that the company would show a net loss for the third fiscal quarter ended March 31.

The *Wall Street Journal* had the story:

"The executive (Clark) said higher material and labor costs and a slowdown in overall construction progress caused the downturn. He added that final figures for the quarter wouldn't be available for several weeks.

"Four Seasons also disclosed that it is changing its method of accounting for franchise fees to conform with the 'more conservative treatment' being recommended for franchised income, further hurting the third quarter results.

"A spokesman explained the accounting change as meaning Four Seasons won't add franchise fees to its earnings until it 'does something substantive,' such as beginning construction of a franchised building. Under previous accounting procedures, franchise fees were added to earnings as soon as the franchise contract was signed.

"Mr. Clark said: 'We anticipate the earnings for the fiscal year ending June 30 will be comparable with the 80 cents a share earned last year."

Clark was still optimistic.

On May 13, the Security Exchange Commission halted all, even over-the-counter, trading in Four Seasons stock.

Thousands of phone calls poured into Clark's office and the pressure mounted.

May 21, Clark, Amos D. Bouse and Tom J. Gray—the three founders of Four Seasons—resigned.

Clark now says the major reason he resigned was because of poor health.

"We had an executive meeting and I thought I had a heart attack," he said in a *Journal* interview. "That's the time I finally got the ultimatum from my doctors—they said I had 30 to 60 days to live."

He was admitted to St. Anthony Hospital where doctors found that he would survive.

Although Clark and Four Seasons attorney John Andrews remained on the board of directors, the rest of the officers were new faces.

James P. Linn, now a practicing Oklahoma City lawyer who previously headed the franchise division, was named president.

Linn was optimistic.

"The company is in good financial condition," he said. "It's good and sound. We have $18 million in the bank and our long-term debts are not excessive."

Toward the end of June, in Linn's first month of presidency, the company began considering filing for reorganization under Chapter X of the Federal Bankruptcy Act.

It was decided that Norman Hirschfield of Oklahoma City should lead the company into bankruptcy.

The move was thought only to be temporary—"to get the company under the federal umbrella."

On June 26, 1970, Four Seasons filed for reorganization under the Bankruptcy Act in the Oklahoma City federal courthouse.

SUPER-SALESMANSHIP ROCKETS CLARK TO TOP

Some men are born with success. Others have to make it themselves.

There are dreams of success in the eyes of all young men—from those who work in the auto repair shops on S. Robinson in Oklahoma City to those who shuffle papers waiting for the big break in the office buildings on Robert S. Kerr or Park Avenues.

Jack L. Clark, the man who built the Four Seasons Nursing Centers Empire, is one of the very few whose dreams came true.

His life story before the company he built filed bankruptcy in 1970, is in the best tradition of Horatio Alger.

"Jack Clark is like a Horatio Alger—or a Walter Mitty whose dreams came true," said a former employee.

"Somewhere along the line the Lord put his hand on my shoulder," explains Clark.

Clark's father was an oilfield worker, a man who now lives in one of the nursing homes his son built. From his earliest days young Clark was taught the virtues of "work—hard work."

Jack L. Clark speaks reverently of his father and of his early training.

"He only had a second grade education but he was a very innovative man. He developed his own oilfield tools."

"All I knew from the beginning was the oilfields," Clark remembers now with his feet propped up on an orange marble table in a room filled with African hunting trophies. "I was roughnecking when I was 12 years old. When I was 16, I was probably the youngest driller in the fields."

As a youngster, Clark was known as a big, rough and hard-to-handle boy with a stuttering problem.

In Classen High School he was in the running for the title of the school's best fistfighter.

"He was big and rough and liked to fight," remembers John Bentley, a classmate of Clark's at Classen. "I remember he had a fight almost every noon hour. It didn't take much to provoke Jack into a fight. Sometimes the best fighters from Central High School would come over and challenge him."

Clark was later to get a short, very successful, taste of organized boxing. "I don't want to brag but I never lost a bout in 15 fights. In fact, I considered turning professional," he says.

He dropped out of Classen before graduating and joined the Air Force.

But apparently the service life helped him and he came back a more mature and responsible fellow. He re-enrolled at Classen where he graduated after one semester. "I graduated with the highest grades (for that one semester) ever received at Classen— all A's except for one A-plus."

After the Air Force and his graduation from Classen, Clark apparently went for a short time to junior college at St. Thomas Military Academy in Minnesota and then spent "two or three semesters at OU."

While he was a student at the University of Oklahoma, at age 22, he married Anne Dunning, the beautiful daughter of Oklahoma City construction man Charles M. Dunning.

His first job after dropping out of college was as an oil company agent on a site near Rawlings, Wyo. Clark remembers it as "the coldest winter ever recorded in Wyoming."

The site was miles from town and Anne Clark was pregnant with Jack Jr., now 22 years old. "She was pregnant and ready to have the baby and I couldn't even get to her," he remembers now.

So he quit his job with the oil company and came back to Oklahoma City with his family. In 1950 he became a milkman with Meadow Gold Dairies.

Clark, the man who started the nation's largest chain of nursing homes, the man who at one time was worth more than $40 million on paper, the man who lives in a home that some value at $2 million, was in 1950 getting up at 4 A.M. delivering milk and butter to Oklahoma City families.

He doesn't remember his years as a milkman with any great fondness. "When you get up in the morning at 4 A.M. with the flu and you know you have a job to do that has to be done, it doesn't come easy."

Both he and his wife remember that period in their lives with a slight shiver but it was a start, and "the family was together."

"It wasn't the only job I could get but it paid well for those times. I didn't want to do it forever but I'll never apologize for it —I never had to apologize to my family," Clark says.

It was the milk-run that began his steady and quick upward mobility.

He built his individual milk-run into "the largest in the city." Then he was promoted to route manager and then built his district into the "largest in the city."

It was obvious the milk business wasn't large enough to hold Clark and he began to experiment with other occupations.

For awhile he was a golf cart salesman. This was the occupation that was later to propel him to a hard-driving "one-handicap."

After a successful stint with the golf carts, the first real test of his salesmanship prowess, he became a sales agent for U.S. Gypsum company in Oklahoma City.

He built a reputation as a "super-salesman." When you ask a man who knew Clark during his reign as president of Four Seasons this is the description that keeps coming back over and over again.

"He was, over and above everything else, with all the bad and all the good, first of all a great salesman," said a former top-executive with the company.

Later his salesmanship was to be given the most severe tests available in a world of salesmen. He was to go and sell doctors on building nursing homes in their small towns, then he was to go and sell the nation's most prestigious and sharp-eyed investors on the future of the company and then many others—from top state officials in Ohio to the leading "financiers" of Europe.

He came to U.S. Gypsum "not knowing which end of the nail to hit" and left breaking "all the company's records as a salesman."

"I remember him as a very good salesman," says former U.S. Gypsum district manager Gary Ensing, now retired and living in Tulsa. "I would say his greatest qualities were perseverance and his great confidence in himself."

Clark says he used to go into prospective buyers' businesses wearing khaki pants and open-collared shirt with his sleeves rolled up. He would go in, commandeer a ladder, and demonstrate the product.

He learned the essential sales axiom: "Never take no for an answer."

"If they said 'no' I wouldn't just walk out the door and give up on the sale. I would ask them why they hadn't bought the product and make them give me a reason.

"When they explained why, I reasoned with them. More often than not, I would make the sale."

Offered a promotion at U.S. Gypsum which meant he would have to leave Oklahoma City—Clark declined.

His boss, Ensing, of whom Clark speaks with great reverence, introduced him into the homebuilding business by helping the young salesman secure loans to build his first two homes.

"I built those two homes," remembers Clark with a touch of nostalgia. "I went there during the day and raked the yards and at night I swept the floors.

"I sold five custom jobs off of one house."

He was on his way. He was on Horatio Alger's doorstep.

"In the 18 months after those first two sales I made $100,000. At that time that was the World's Fair to me."

He had built a successful homebuilding career in 1961 when Tom Gray, his half-brother then living in Texas, approached him and fellow homebuilder Bud Bouse with the idea of building a nursing home.

Gray had converted a motel in Henrietta, Texas, into a nursing home and in Clark's words "saw the great need for skilled nursing centers."

They built the first nursing center in Odessa, Tex.

Once started, Clark's company grew at a rapid rate unequaled in American business.

Soon top executives and investors were praising Clark as a great leader and a major innovator in business techniques.

"Jack Clark of Four Seasons was the most impressive corporate head I've ever met," remembers David O. Ehlers, president of the Gibraltar Growth Fund. "He worked hard all the time and seemed to speak with the aura of truth. Much of what he said was true."

Just before the bankruptcy petition was filed by the company, *Business Week* magazine delivered its own eulogy of Four Seasons:

"In its heyday, the company was considered one of the best managed in the industry. Clark was a pioneer in standardized nursing home design and construction techniques that permitted employe-to-patient ratios to be lowered and a single head nurse to keep an eye on four corridors of patients. He also came up with a novel financing plan that brought in physicians' groups as major investors. These doctors still refer patients to Four Seasons."

While the company was going strong there seemed no end to the praises that were being heaped on Clark.

But the business world is fickle. It compares in this respect to the world of athletics.

They booed Mickey Mantle in Yankee Stadium after he lost his legs.

They booed Jack Clark on Wall Street after Four Seasons started its downward trend.

Before that, when Four Seasons was $100 a share and ready to split, when the nursing home industry was the hottest thing going, when investors were reaping huge profits and coming back for more, nothing was too good for Clark, the darling of Wall Street.

He was the "most impressive corporate head" people had ever met.

He was a "super-salesman" among super-salesmen.

He was elected one of the first directors of the American Council of Health Care Centers.

He was invited to speak before a special meeting of the New York Society of Security Analysts.

He was the king of the mountain, the man credited with "revolutionizing" the nursing home industry through pure concentration of business brilliance and hard work.

After the fall of the company came the lawsuits. Among the plaintiffs' names you could see the professional litigants, the "ambulance chasers" of securities trials. The men and the attorneys who follow securities cases around the country hoping to win a class action judgment against former officers or the remains of the company.

And along with the lawsuits came the agents of the Securities Exchange Commission, the FBI and postal inspectors. Asking questions.

Questions like:

"Who does a certain person play golf with? Where did Jack Clark gamble?

"Who'd they take along on those airplane rides?"

Noises of grand jury action began coming from the U.S. Attorneys' office.

Clark's private life was ruined.

The man who began the industry, became to some the man who deceived the industry.

Angel or demon, genius or fool, take your choice.

"What happened to these companies, to these men?" philosophized David Ehlers. "All of sudden former geniuses looked like jerks, and the jerks, who had kept the cash in the till, looked like geniuses."

There are two sides to men like Clark.

On one hand there is the man who says: "Some would say our senior citizens are too old to demonstrate, too infirm to protest, too tired to turn-on. Others might say perhaps they're just too smart. Whatever the reason, one thing is clear: 20 million people must not be forgotten."

And: "Our technological brilliance will allow us to fly to the moon next week; yet, we still are faced with the age-old question of how to satisfy our social and moral obligations to the elderly."

On the other hand:

City furniture store owner Bill Bentley describes Clark: "He is capable of holding a $30,000 poker hand and calling it—and that could be all the money he had. If he was a wildcat driller he would be the same way."

"He is an egotistical braggart," said one former top official in a related company.

"Egotistical" enough to ask James P. Linn, former head of the Four Seasons Franchise division and president of Four Seasons after Clark resigned, that he be made "senior U.S. Senator" from Oklahoma.

Egotistical enough to do all that, but naive enough to think that he would be "senior senator of Oklahoma."

Egotistical enough to reportedly have lectured the worldly "financiers" of such European banking houses as Banque Rothschild, Credit Commerciel de France and Kreditbank Luxembourgeoise, on "good and bad" wines while he was in Europe, but naive enough to believe he was impressing them and smart enough to sell them $15 million in debenture bonds.

One minute he is negotiating on the phone with a man who wants to sell him a jet airplane, and next, as happened just recently, he loans $25,000 to a young man he barely knows to deal in the commodities market only to find weeks later that his investment has dwindled to nothing.

He is as elusive as a butterfly, as mysterious as F. Scott Fitzgerald's Jay Gatsby, as materialistic as Sinclair Lewis' Babbitt— but through it all, a great historical character.

THIS IS THE HOUSE THAT JACK BUILT

"This is the house that Jack built."

—Old Nursery Rhyme

The house that Jack L. Clark built resembles a huge stony mausoleum constructed in honor of the Unknown Soldier or a South American liberator.

It sits, in all its frowning expansiveness, on Grand Boulevard across the street and almost within putting distance of the Oklahoma City Golf and Country Club.

The cost of the home is difficult to estimate.

U.S. District Judge Luther Bohanon in that controversial Nov. 2 federal court hearing placed the value somewhere in the neighborhood of $500,000.

"The court," Judge Bohanon said, "has positive knowledge that Mr. Clark has built out of the proceeds he received from his wrongful, illegal and shameful and disgraceful acts, a half-million dollar home."

But the judge's estimate seems to be considerably off the mark. Clark himself admits that it cost more than $1 million and a former close associate of his runs the figure up to around $2 million.

Regardless of the cost and the cold forbidding exterior of the home, the interior is a visual field-trip, full of marble, expensive French cut-glass, living room moats and an unequaled collection of "objets d'art."

The first thing that strikes you after the drive up the long circular driveway is the huge pair of carved wooden doors that rest in the center of a polished marble porch. The doors are at least ten feet high; they are the kind that ransacking armies would have to crush with huge pilings.

The whole house, in fact, resembles a fortress.

Built in a squared-off semi-circle with all windows facing into a courtyard, the interior is protected by tall windowless stone walls on three sides and by a ten-foot high stone barrier on the fourth.

The first thing you see when you enter is a small maze-like moat in the entrance hall with circulating water that is warm to the touch. Through the moat you see a dazzling snow-white living room.

To the right is a dining room with a long twelve-chaired table. One of the chairs in the sparkling-new dining room set still has the factory plastic cover.

Once inside, there is a wealth of natural light. The interior walls are simply huge glass sliding doors all of which open into the courtyard and the swimming pool area.

The pool is more of a reflecting pond than a swimming spot. It is so well-designed and built that it seems you would disrupt its serenity by splashing and cavorting in it.

If you stand near the pool in the center courtyard area you have a full view of most of the rooms and their interiors. You see that where it is not rough-stone or glass, practically everything is shiny marble of various shades and colors.

You see a master bedroom decorated in alternating subtle and bright turquoise colors with strategically placed mirrors.

On one flank of the ultra-white living room is what the Clark family calls the game room. One of the few rooms in the house that looks slightly "used," the game room is furnished in a semi-circle of soft comfortable sofas and chairs around a translucent white glass table with submerged lights that shine up through cut-glass ashtrays.

Its most distinguishing feature is a fireplace with a huge bronze-sculpted mantle that reaches to the top of the ceiling.

The fireplace is one of the touches engineered by Arthur Elrod, the Palm Springs interior decorator with the Midas touch.

Elrod, decorator for such Hollywood personalities as Bob Hope, is one of the most expensive if not the most sought-after of America's interior consultants.

"When you use Arthur Elrod," says one man close to the source, "you should be prepared to spend $500 for an ashtray. An Elrod home is a several hundred thousand dollar investment."

Both Clark, as president of Four Seasons Nursing Centers of America, and his close friend and vice president of Four Seasons, Amos D. "Bud" Bouse had their homes done by Arthur Elrod.

Although figures aren't available, estimated costs for Elrod's job on the Clark home range from $300,000 to a slightly more inhibiting $750,000.

Elrod's own home, shooting background for many Hollywood

movies in need of an elegant setting, can be seen in all its luxury in the James Bond film, "Diamonds are Forever."

Practically one whole wing of the Clark home is taken up by combination trophy room and office.

When Clark resigned from the company in May, 1970, he became just another wealthy man without a company, and without an office. Particularly since the fraud allegations began pouring in, Clark has used his home as his office.

And his office within the home is adjacent to the trophy room.

There is probably no other room in the American Southwest quite like Jack Clark's trophy room.

Mounted and stuffed along the walls and in pouncing positions on the floor are a great variety of African animals.

Included in the incredible montage are two fully stuffed and dressed lions, two cape buffalo, antelope, gazelles, boars, impalas, topi, a wildebeest (gnu) and many others. Above his desk in the corner are five positively huge largemouth bass caught by Clark and his wife at a lake in Mexico.

It's enough to make any big game hunter green with envy and any naturalist cringe with despair.

The two stuffed lions are in the center of the floor. One is in a pouncing position and looks like the model for the Dreyfus Fund lion.

The cape buffalo, gentle as India's sacred cows in appearance, were reported by Clark to be the toughest animal in Africa to bring down.

"You can't turn a cape buffalo," he says. "You can turn a lion and you can turn an elephant, but you can't turn a cape buffalo. They just keep coming."

Clark tells the tale of how he bagged one of the lions (a son shot the other). He and the family hired the same guide who takes "Gloria and Jimmy Stewart" when they go on safari.

They were in Tanzania on sort of a search and destroy mission for the "topi." They saw the hoofed animal and Clark was prepared to fire when the guide yelled in Swahili, "lion!"

The lion came at Clark and he managed to "turn him" with a low-powered rifle. The lion retreated to the high grass. Clark went in after him, and finally bagged the beast within whites-of-the-eyeball distance.

Another close associate of Clark's tells a less flattering tale.

"Jack had hired a professional photographer to come along and take pictures of the hunt. They go into the bush looking for lions. They see one there swatting flies with its tail. Jack climbs a tree and shoots it."

A recent convert to hunting, Jack Clark has long been known as a great lover of fishing—especially for bass.

He still says fishing is his first love.

"In fact, I'm in the process now of writing a book on fishing. Just recently I tried to buy a bait company."

But for the time being anyway, Jack Clark is biding his time.

With rumors of possible criminal charges ready for the indictment process any day now in the Southern District of New York and almost more civil fraud cases than there were stockholders, he spends much of his time behind his huge curved orange marble desk beneath the five positively huge largemouth bass, next to the Dreyfus Fund lion, just across the reflecting-pond swimming pool from the sparkling white living room next to the heated moat, through the mammoth wooden doors within putting distance of the country club on Grand Boulevard . . . in the house that Jack built.

FOUR SEASONS SURVIVING ITS PROBLEMS

Modest Profits Expected for Reorganized Firm

No one knows better than Oklahomans that a good farmer can grow a crop from even the poorest soil.

No one knows better than Americans that freewheeling means can sometimes result in good ends.

The 19th Century "robber barons" are not remembered for their saintly ways, yet these men, the John D. Rockefellers, the Jay Goulds and the James J. Hills, built the railroads and drilled the oil wells that made this country what it is today.

Jack L. Clark and the men who founded Four Seasons Nursing Centers of America have been accused in lawsuits and from the federal bench of using high-handed methods to perpetrate a fraud on the American people.

On this day evidence is being prepared to present a criminal case against former Four Seasons officers in the Southern District of New York, in New York City.

But when the dust settles and the litigation grinds its way toward resolution, Four Seasons may come out of the whole thing with a polished image.

A hint of that possible eventuality is found in the relative success enjoyed by the remains of the company now under reorganization.

In hearings on a proposed final plan of reorganization held in November, Four Seasons trustee James R. Tolbert III, a local corporate consultant who has brilliantly managed the myriad of company affairs since February, 1971, predicted first year net earnings for the company after reorganization of $1.2 million.

Tolbert forecasts anticipated gross earnings of the corporation of $15.7 million for the same period.

The company has gone from the 45 nursing homes it was operating when it filed for bankruptcy reorganization to 26 operating nursing homes and two child care centers.

These 26 nursing homes, Tolbert reports, are "in the aggregate" doing well and the trustee is "pleased with the progress" of the child care centers in Denver and Atlanta.

The nursing homes have gone from a monthly operating loss of $100,000 when Tolbert took over in February, 1971, to a monthly net profit of between $65,000 and $70,000.

"In addition," Tolbert said in a recent Journal interview, "the reorganized company will have a portfolio of real estate assets made up of partially completed nursing homes and child care centers and undeveloped land. These should provide a base for expanded operations whether in the nursing home field or in some related or other field."

One of Tolbert's first executive actions when he took the trusteeship from Norman Hirschfield was to sell properties and facilities the management deemed to be marginal or hopelessly tangled in finances.

"We sold the properties for only three reasons," Tolbert said: "They were either partially built properties that were deteriorating because of the elements, properties that because of the way in which they were financed were burdensome and properties that were necessary to dispose of because of third party interest.

"My goal was to maintain as many options as possible for the reorganized company."

The trustee reports that the company has "just about broke

even" on their property sales. In some cases a profit has been made.

For example, 200-bed nursing homes in Tucson, Ariz., and Elk Grove, Ill., were sold individually for $1.5 million.

The Tucson operation has become a county-operated nursing home and the one in Illinois is operated as a hospital annex.

Tolbert reports that the company is watching closely the eventual use of the facilities by the buyer groups.

There is a strong indication from the sales of potential growth areas in "specialized health care, facilities for the mentally retarded and limited use and psychiatric hospitals."

The administration of the nursing home enterprise itself has been drastically reshaped, beginning with staff cuts by Hirschfield and continued by Tolbert.

Overall, the central office staff has been cut from 470 to 38 persons. No one who was prominently involved with the original Four Seasons operation is still on the office payroll.

The administration has been decentralized through the use of a district manager system. Each district manager is responsible for from five to eight homes.

This system allows for a much great accountability than the original management program.

Tolbert's task when he signed on as trustee was to discover if a reorganized company could be a viable business. The figures show that Four Seasons is that, and all indications are that the corporation founded on the dreams of a few Southwestern home builders will remain a prominent fixture in the industry.

The company may never approximate the vision of Jack L. Clark as one of the world's major corporations, but there at least will be something left for his efforts.

"My wife and I have talked it over," Clark said recently, "and decided that if we did all this and got all this accomplished, then if I have to go to jail or whatever they do to me doesn't matter."

Clark says he is still very much intrigued with the nursing home and general health care field. At one time, he said recently, he entertained hopes of being renamed Four Seasons president.

He says he is tired of his business dormancy and is ready to start building once again.

"I predict that I will be building new facilities within 90 days," he said a month ago.

A nursing home that he and his wife personally funded with $200,000 is presently under construction for the Westminster Presbyterian Church, 4400 N. Shartel.

Meanwhile, a plan for reorganization is nearing finalization in federal court.

U.S. District Judge Luther Bohanon, with great praise on the trusteeship of Tolbert tentatively approved the plan in November.

Judge Bohanon referred the proposed plan to the Security Exchange Commission for study and its report is expected any day.

Since Grant Guthrie, chief counsel for the SEC out of Chicago, worked closely with Tolbert in forming the plan, the agency is expected to give it a favorable review, asking for few if any revisions.

Once the SEC report returns, Judge Bohanon must first give it his final approval before copies will be mailed to the some 20,000–25,000 unsecured creditors and "creditor-stockholders" with interest in the company.

The plan is basically centered around two classes of creditors —the unsecured creditors, who number somewhere in the neighborhood of 6,000, and the "stockholder creditors," who are those people who lost money on the purchase of Four Seasons Nursing Centers of America and Four Seasons Equity stock from the day the companies were founded to July 22, 1970, the day Equity filed for reorganization.

The "stockholder-creditor" class is the most controversial part of the reorganization plan.

Under the plan, this massive group of former stockholders— whose potential claims have been estimated from between $60 million and $190 million—will be granted common stock in the reorganized company based on one-third of the new company's equity.

This class, Tolbert explained, was a "compromise" created to offset the spectre of stockholder fraud suits, of which there are several which could delay a proper reorganization.

The opposition is coming basically from two areas—the state of Ohio, and those who bought Four Seasons or Equity stock after the July 22 deadline.

Ohio, which originally loaned Four Seasons $4 million, claims it cannot legally accept common stock in a reorganized company.

The after-deadline stock purchasers, who reportedly include many famous "high rollers," would literally be left with nothing under the plan. These are people who are gambling that the re-organization plan will fail and the outstanding stock will once again be traded at a higher rate.

After the mammoth job of mailing the plan and other items to the main classes of creditors is completed, each separate class will vote on the approval of the plan.

Each unsecured creditor will have a vote power relative to the amount of money his claim represents in the whole class. Each stockholder-creditor would have voting power dependent on the percentage amount of loss his claim represents in his whole field.

Each class separately must approve the plan by a two-thirds majority before it can be ratified.

If the plan is approved by both major groups then it will be sent back to the judge, who will appoint a board of directors for the new company. The unsecured creditors will be issued stock in the new company roughly on the basis of one stock for every $7 claimed.

The stockholder-creditors will be issued stock on a pro-rata basis reflecting their percentage interest in their class.

From this point the company will begin to operate as a normal business enterprise. The stockholders slowly will evolve to the point where they elect their own board of directors.

Tolbert, who left a prosperous business of his own to act as trustee, says he is willing to remain with the company for up to 18 months after final reorganization.

If the reorganization scheme follows the outline, it will be one of the quickest ever done through the courts of this country.

Four Seasons once again will be on its own.

All the good and all the bad that marked its history will be left behind. Jack Clark and the other founders will be somewhere else.

But Four Seasons will not be forgotten.

[End of series]

Four Seasons Group Indicted

Clark, 7 Others Accused of Fraud

Jack L. Clark, the Oklahoma City multi-millionaire who forged Four Seasons Nursing Centers of America into a high-flying glamor corporation of the late 1960s, and seven other men were

indicted Wednesday by a New York federal grand jury on charges
of massive securities fraud conspiracy.

After a ten-month probe into the financial dealings of Four
Seasons, the grand jury returned a 65-count indictment against
Clark, the former Four Seasons president and chairman, former
director Tom J. Gray, former franchise subsidiary president and
city attorney James P. Linn, three local Arthur Anderson accounting firm partners and two top officials with the major Wall
Street investment banking firm Walston and Company.

Assistant U.S. Attorney Gary Naftalis, who presented the case
to the grand jury, said Wednesday "it is probably the biggest
security fraud case ever filed" in that it is among the first to deal
with "rich, powerful and influential people."

In a statement issued following the indictments, Whitney North
Seymour Jr., chief U.S. attorney for the Southern District of New
York, hailed the indictment as "the first criminal fraud charge
ever filed against high officers of a major Wall Street investment
banking firm and the second such indictment ever filed against
partners of a national accounting firm."

All of the defendants and alleged co-conspirators contacted
Wednesday denied the allegations set forth in the federal indictments.

The U.S. attorney's office estimated the amount of losses absorbed by investors in the now-defunct Four Seasons firm to be in
the area of $200 billion and the net gains by insiders in the $21
million range.

The one conspiracy charge naming all eight defendants charges
that they: (1) conspired to defraud the purchasers of Four Seasons
stock by fraudulently reflecting the company's earnings; (2) defrauded the state of Ohio out of $4 million by using a falsely
certified financial statement to obtain a loan; (3) defrauded European investors out of $15 million through the sale of debenture
bonds; and (4) filed false financial statements with the American
Stock Exchange and the Securities Exchange Commission.

Indicted on the securities fraud conspiracy charges Wednesday
were Clark, 46, of 2305 NW Grand Blvd.; Gray, 57, of Wichita
Falls, but now reported living in Spain; Linn, 46, of 1605 Wilshire
Blvd.; Kenneth J. Wahrman, 38, of 3012 Red Rock Circle, partner
in Arthur Anderson and Co., accounting firm; Edward J. Bolka,
41, 2312 NW 115, Arthur Anderson partner; Jimmie E. Madole,
1416 NW 104 Terrace, Arthur Anderson employe; Gordon H.

McCollum, Paradise Valley, Ariz., former director of Four Seasons and vice president of Walston and Co. investment banking firm, and Glen R. Miller, Glenview, Ill., considered a top executive with Walston.

U.S. District Judge Lloyd F. MacMahon accepted the indictment in New York and ordered an arrest warrant for Gray after Naftalis told him the defendant was living in Spain and might not return to the U.S.

The eight defendants have been ordered to appear for pleading hearings in New York Jan. 2.

In addition to the eight regular defendants, four other citizens, including Oklahoma City banking figure Bill P. Jennings, executive vice president of Fidelity Bank and former director of Four Seasons Equity, and John W. "Jack" Johnston, Quail Creek developer and former president of Equity, were named as co-conspirators in the case.

Named as co-conspirators, which itself is not a criminal charge but connects those named as part of any alleged conspiracy, were Johnston, 11105 Blue Stem Road; Jennings, 1313 NW 85; Larry D. Hunt, Arthur Anderson employe; Kale Kenneth Kilfoy, 1208 NW 88, former Four Seasons construction division employe; Frank J. Crimmins, New York City, former exchange representative of Walston and Co. for Four Seasons; the late Amos D. "Bud" Bouse, former Four Seasons vice president killed in an Oct. 21, 1971, plane crash; and Arthur Anderson and Co.

Under the leadership of Clark and Bouse, Four Seasons Nursing Centers of America grew from a "mom-and-pop" nursing home operation in 1966 to a major national corporation worth several hundred million dollars before it entered Federal Chapter X bankruptcy in June, 1970.

During its meteoric rise it became the "darling of the American Stock Exchange" in one observer's words and its executives were wined and dined by some of the country's foremost investors.

Its stock was rated blue chip by the national credit office of Dun and Bradstreet and rose from $11 per share to more than $100 per share, split 2–1, and rose again.

Seymour's statement Wednesday said the federal indictments were a result of a probe into "the collapse and bankruptcy of Four Seasons."

"Four Seasons was one of the glamor stocks of the American Stock Exchange during late 1969 and early 1970 before it suddenly went bankrupt, causing losses of hundreds of millions of dollars to the American public," the statement said.

The American Stock Exchange earlier fined defendant Miller $10,000 and suspended him from the exchange for his dealings with Four Seasons and fined Walston and Co. $75,000, the largest fine ever levied by the exchange.

The federal indictment revealed two previously uncovered charges against Four Seasons officials and agents.

For one, the indictment claims that in August, 1969, "when the Arthur Anderson audit of Four Seasons revealed that the company had not reached its earning projections" Clark and Linn "manufactured millions of dollars of false, fictitious and non-existent construction costs" to cover the missing money.

The second new accusation listed in the indictment is that Clark, Gray, Bouse and McCollum began in late 1969 to sell their personal stock through "secret numbered accounts" when the Four Seasons financial position became precarious.

The indictment claims that Four Seasons Equity Corp. was a "captive customer to which Four Seasons Nursing Centers of America would sell large numbers of unprofitable nursing homes for the purpose of falsely inflating its earnings."

The charges came, as predicted in a long analysis of the Four Seasons empire appearing in the *Oklahoma Journal* last March, under securities fraud provisions of the Securities Acts of 1933 and 1934, under federal mail fraud statutes and filing false financial statements provisions of the U.S. Criminal Code.

The defendants face a possible maximum sentence if convicted on the conspiracy counts of five years in prison and $10,000 fines; five years in prison and $1,000 fine on the mail fraud counts; and two years and $10,000 fines on the false financial filing charges.

Naftalis said he felt like a "tired and worn out old attorney" Wednesday after the indictments were returned.

He praised the 2½ years of investigative work done on the case by SEC agents Ben Simms and Cecil Mathis and Postal Inspector Ken Ishmael.

DEFENDANTS DENY ANY WRONGDOING

Charges in a federal grand jury indictment against former officers and agents of Four Seasons Nursing Centers of America were denied by all defendants contacted Wednesday and faced strong countercharges from the chairman of Arthur Anderson and Co., a national accounting firm which had three partners named in the indictment.

Anderson Chairman Harvey Kapnick charged in a prepared release that the U.S. attorney's office in New York had refused to allow testimony from a specially hired polygraph expert to come before the grand jury on behalf of Anderson partners Kenneth J. Wahrman, Edward J. Bolka and Jimmie E. Madole.

"The refusal of the United States attorney to grant these fair requests is unwarranted and unjustified," Kapnick stated. "No rational explanation supports this refusal. As a result, the men charged in today's indictment were denied a fair opportunity to present their side of the case to the grand jury."

"The charges will be defended vigorously," Kapnick stated. "We plan to ask the court for an immediate trial date." He said the three men will remain with the firm.

City attorney and former Four Seasons Franchise president James P. Linn said Wednesday he "was astonished and horrified that my name was included in the indictment."

"It is unbelievable to me that my name would be included," Linn said. "I'm going to resist—I'll tell you that." Linn, former Hanford, Tex., county attorney, said he would represent himself in the New York federal court.

Former Four Seasons president and chairman Jack L. Clark was in Oklahoma City Wednesday but could not be reached for comment. Clark's local attorney, R.C. Jopling, said Clark "is not ready yet" to make a statement but possibly would do so Thursday.

Clark is represented nationally by the law firm of Manny Cohen, former chairman of the Securities Exchange Commission, and Arthur Mathews, former chief prosecutor of the SEC.

Reaction to the naming of Fidelity Bank executive Bill P. Jennings as a co-conspirator came as the indictments were officially announced.

First, the law firm of former Secretary of Defense Clark Clifford issued a memorandum on behalf of Fidelity Bank chairman Jack T. Conn which asserted the status of "co-conspirator" means that Jennings is not a defendant, "he is subject to no penalties of any kind growing out of the alleged conspirational activities of the defendants" and that the designation has "recently become so common in federal practice that virtually no stigma attaches to those so named."

Jennings himself said in a statement that he was "astounded and chagrined that I have been named as a co-conspirator. I realize, however, the designation does not charge me with any crime; that the practice of naming numerous co-conspirators in antitrust and SEC matters has found increasing favor by the government as an aid in its prosecutions.

"The SEC and the Department of Justice have devoted two and one-half years in examining every facet of the Four Seasons debacle," Jennings said. "I am gratified after that exhaustive inquiry I have been exonerated from any charge of criminal complicity and that my conduct has been vindicated."

Jennings said he made a "substantial" investment in Four Seasons Equity, and "I, too, lost my money."

Fidelity Bank Chairman Conn issued the following statement supporting Jennings:

"Fidelity was the principal bank of the Four Seasons entities. We assigned those deposit relationships to Bill P. Jennings, executive vice president of the bank. With our permission Jennings served as a member of the board of directors of Four Seasons Equity. He was an outside director and had no part in the management or day-to-day operations of the company.

"In all Jennings' relationships with the Four Seasons companies, we find no evidence of wrongdoing."

The Auto Towing Caper

Peter Benjaminson's investigation of a local towing company for the *Detroit Free Press,* published June 9–11, 1971 and reprinted here with permission, illustrates how much valuable information can be obtained from public records, how the publication of one story can lead to a strong follow-up the next day, and how an investigative story can produce substantive results. An explanation of the research that went into these stories can be found at the end of chapter 6.

GOOD CARS TOWED AWAY

Ex-Felon Has City Permit

A local wrecking firm has been the target of complaints by Detroit residents that it towed their automobiles from in front of their homes even though there was usually little wrong with them and they were not abandoned.

The president of the company—authorized by the Detroit Police Department to remove abandoned automobiles from city streets and then strip, sell, or destroy them—was convicted in 1961 of receiving stolen property worth more than $10,000.

When applying for a wrecking yard license two years ago, the man—John Soave, president of Kercheval Used Auto Parts & Wrecking Co. Inc.—apparently hid his felony conviction from public officials. City ordinances require disclosure of such information.

One of the founders of the Kercheval Co. itself was a man indicted by a federal grand jury for conspiring with an alleged Mafia leader in an illegal gambling operation.

The company, which has its yard at 11851 Kercheval, is being investigated by the Internal Revenue Service.

The police unit responsible for turning over abandoned automobiles to private wreckers, the Auto Recovery Bureau, is also being investigated, by the Detroit Police Department Special Investigation Bureau, which investigates possible police infractions.

The Common Council is looking into the whole question of procedures for dealing with abandoned vehicles at 10 a.m. Wednesday.

Two city ordinances allow a policeman to authorize a licensed wrecking firm to tow away a vehicle that he believes has been parked on a public street for 48 hours or more, that he judges to be worth less than $100, and that he thinks "reasonably appears" abandoned.

But the complaining citizens say that their cars were in good shape and that they had to pay the Kercheval Co. towing and storage fees to get them back or let the yard strip and scrap them.

Mrs. Cornelius Proctor said she was inside her home at 5256 Larchmont one Saturday last March and didn't hear the tow trucks arrive. Her car, a 1962 Mercury, was parked at the curb in front of her house. When she came out later in the day, it was gone.

Although Mrs. Proctor admitted that the car had been parked in the same spot for "a day or two," she said she was using it frequently and had recently paid $36 for a new battery for it. Inside the car were her husband's tools and fishing tackle.

She called the police and told them her car had been stolen. The police checked with other police units and then told her to call the Kercheval Co. The firm told her she would have to pay a $10 towing fee and $1 a day storage charge to get her car back.

Arguing that "there must be some way to get my car back, without paying all that money," Mrs. Proctor refused to pay anything. The Kercheval Co. still has her car.

On the same day that Mrs. Proctor's car was picked up, a Kercheval truck also towed away a 1962 Corvair parked in front of the home of its owner, Emett Grimmett of 5008 Pacific.

Grimmett said he had driven to a church fellowship meeting the night before, then woke up Saturday morning and found his car gone. The Kercheval Co. had it.

Instead of paying the company, Grimmett called Councilman Ernest Browne Jr. Browne called police officials, and the following Tuesday the police returned Grimmett's car.

Maxey Reid's 1962 Cadillac had been sitting at the curb in front of his house at 1232 Meadowbrook for several weeks last fall. He had left it there, he said, because it had been damaged in an accident and he was waiting for an insurance adjuster to arrive to estimate the damage.

When a Kercheval Co. tow truck, accompanied by a Detroit police officer, came to pick it up, Reid objected, showing them his title and registration and telling them about his dispute with the insurance company.

According to Reid, the truck took it anyway. He said that he had to pay $37 to get it back and that it had been further damaged during towing. He has appealed to the council for a refund.

Nathaniel Mitchell Jr. said he had the same experience when the Kercheval Co. came to tow away his car. He said he had spent about $60 to fix up his 1962 Dodge and was trying to save enough money to buy an alternator. His car had valid Michigan plates and was in good condition except for the engine.

But Mitchell said that when he showed his papers and told the Kercheval crew his story, "they just went on doing what they were doing. They were in a hurry to get away."

Soave said Tuesday that his firm tows away any "inoperable" car or any other car parked more than 48 hours in the same spot, when authorized by the police, in the city's Fifth (Jefferson-St. Jean) and Seventh (Mack-Gratiot) precincts on the east side. Soave said: "I don't understand why I'm being attacked just because I pick up cars for the Police Department."

According to court records, Soave was convicted of receiving stolen property in 1961 after originally being charged with grand larceny for allegedly stealing a refrigerator van containing $12,000 worth of meat from a Detroit packing house.

But he was sentenced to three years probation and ordered to pay $100 in court costs after he pleaded guilty to the lesser charge.

Soave said Tuesday that he "did at one time buy stolen property from someone" but said that he "didn't know it was stolen."

When Soave applied to the Detroit Police Department in 1969 for a license to run a wrecking yard, he did not answer the question on the application that asks if "the applicant . . . has ever been convicted of a felony or misdemeanor . . ."

He said Tuesday that "that conviction was 10 years ago" and that he "didn't remember whether he told police about it."

Under city ordinance, licenses may be granted by cities to persons wishing to operate wrecking yards if they are of "good moral character."

The law also allows the mayor to revoke or suspend a license if the applicant falsifies "any material fact" in his application.

Soave's application was approved in writing by Auto Recovery Bureau Inspector Joseph Nufer and Detective John Urish. Neither was available for comment Tuesday. Nufer retired from the force six months ago and was said to be touring the West Coast.

A police spokesman said that, with Nufer unavailable, the department was unable to say why Soave's application was approved.

One of Kercheval's original incorporators, Peter Cilluffo, was indicted by a federal grand jury in 1966 for conspiring with alleged Mafia boss Matthew (Mike) Rubino to run an illegal gambling operation.

Rubino was identified as a Mafia leader by former Detroit Police Commissioner George Edwards at a U.S. Senate Crime Committee hearing in 1963.

The case against Cilluffo was dismissed in 1968 by the late U.S. District Judge Theodore Levin because of new U.S. Supreme Court decisions which Levin said invalidated the evidence against him.

Cilluffo was not available for comment Tuesday, but Soave said he bought out Cilluffo's interest in the wrecking firm two years ago.

Ex-Policeman Bares Tow-Away Firm Link

A former member of the Detroit Police Department's Auto Recovery Bureau (ARB) admitted Wednesday that while he was on the force he was co-owner of a private wrecking firm authorized to tow away vehicles the ARB decided were abandoned.

The retired policeman, George Hacquebart, also admitted that in 1968 he sold his one-half interest in Kercheval Used Auto Parts and Wrecking Co., Inc. to Peter Cilluffo, then under indictment by a federal grand jury for conspiring with an alleged Mafia boss, Matthew (Mike) Rubino.

State incorporation records show that Cilluffo and Hacquebart became co-owners of the firm—each owning 5,000 of its 10,000 shares—in October, 1967. Hacquebart said his stock was later held by his wife.

Hacquebart said that after he became a co-owner, the Police Department authorized Kercheval to tow away abandoned vehicles for a fee. Five firms in the Detroit area, including Kercheval, have such authorization.

Asked if he saw any conflict of interest in his dual role as part owner of a firm involved in auto towing and as a policeman in the Auto Recovery Bureau, Hacquebart said: "But John Nichols and city attorneys knew all about it."

Nichols, now Detroit's police commissioner, was appointed superintendent of the department a few months after Hacquebart became a part owner of Kercheval.

"I don't really recall," Nichols said Wednesday when asked if he knew of Hacquebart's ownership. But Nichols said it "possibly could be true" that he knew at the time of Hacquebart's involvement in the firm.

Nichols also said: "If city attorneys didn't see it as a conflict of interest, why should I?"

Hacquebart would not specify which of the city's attorneys knew about his business connections.

The firm has been the recent target of complaints by Detroit residents that it towed their automobiles from in front of their homes even though the cars were in working order and were not abandoned.

It is up to the discretion of individual ARB policemen under city ordinances to decide which automobiles are "abandoned" and ought to be towed away and which are not.

The complaining citizens had to pay the firm, located at 11851 Kercheval, towing and storage fees to get the cars back, or let the firm scrap and sell them.

The *Free Press* reported Wednesday that the Kercheval Co. is presently run by John Soave, an ex-felon who concealed his record from the police when applying for a wrecking license.

City ordinances require disclosure of such information.

One of the two policemen who approved, in writing, Soave's application for a license was Detective John Urish, indicted by a Wayne County citizens grand jury last month for accepting a bribe.

The alleged bribe was in return for getting charges dropped in a fraudulent car-purchase case in 1965. Urish, who retired in July, 1970, was known as "Mr. Auto Squad" for the techniques and equipment he developed to detect erased and obliterated numbers on stolen autos.

Hacquebart, who retired from the force in August, 1969, said he sold his Kercheval Co. stock to Cilluffo in March or April of 1968.

Cilluffo had been indicted by a federal grand jury in 1966 on charges of conspiring with Rubino to run an illegal gambling operation.

Charges against Cilluffo were dismissed in June, 1968, by the late U.S. District Court Judge Theodore Levin after Levin said new U.S. Supreme Court decisions invalidated the evidence against the alleged conspirator.

Rubino had been identified as a Mafia leader by former Detroit Police Commissioner George Edwards at a U.S. Senate Crime Committee hearing in 1963.

The Kercheval Co.'s Soave said Tuesday he bought out Cilluffo's interest in the firm two years ago.

After testifying at a Common Council hearing Wednesday, the present ARB chief, Inspector Ara Bezian, jokingly asked reporters: "If you were on the beat like me, wouldn't you be tempted to take payoffs from the Mafia?"

Bezian also said he "wondered why Elliot Ness died so poor. Look at all the opportunities he had to make money."

Bezian told the councilman that some tow truck operators cruise the streets late at night, pick up cars they think are abandoned, and then scrap them, all without any police authorization.

But Bezian said after the meeting that these operators—whom he called "hawks" or "midnight requisitioners"—really didn't get very many cars and that he mentioned them at the council meeting "to cover our tracks."

Under criticism at the meeting from Councilman Ernest Browne Jr., Bezian admitted that his men have had approximately one confrontation a week with citizens who claim to own, or who claim to know the owners of allegedly abandoned automobiles being towed away.

"This happens especially on weekends when people are home," Bezian said.

Councilman Carl Levin asked Bezian and City Attorney Thomas Gallagher several times why private wrecking yards which tow abandoned vehicles for the police are not hired by contract under competitive bidding procedures.

Gallagher agreed to study Levin's proposal but after the meeting Bezian called it "ridiculous."

Probe Ordered into Towing Firm

City to Study Police Tie-In

Mayor Gribbs ordered a full investigation Thursday into the police department's relationship with an auto towing firm after the *Free Press* revealed that one of the firm's owners was a policeman supervising the towing away of abandoned automobiles.

And a police department spokesman said that the officer, who left the force two years ago, "was either lying to us before or is lying to the *Free Press* now" concerning his role in the firm while he was still on the force.

Retired Detective Lieutenant George Hacquebart admitted Wednesday that he was co-owner of Kercheval Used Auto Parts and Wrecking Co., Inc., while he was serving on the police department's Auto Recovery Bureau.

The firm was not authorized to tow away automobiles by the police department until after Hacquebart became a co-owner.

Under city ordinances, it is up to the discretion of individual auto-recovery policemen to decide which automobiles are abandoned and ought to be towed away and which are not.

The mayor directed Chief City Attorney Michael Glusac to "investigate the facts surrounding the Kercheval Co. and make a recommendation with reference to its license."

City ordinances allow the mayor to revoke or suspend a wrecking yard's license if the applicant falsifies "any material fact" in his application.

The *Free Press* revealed that the Kercheval Co. was now operated by an ex-felon, John Soave, who concealed the facts of his conviction from the police when applying for a wrecking yard license in 1969.

Such concealment is illegal.

According to documents released Thursday by the police, Hacquebart wrote the then Deputy Chief of Detectives, George Bloomfield, in 1968 that his involvement with the Kercheval Co. was minimal.

He said that when the corporation was formed in October, 1967, 5,000 shares of stock—10 percent of the issue—were issued to his wife.

But state incorporation papers show that only 10,000 shares of

Kercheval Co. stock were ever issued—5,000 to Hacquebart himself and 5,000 to Peter Cilluffo, who was under indictment by a federal grand jury at the time for conspiring with an alleged Mafia boss.

City Hall sources said that by the time Hacquebart wrote his letter in May, 1968 he could have transfered the shares to his wife.

But they noted that the size of the shareholdings represented a substantial interest in the firm.

Cilluffo was indicted by a federal grand jury in 1966 on charges of conspiring with Matthew (Mike) Rubino to run an illegal gambling operation.

Charges against Cilluffo were dismissed in June, 1968 by the late U.S. District Court Judge Theodore Levin, who said that a new U.S. Supreme Court decision invalidated the evidence.

The Kercheval Co. has been the target of complaints by Detroit residents who claimed that their automobiles were towed from in front of their homes even though they were in working order and hadn't been abandoned.

AUTO FIRM LOSES CITY WORK

Subject of Controversy

Detroit Police have ceased doing business with Kercheval Auto Parts and Wrecking Co. Inc.

The firm, one that worked with police in towing away abandoned autos, had been accused in June by several residents of towing away cars that were not abandoned and then charging the car owners fees for recovery.

The city at that time retained the company's services despite the complaints.

The recent police action came following the arrest on Oct. 7 of Kercheval's president, John Soave, on charges of receiving and concealing stolen property worth more than $100. The charges against Soave, however, were dismissed Oct. 15 when the owner of the property refused to press the case and "accepted restitution."

An investigation into the complaints in June revealed that the towing firm at one time had been half-owned by a policeman who had also been in the department's Auto Recovery Bureau. The officer, now retired, was Lt. George Hacquebart.

Soave, who had been convicted in 1961 of receiving stolen property, was arrested after police said they found about $4,000 in allegedly stolen tools on the Kercheval Co.'s lot at 11851 Kercheval. The tools were traced to a nearby garage where they had been stored by the owner of a defunct body shop, Philip Stanley.

When Stanley did not press charges, Soave was released from bond and the case dismissed from Recorder's Court.

Soave's firm had been one of several companies authorized by the police to tow away abandoned automobiles, then either keep the cars or charge their owners for towing and storage.

Land-Use Planning

In chapter 7, we discussed a recent investigation of privileged information and possible conflicts of interest in land-use planning. The following article by Remer Tyson and David Anderson, published by the *Detroit Free Press* November 11, 1974 and reprinted here with permission, was preceded by a story accusing the Republican candidate for lieutenant governor of accepting unusually large campaign contributions from suburban Detroit land developers who benefitted from his votes on zoning and related land-use matters.

After the initial story ran, Michigan Governor William Milliken was asked to have Damman make his tax returns public, as the governor and his opponents had. The tax returns showed Damman owned a part interest in land throughout Troy. One of Damman's business partners then gave reporters company records showing the location, purchase price, and terms of the firm's land holdings. Only one confidential source was used in developing the information. The accounts of Damman's activities as they related to his land holdings came from examining Troy city council minutes, listening to tapes of city council meetings, and interviewing Damman's colleagues on the city council.

Early in 1975, the state attorney general held that although Damman had acted to preserve the value of his land, he broke no law in doing so because there was no Michigan statute preventing part-time city officials from voting in conflicts of interest. In August, 1975, at the urging of Common Cause, such a law was passed.

PROBE CONFIRMS DAMMAN'S LAND ROLE

A continuing investigation by the *Free Press* confirms that Lt. Gov.-elect James J. Damman, as a Troy city commissioner, helped draft and voted for land-use plans while owning an interest in property directly affected by those plans.

The investigation, which began in mid-September, has included an extensive survey of public records in Troy and lengthy interviews with Damman, his attorney, two attorneys acting as Gov. Milliken's investigators, and numerous planning consultants and Troy city officials.

The investigation shows that:

Damman participated in public and private meetings between the Troy City Commission and the Troy Planning Commission at which future plans for land use in the Oakland County suburb were discussed and modified.

Damman voted in public meetings on those plans while holding a direct financial interest in land affected by the plans, in apparent violation of the conflict-of-interest clause of the Troy city charter.

Damman's land interests were not known to his fellow city commissioners or the general public when he was helping shape the land-use plans. Among Damman's partners at the time were the city attorney and two former city commissioners.

Earlier *Free Press* stories reporting Damman's land investment activities while a city commissioner were correct. Those stories became a major issue in the Nov. 5 election when they were disputed by Damman, who in turn was defended by his running mate, incumbent Gov. Milliken.

A statement raised in Damman's defense and issued in a formal report by Milliken 72 hours before election day was incomplete and thus inaccurate in its description of Damman's role in helping shape Troy's land-use plans.

A spokesman for Gov. Milliken, who along with Damman defeated the Democratic ticket of Sander Levin and Paul Brown in the Nov. 5 election, declined comment late Tuesday.

Damman has insisted and continues to insist that he is innocent of any wrongdoing.

Acknowledging that he does not recall some of the events during his term as a Troy city commissioner, in 1969–70, Damman maintains that he never knowingly acted to abuse his office or improperly profit from it.

The key story in the Damman controversy was published in the *Free Press* on Thursday, Oct. 31, five days before election day. The essential paragraphs of that story said:

"State Rep. James Damman, the Republican candidate for lieutenant governor, and four other past and present Troy city officials were helping to draft a new master plan for Troy while buying undeveloped land that stood to greatly increase in value once the plan was approved.

"Before the final plan was adopted, the land investment company that Damman and the others had quietly formed in late 1967 was used to purchase, under a variety of methods, more than 30 parcels of land in areas made potentially more valuable by their own recommendations and those of the city planners hired by the Troy City Commission."

Damman's defense, as outlined by Milliken and the two attorneys acting as Milliken's investigators, Lawrence Lindemer and David Dykehouse, was essentially that Damman was not on the City Commission at the time it considered a plan that affected holdings of Lincoln & Co., the firm in which Damman was a partner. The governor said that he and his staff had examined "all relevant documents available to us."

The governor's report also said that since the contents of the "plan in question" became public knowledge before the investment firm made their purchases, "the allegation that land purchases were made on the basis of 'inside' information not available to the public" was not substantiated.

The key portion of the Damman statement said:

"The plan was made public on June 10, 1968, and adopted, after public hearings, on March 31, 1969. Mr. Damman did not become a member of the Troy City Commission until April 1969. He had no part in the deliberations, public or private, leading to the adoption of the plan."

The *Free Press* investigation shows that the Troy City Center Plan referred to by Milliken as "the plan in question" was not generally known to the public until more than seven months after the June 10 date cited by the governor.

At the time that plan was being debated, in private study sessions among city officials, Damman's partners in Lincoln & Co. included two city commissioners, Glen Houghten and Ben Jones, and the city attorney, Stanley Burke.

Milliken's rebuttal, in focusing on the City Center Plan, omitted the fact that the Troy master land use plan underwent a series of major amendments and proposed changes during Damman's tenure as a city commissioner from April, 1969, through December, 1970.

The governor's report failed to say that a new land-use plan submitted to the Troy city commission after Damman was a commissioner would have downgraded land owned by Lincoln & Co. to single-family residential use, diminishing its potential value.

This new plan was known as the Big Beaver Corridor study, done by Troy planning consultants Vilican-Leman Associates Inc.

Damman participated in the series of non-public meetings at which the new plan was revised. In that process, the portion of the plan affecting Lincoln & Co. land was dropped, thereby maintaining the land in an office-commercial classification. Damman then voted to adopt the modified plan in apparent violation of the Troy city charter, which states:

"No member of the (city) commission shall vote on any question in which he has a financial interest, other than the common public interest."

Asked about Damman's role in the planning process after he became a city commissioner, Lindemer and Dykehouse said that they were not aware of the proposal that would have changed the City Center plan at the time they prepared their report for Gov. Milliken or of Damman's participation in the sessions which dealt with the proposal.

Meeting voluntarily with the *Free Press* last week, Damman acknowledged participating in the study sessions that led to the adoption of the Big Beaver plan, although he said he couldn't remember any details of the meetings. He also said he was aware of the August 1969 Vilican-Leman report that was later revised in the meetings and acknowledged voting on the final plans.

He maintains, however, that these official activities, despite his land investment interests, were above reproach.

Damman said that neither he nor any of his partners ever discussed or used any knowledge they gained as public officials in their dealings as a private real estate group.

"I'm not suggesting there's no possibility of impropriety when someone who is on a governmental body invests in real estate in the city," said Damman. "To suggest otherwise would be terribly naive."

Damman said he never felt it necessary to raise the question of whether his land dealings would constitute conflict of interest, even though during this same period of time he says he did raise the question on a zoning vote before the commission.

In early 1970, before voting to approve a rezoning that would affect a proposed shopping center in which he was negotiating for a lease, Damman says he asked City Attorney Burke whether that disqualified him under the city charter.

Burke says he ruled that, since Damman was not the owner of any of the shopping center property, only a prospective lessee, Damman could vote.

Burke, it is now known, was at the time a partner of Damman's in Lincoln & Co., along with former Commissioners Houghten and Jones and Tax Review Board member Roger Blackwood.

Damman himself made the motion on at least one occasion that another commissioner, Sherwood Shaver, disqualify himself from voting. Shaver did so.

The existence of the land investment firm became generally known only after Damman made public his income tax returns for the period 1967 through 1973.

Free Press reporters asked for the returns in an interview with Damman Oct. 8, but Damman refused to disclose them at that time.

Damman released them on Oct. 25 after the *Free Press* asked Gov. Milliken to intercede.

The tax returns also reflected Damman's membership on the board of directors of Real Estate One, a large midwestern real estate company based in Michigan.

Neither company had been mentioned on a financial disclosure statement issued by Damman in August, after his confirmation as the GOP lieutenant governor candidate.

Damman explained the omission by saying that he had sold his share of Lincoln & Co. to his brother, Robert, in July, for $16,000, because he could no longer afford the $100-a-month payments. At that time, he had invested about $9,000, he said, over six-and-a-half years.

He stressed that his sale of the partnership was not out of any concern for appearances.

Robert Wilmoth, an attorney for Real Estate One who sponsored Damman for the board of that company, said Damman resigned that position last summer, however, at Wilmoth's suggestion after being picked to run by the governor.

"It wouldn't look good," Wilmoth said, for the lieutenant governor to be on the board of a large real estate firm doing business in the state.

Damman said the only income he received from Real Estate

One was a $100 fee for each of the three or four board meetings he attended each year.

Wilmoth, formerly the attorney for Damman Hardware Co., has been retained by Damman in the Troy investigation.

The existence of Lincoln & Co. and the role of Damman and the others in it came as a surprise to Troy city officials.

Asked who would have known of the company while Damman was in office in Troy, Lindemer replied "the Macomb County clerk." The partnership was registered in Macomb County with an address in Warren, that of the business offices of one of the partners, Roy Beach.

Asked the same question, Damman answered: "Certainly our wives all knew about it . . . children . . . secretarial help in the various offices. . . ."

The partners in Lincoln & Co. have stressed that the investment group was largely social and that business matters were always secondary to fellowship among the 12 original members.

Damman moved to Troy in 1966 and quickly established a place among the city's business and civic elite.

Damman became a political protege of City Commissioner Houghten, who sponsored Damman's appointment to the city's hospital study commission in December 1966 and to the Troy Zoning Board of Appeals in July 1967.

Houghten was also the organizer, early in 1967, of a poker-playing and investment club that quietly bought land within areas of Troy that would be designated for intensive development by city officials in a massive rewriting of the city's master land use plan.

The poker players became a legal partnership called Lincoln & Co. in October 1967, and its 12 members included seven men who served in elected or appointed city posts during the period 1967 through 1970. Among the players were:

Three city commissioners—Damman, Houghten and Jones. Houghten and Jones left the council as Damman joined it in April 1969. All three helped to shape the city's land use plans which, among other things, had a direct impact on the value of land which they would own.

City Attorney Burke, who advised city officials on legal aspects of the land use revisions and who owns other land in the center of Troy apart from his share in Lincoln & Co.

Roy C. Beach and Charles Paes, who were members of the city's

Commercial and Industrial Development Committee, which was appointed by the City Commission. Beach was nominated for his appointment by Houghten.

Joel Garrett, a well-connected Troy realty company owner who is the operating partner in at least three other investment partnerships in addition to Lincoln & Co. Garrett's other partnerships include a current Troy commissioner, Shaver, who was elected with Damman, and Ronald Chapman, an assistant city attorney and one of Burke's partners.

Houghten said he organized the Lincoln group as a social and investment club, formed to buy and sell anything that would turn a profit.

"The way I put it," he said, "was if we could buy a dead horse for $12 and sell it for $25, we'd do it. It wasn't just to buy land."

However, from the time Lincoln was formed until Houghten, Jones and Damman had left the City Commission, the partnership invested only in Troy real estate, all of it in areas affected by changing city plans.

The overall master land-use plan for Troy was drafted between early 1968 and early 1971. Damman was a Troy city commissioner from April 1969 until December 1970. He took a seat in the State House of Representatives in January 1971 and is completing his second term there this year.

Altogether, from February 1968 through January 1970, the partnership bought 37 parcels of land in central Troy at a total price of $96,933, according to unaudited Lincoln & Co. records furnished by Damman.

Their first purchase resulted in a quick 50 percent profit when they resold it 13 months later for $32,000. The remaining properties still held by Lincoln & Co. have increased in value 350 percent, according to information supplied by Garrett.

The partnership also took special steps in doing business that had the effect of making Lincoln & Co. virtually unknown except to the partners themselves.

Lincoln & Co. did not register most of its land transactions at the Oakland County courthouse.

The 12-member group filed as a legal partnership in Macomb County and listed as its business address a welding plant in Warren owned by Beach.

Landowners, including the Troy School Board, who sold property to the group did not know they were dealing with a land company whose members included several city officials. They thought they were selling to Beach or Paes as individual purchasers. Their names appeared on the Troy tax rolls as the owners of the Lincoln properties.

Other city officials said they were unaware that some of their colleagues were buying land while they were helping to plan the future business core of Troy.

Damman said there was no intent to keep Lincoln & Co. a secret but that "It was simply not the kind of thing that was normal table conversation."

Damman said the Lincoln & Co. partners met about once a month and that all the group's purchases had nearly unanimous approval from the members.

Beginning in September 1967, Lincoln & Co. began accumulating investment capital by assessing each of its 12 members $100 a month.

During the period in which Lincoln & Co. was formed a number of city commissioners, Houghten and Jones among them, were pushing hard for a planning study that would lay out a highly concentrated downtown core.

The vision was a downtown core surrounding the city hall, police station and library that would distinguish Troy from Detroit's other sprawling suburbs. Even members of the commission's "home owners bloc" favored the study as a means of keeping high density developments out of quiet residential neighborhoods.

In February 1968, the city hired the planning firm of Crane, Gorwick & Associates to design a new downtown. The project became known as the Troy City Center plan.

On Aug. 9, 1968, Beach, acting for Lincoln & Co., bought four acres of residentially zoned property on Livernois, north of Big Beaver Road, from Theophilus Cyzio for $22,000. The land is now valued at $60,000, according to unaudited Lincoln & Co. records.

Damman said last week that the purchase was recommended to the partnership by Beach and that Lincoln & Co. bought the parcel because the members knew that the new City Center plan would upgrade the intended land use from residential to office-commercial.

But Damman insisted that the partners did not act on inside information. In an interview Thursday, Damman could not recall when the City Center plan was made public, but he insisted the proposed land use on Livernois was publicly known when Lincoln & Co. acted.

Gov. Milliken, in a statement Nov. 2, asserted that "all purchases made by the partnership of land within the boundaries of the City Center Plan were made after that plan became public knowledge."

Milliken claimed the plan "was made public on June 10, 1968."

A *Free Press* investigation disclosed there was no action making the plan public on June 10. The City Center plan wasn't published, all available records indicate, until early 1969.

Before that date, according to city planning officials and consultant Victor Shrem, there were no maps or documents available to the public to show the land uses being developed in the City Center plan.

The plan was developed during 1968 and early 1969 in a series of private "study sessions" involving the City Commission, the Planning Commission and city staff.

Schrem made a major presentation in late May on the completed land use phase of the plan in a study session in the basement conference room of Troy City Hall. He showed the city officials colored maps of the proposed land uses in the City Center area.

The planner said he retained custody of the maps and they were not made public until the study was completed and published in booklet form in early 1969.

On June 11, 1968, the planning commission in a public meeting approved an $11,000 payment to Shrem for completing the first phase of the City Center plan. There was no discussion of the plan.

On June 17, the City Commission approved the payment in a public meeting. The entire action took 50 seconds of City Commission time, according to tapes of the meeting listened to by the *Free Press.*

A week later at another council session, when former City Manager Paul York told the council that changes in the City Center plan were being proposed by the planning commission, one councilman, unidentified on the tapes, declared:

"I don't think that these plans ought to be brought out here at a public meeting."

Cyzio, a Hazel Park factory worker, told the *Free Press* he knew nothing about proposed land use changes on his Livernois property at the time Lincoln & Co. bought it.

Cyzio said he asked city officials just before the sale whether it would be possible to change the land use on the property from residential to commercial and wasn't told that the proposed City Center plan would do just that.

"They said it was residential. If enough residents signed a petition, probably it could be changed," Cyzio recalled.

"I got mad with the city fathers, they gave me such a hard time," he said. "I put it up for sale."

Cyzio listed the property with Chamberlain Realty in Royal Oak, which sold it to Lincoln & Co.

"There was only one man on the contract—Roy Beach. I never heard of no Lincoln. I was surprised Mr. Damman was included in the syndicate. He was a city father, wasn't he?"

Cyzio said, "A thing that struck me kind of funny was that when I sold it, in the near future they put up a big sign that said 'For Sale, Commercial.' I was surprised because I was told distinctly by the city fathers that it was residential."

Cyzio said the sign, which belonged to Ladd's Realty, came down some time later.

Damman was not yet a city councilman when the City Center plan was approved publicly March 31, 1969. Houghten and Jones, who had supported and helped shape the plan, voted for its approval as their last major act as city councilmen.

Jones was not running for re-election that spring, and Houghten was defeated in a race for mayor in the April 7 city election.

The council was divided at the March 31 meeting over land uses in the plan, and some councilmen wanted another meeting. But Houghten, arguing for immediate action, said:

"I just think you ought to get it off dead center, Mayor. You keep having meetings." Noting that Jones was "instrumental" in pushing the plan, Houghten said, "I think that if the commission agrees on the plan that they ought to give Jones the pleasure and honor of letting him sit here while it's approved."

Jones responded, "Thank you, Glen. I'm sure it will change in time, but the idea should get started. You can't steer a car unless it's moving."

Damman was elected to the council April 7 and took office April 14, 1969.

Within a short time Lincoln & Co. purchased two more parcels in the core city area. On May 1, 1969, the partnership bought a parcel on Troy Street just north of Big Beaver (Sixteen Mile Road), the main east-west thoroughfare of Troy. That summer they purchased 14 vacant lots from the Troy School Board on Starr Drive in the southeast corner of the core area.

At the time, another major Troy planning study was under way that was destined to affect all three of the Lincoln & Co. holdings in Troy.

That report, known as the Big Beaver Corridor Study, included a mile-wide swath of Troy running from Crooks on the west to Rochester on the east. It was prepared by Vilican-Leman & Associates Inc., a Southfield planning firm.

When the Big Beaver study was given to Troy officials it recommended a number of major changes in the City Center area which is at about the mid-point of the Big Beaver Corridor.

One of the changes proposed by Vilican-Leman, who were at the time Troy's official planning consultants, downgraded the Livernois and Troy Street properties owned by Lincoln & Co. from office and commercial back to residential.

Another Vilican-Leman proposal would have eliminated the planned "Ring Road" which would have circled the downtown area and cut through two of the properties owned by Damman and his partners. Such a road, lined as it would be with shops and offices, would have inevitably made the Lincoln & Co. land more valuable.

The Vilican-Leman recommendations, if adopted by the city commission, would have greatly reduced the potential value of all three properties owned by Lincoln & Co.

But when Damman and the other Troy commissioners voted to approve the Big Beaver Corridor plan on Nov. 3 and again on Nov. 10 in 1969, the study had been changed to preserve the earlier recommendations of the City Center plan.

The ring road was back in place and all three properties owned by Lincoln were again designated for office and commercial use.

The Big Beaver Corridor future land use map approved by the city commissioners was drafted in a series of non-public "study sessions" and special public and private joint meetings.

Damman said he doesn't recall "any discussions about the City Center area" nor could he recall any specific recommendations made at the sessions that affected areas where his property was located.

The Big Beaver Corridor plan, as approved by Damman and other councilmen, was essentially a compromise between the earlier Crane-Gorwic proposal of a concentrated downtown and the

Vilican-Leman proposal for a strip of high density development limited to the areas immediately adjacent to Big Beaver Road.

Damman also was asked why Lincoln & Co. purchased the small Troy Street lot. He said the partners realized the lot would have to be acquired by anyone who wanted to develop the shallow parcel in front of it fronting on Big Beaver.

Damman said, "It was projected for office use (in the City Center study but not in the Vilican-Leman plan). It was a key parcel."

Planning Consultant George Vilican said his firm opposed the City Center concept as impractical. "I told them it was a damn dumb thing to do. They were taking one piece of real estate and saying that's where all the development was going to be."

Vilican added, "On Big Beaver we had several meetings (with the city council and planning commission) before there was any public discussion. It was highly argumentative.

"They chose to stick with the City Center and rejected our recommendations in this area."

But Vilican said he could not say exactly when that decision was made or which city officials argued for it because his firm was excluded from attending some of the meetings.

Lincoln & Co. records provided by Damman show that the Starr Drive property was purchased from the Troy School Board on July 25, 1969. Damman's attorney, Wilmoth, said Lincoln & Co. minutes show the group did not discuss purchasing the land until July 10.

But the minutes of the Troy School Board show the board voted to accept an offer-to-purchase the land by Beach, a Lincoln partner, on June 25, 1969. The sellers in the Lincoln & Co. transactions thought they were selling to individual buyers, not Lincoln & Co.

The difference between the dates is crucial to Damman. For on July 7, 1969, Damman voted not to assess Starr Drive property owners for sewer and water mains.

Wilmoth said that Beach had actually bought the land for himself and didn't decide to offer it to the partnership until after Damman voted. He cites a copy of minutes of the July 10, 1969 Lincoln & Co. meeting, that purported to show that Beach sold the land to his partners for the same price, down payment and interest at which school records show he bought it from the school board.

Garrett, who acted as the real estate broker, collected a $1,690 fee from the school board on the transaction.

In the first two years that Lincoln & Co. owned the property, its $3,000 annual payments to the school board were made with checks from the personal account of Mr. and Mrs. Roy Beach.

In 1972, the school board began receiving checks written on a Lincoln & Co. bank account.

By its unanimous vote on July 7, 1969, the city commission had rejected the petition of Mrs. Edith Beier and one other property owner to install water and sewer mains. Mrs. Beier owned 20 vacant lots along the street.

Former City Manager York recommended against approving the project because it was sought by owners of vacant land rather than homeowners.

Damman commented at the council meeting, "I think that's the critical thing. It's all vacant property, and I also note that this falls within the City Center, and the whole picture could change."

Damman acknowledges that he voted to deny the sewers, but said it was the Troy city commission's policy then not to approve sewer lines that would serve primarily vacant parcels of property.

The council's action saved Lincoln & Co. from having to pay a special water and sewer assessment on its vacant lots.

The rejection of the project by the city council also paved the way for Lincoln & Co.'s next big land purchase.

Mrs. Beier's son, Dean C. Beier, said his mother wanted sewer and water service on Starr Drive in order to improve her vacant property. When the project was rejected, Beier said, he decided to sell the land.

On Dec. 10, 1969, Beier signed an agreement to sell the property to Paes, one of the Lincoln partners. Beier said the sale was handled by Ladd's Realty Inc., of which Garrett is president.

Beier said he knew nothing of Lincoln & Co. at the time of the transaction.

Damman told the *Free Press* he didn't remember voting to reject the sewer project or being aware that Lincoln & Co. had an interest in Starr Drive at the time.

He said, "I frankly didn't recall the assessment at all, but it wouldn't have made any difference."

To date Lincoln & Co. still owns the properties on Livernois, Troy Street and Starr Drive.

In the last few years the partners have been repeatedly late in paying their property taxes and records in the Oakland County Assessor's Office show the partnership owes nearly $3,400 in unpaid property taxes.

The partnership did not pay property taxes for nearly two years on the Starr Drive land bought from the school board because the transaction was not recorded by Lincoln & Co. or reported to the city tax assessor by school officials.

Damman said the taxes have not been paid because of "cash-flow problems" and because the interest penalty on unpaid property taxes is only six percent—far less than it would cost to borrow money from private sources.

He said, however, that as a state legislator he voted for a bill that would raise that penalty to a level that would discourage non-payment of taxes.

Michigan Attorney General Frank Kelley began an investigation into the activities of Lincoln & Co. shortly after the *Free Press* published its first account of Damman's and other city officials' interest in downtown Troy.

The probe is continuing. Two lawyers assigned to the case have met with a number of past and present Troy officials and have sought documents and information from the attorneys Gov. Milliken assigned to defend Damman prior to the election.

Ethics in Journalism

The problem of ethics in journalism is, as we have said, one subject newspapers rarely touch. The following article by Bob Wyrick and Pete Bowles, published by *Newsday* October 26, 1972 and reprinted here with permission, is quite unusual. It supports a contention often disputed by editors: that one newspaper can and should publish articles about the doings of competing newspapers and their employees. It is also an example of the sort of investigation that only reaches print when a reporter decides to look critically and in detail at the implications of facts "known" to many.

The story abounds with the rationalizations encountered daily by investigative reporters. But in this case, it is reporters who are the subjects of the investigation and who are trying to justify moonlighting for the same politicians they cover during the day. The story demonstrates the use of a computer by investigative reporters to match up newspaper employees with the state payroll. In one respect, however, the story is not unusual. It is written with little drama and crammed full of details, many of which are dropped on the reader early in the story. The article, therefore, illustrates the pitfalls of assuming that an audience will be as interested in a particular investigation as the reporter who researched and wrote it.

The story was originally Wyrick's idea, both reporters said in recent interviews. Wyrick came to *Newsday* after working on a small Florida newspaper. Assigned to the press room in the State Supreme Court building in Mineola, Wyrick noticed, in his words, that other reporters "would write press releases at night for the politicians they covered during the day and sometimes printed their own releases." According to Wyrick, this dual-employment practice "was common knowledge, but no one gave a shit. It seemed like just no one cared."

Although initially shocked at this practice, Wyrick said, it took him two years to get around to proposing a story on the subject.

He sent a memo including documentation of a couple of cases to his editors and asked permission to do the story. He knew, he said, that the story "had a potential to involve *Newsday* people as well as others" and that "the editors at *Newsday* were friends with the editors at other papers." He also knew that management might "think it very touchy to have staff morale screwed up by a guy poking around." But, to Wyrick's surprise, he was given the go-ahead on the story shortly after he sent in his memo.

Wyrick said he and Bowles gathered the names of some staffers on the other papers from newspaper union membership lists. They already knew—from first hand observation or reliable tips—of many of their fellow reporters engaged in dual political employment.

Wyrick said that he and Bowles then "talked to a lot of these guys on the take and asked them who else was on the take. We would lay a piece of paper in front of them (a press release) and ask, 'Did you write this?' If they said yes, we then said, 'Are you so generous you did it for free?' They were ratting on each other. I don't have any respect for any of them. They shouldn't have been newspapermen in the first place."

The Wyrick-Bowles technique uncovered many dually employed journalists, but it also missed a couple, according to Wyrick. One of them, he said, was a man who at that time was a *Newsday* political writer in Suffolk County. "I asked him if he knew of any reporters on the take," Wyrick said, "and his answer was no. I didn't ask him about himself. He was highly respected." But recently, according to Wyrick, two other *Newsday* reporters revealed that this same man had been paid $7,000 or $8,000 annually by a local political boss. The payments came to light during a law suit when some old Republican Party records were examined, Wyrick said.

Wyrick said the ethics story was written three or four times. "There was a lot of writing by committee," Wyrick said. "But, I don't think it had anything to do with fear. There was a lot of writing by committee at *Newsday.*" In the rewriting, however, what Wyrick sees as an important fact was inadvertently left out: Stan Hinden, the former *Newsday* political editor who was paid for writing stories for the civil service union newspaper, had written permission from his boss to do so.

According to Bowles, the original idea behind the *Newsday* exposé was to write a story about all the reporters in both the New

York State and New York City areas who were paid kickbacks
and fees by various businesses, as well as about those reporters
who worked for politicians. For instance, Bowles said, one airline
offered free trips to Australia to those reporters who boosted
tourism by placing photographs of Australian bathing beauties in
the paper. Also, Bowles said, the American Cigar Institute offered
compensation to reporters and editors who successfully placed
photographs of cigar smokers in their newspapers. Finally, Bowles
said, the two decided to focus their attention on reporters in their
own bailiwick—Long Island—who were working for politicians
they were supposed to be covering objectively.

Bowles said that he and Wyrick requested and received from
the state government the records of anyone who had been employed by the joint legislative committees in Albany, because,
according to Bowles, "we were told that many of these were
no-show jobs" and that many were held by reporters. This list was
one of those run through the computer, as the story explains.
Bowles said the two *Newsday* reporters also obtained, from sym-
pathizers, lists of employees of other newspapers, and, directly
from *Newsday*'s management, lists of its own past and present
employees.

Both reporters said that most of their information was obtained
directly from fellow reporters who had known about the dual-
employment practice for years and from the politicians involved.
Not all their fellow reporters were cooperative. "There was lots
of mistrust in our office. Some people thought it was a dirty deal
for us to be going after other reporters," Bowles said. "When the
story came out, lots of people were relieved that we only went after
people who had been working for politicians," and not people
holding non-political governmental jobs. Some people whose jobs
were in such gray areas were eliminated from the story, Bowles
said.

Bowles insists that the story as originally written was "much
harder than it finally came out. The editors worried about running
it and wanted it rewritten a number of times. They may have been
getting pressure from other papers who didn't think it was fair for
our newspaper to attack their reporters. . . . Finally, they made
us put a feature lead on it."

Bowles detailed one example of friendship's altering the content
of the story. According to Bowles, *New York Daily News* Editor
Mike O'Neill was a friend of the *Newsday* editor in charge of the

story, David Laventhol. "O'Neill refused to be interviewed by us," Bowles said. "But because of his friendship with Laventhol, he was able to give Laventhol a printed statement (on dual employment) which was included in the story. It wasn't right," Bowles said. "Other people wouldn't sit down for an interview and we reported in the story that they refused to discuss the matter with us." They weren't allowed to submit prepared statements. Bowles said, however, that there were other apparent pressures that Laventhol resisted, such as telephone calls from the *Long Island Press,* many of whose dually employed reporters were mentioned in the story.

Several years later, *Newsday* published three follow-up stories which clearly show the value of pursuing an investigation, no matter how unscathed a subject may initially appear. The first of these articles on former Nassau County Family Court Judge Martin Ginsberg was written by Brian Donovan (February 8, 1975), the second by Dan Hertzberg (March 1, 1975), and the third by Bradford W. O'Hearn (March 13, 1975).

Newsmen Holding Paid Political Jobs, a Survey Reveals

[*Newsday* reporter Bob Wyrick spent three months looking into the relationship of the press and politicians on Long Island. Reporter Pete Bowles worked with Wyrick and finished the investigation when Wyrick took a leave in late September for a year's study at Harvard University as a Nieman Fellow.]

Readers regularly find stories in their daily newspapers about the pronouncements and activities of government officials and politicians. What they may not realize, however, is that some of those articles are written or edited by journalists who receive second salaries from the people they write about.

A *Newsday* investigation has identified a tradition of newsmen accepting paid political jobs. The survey was confined to Long Island and to the major daily newspapers here: the *New York Daily News,* the *Long Island Press,* the *New York Times* and *Newsday.*

The *Newsday* survey found that:

Two newsmen currently are receiving second salaries as govern-

CHECKING A GOP CLAIM

In the course of the *Newsday* survey, several Republican officials said that some *Newsday* reporters and editors had been paid secretly in recent years for political work by placing their wives' maiden names on Joint Legislative Committee payrolls in Albany.

Newsday asked for the names of those allegedly involved so that they could be included in the story, but the officials refused to name any. "You're going to get the [names of the] *Newsday* guys," said Bob Ryan, director of communications for Nassau County Executive Caso. "Because when you come out [with a story on the survey] the other papers are going to use them to embarrass you." Ryan, however, said that his statement did not mean he personally would furnish the information to other papers.

In an attempt to check out the Republican claims, *Newsday* used an IBM 360 computer to match the names and addresses of every current and former Newsday editorial employe against the names and addresses of all New York-area persons listed on all the State Joint Legislative Committee payrolls available back to 1965. The computer also was fed the names and addresses of employes from other newspapers who had worked in the Long Island area. The computer was programmed to identify matching addresses even when the names were different.

In checking the names of 700 newspaper employes against the 2,100 New York-area employes on the Joint Legislative Committee payrolls, no *Newsday* employes were found. But five reporters and editors from other newspapers were found.

mental public relations aides, and 16 others have held second jobs in government or politics in the last 10 years. Seven of the 18 have since left their newspapers for full-time public-relations work, six with Republican administrations or political organizations.

At least seven of the 18 involved actually wrote or edited stories for their newspapers about the subjects from whom they were receiving a second salary. Four of the 18 received $10,000 or more a year in extra money from their political jobs.

About half of the 18 newsmen were getting two salaries without the permission of their newspapers, including at least one who disguised his involvement behind his wife's name.

Long Island political candidates employed working newspapermen during campaigns on at least 30 occasions during the past decade. The candidates included such powerful political figures as Nassau County Republican Chairman Joseph Margiotta; Assembly Majority Leader John E. Kingston (R-Westbury); Glen Cove Mayor-Supervisor Andrew J. DiPaola, a Democrat who has received both the GOP and Democratic nominations for the State Supreme Court; Huntington Town Supervisor Jerome Ambro, also a Democrat; former Nassau County Executive Eugene Nickerson, a Democrat; Rep. Norman Lent (R-East Rockaway), and former Assembly Speaker Joseph Carlino (R-Long Beach).

As many as 11 newsmen were on double payrolls at one time during the 1967 election campaign, the peak period for such moonlighting in recent years. The practice appears to be declining. Political leaders of both major parties said that no newsmen had been hired for this year's campaign, mainly because of concern over the publication of the *Newsday* survey. Another reason given was that there was a substantial number of former newspapermen working in political or governmental jobs now. The two reporters in the *Newsday* survey still holding dual jobs are in governmental, not political, posts.

The *Newsday* survey was conducted against the backdrop of recent challenges to the credibility and objectivity of newspapers and other media. The 12-week survey included about 150 interviews and involved the use of an IBM 360 computer. In addition, hundreds of payroll records and documents listing political campaign expenditures were examined. The survey was limited to an attempt to identify cases involving reporters and editors being paid for doing political or governmental work, and thus did not deal with practices where ethical questions are less clear cut—

such as a newsman who does such work on the side but is not paid for it, or one involved personally in local civic issues, or one moonlighting for nonprofit organizations or educational institutions. For instance, Stan Hinden, former *Newsday* political editor, was paid for writing stories for the *Civil Service Leader,* a publication of the Civil Service Employees Association. He was succeeded in that part-time job by Bill Butler of the *Daily News.* Also several *Newsday* reporters and editors, and a *Long Island Press* editor, have moonlighted (some still do) for Long Island colleges and charitable drives and institutions.

The two newsmen in the survey who currently are on government payrolls are: Harry C. Schlegel, an assistant city editor responsible for political assignments at the *New York Daily News* who also receives $900 a month as research director for the Joint Legislative Committee on Interstate Cooperation; and Sherman Phillips, a *Long Island Press* reporter who is registration supervisor at the Nassau County Board of Elections.

The six former journalists who now work for Republican administrations or political organizations are: Richard Miranda, who worked for a number of candidates while employed as a reporter at the *Press;* Tony Panzarella, who served as an aide to several Republicans, including Assembly Majority Leader Kingston, while writing for the *Press;* Gene Turner, who took a job with Margiotta while with the *Press;* Stan Pakula, who directed political campaigns while working at the *Press;* Robert McDonald, who was employed by a Nassau County agency while he was a reporter at the *Daily News;* and Robert Ryan, formerly of the *Press* and the *New York Herald Tribune,* who worked for Glen Cove Democrats and Huntington Republicans during his reporting career.

Frank Krauss, who is now a partner in a public relations firm, worked for former Assemblyman Martin Ginsberg (R-Plainview) while he was employed as a reporter at the *Daily News.* Krauss hid the fact by using his wife's name for the work for Ginsberg.

The remaining nine who showed up in the *Newsday* survey are:

Arnold Friedman, assistant managing editor of the *Press,* who was on the payroll of Rep. Seymour Halpern (R-Jamaica); former *Newsday* night photo editor Bill Sullivan, who was paid to try to get pictures of certain Republicans into the paper; Grover Ryder, Nassau County bureau chief for the *Daily News,* who until last year was on the Huntington Town payroll; Dick Wettereau, night

city editor for the *Press,* who worked for the North Hempstead
GOP from 1959 through 1968; Henry McCann, a news editor at
the *Press* who worked for former Assemblyman Jerome McDougal Jr.; Frank Mazza, a *Daily News* reporter who worked in a
number of Democratic campaigns; Bernard Rabin, a *Daily News*
reporter who once held a Long Beach city job; the late Ben White
of the *News,* who was a key adviser to Nassau Democrats; and the
late Dick Prussin of the *Press,* who served on a joint legislative
committee for seven years.

Most of the newspapermen involved in the practice said the
outside jobs did not interfere with their ability to give their readers
a fair and objective story. "They sold their pen; they didn't sell
their soul," said Bob McDonald, a former *News* reporter who is
now press secretary to Nassau GOP Leader Joseph Margiotta and
who also had outside accounts while working for the *News.* But
another of the 18, former *News* reporter Frank Krauss, said he felt
the abuse of the system of taking outside political work "was not
what you wrote good about a guy—it was the bad things you knew
about and never wrote."

Some politicians think differently. Alexander J. Brandshaft,
chairman of the Huntington Republican Committee, put it this
way: "If we bought a $5,000 advertisement, it's not as good as one
news story from a reporter. A paid political ad, no matter what
you say, is still a paid political ad."

The concept of ethics in journalism has evolved slowly. The
earliest American newspapers were frankly partisan and touted
the politicians they favored in the news columns while either
ignoring or vilifying their opponents. A more objective type of
reporting emerged during the Civil War, and by the turn of the
century it had become a firmly implanted practice in American
journalism to separate editorial opinion from straight factual reporting of news.

Guy Ryan, president of Sigma Delta Chi, the national professional journalism society, said recently that he was surprised that
any newspaper would allow its reporters and editors to work for
politicians. "There's a danger in trying to serve two masters," he
said. "A newsman not only has to play it straight but make it
appear that we are playing it straight."

Long Island Press editor Dave Starr has declined to be interviewed about *Press* reporters who had political jobs. On March 16,
Starr issued a policy statement to his Nassau staff stating that

outside work was permitted as long as it "cannot be misinter-preted—to any degree—as influencing the news judgment or editorial policy of the paper." The memo also said, ". . . public relations work for an elected official or a political leader or a business firm could lead to charges of favored treatment."

Daily News Managing Editor Mike O'Neill said: "The *News* has always opposed any outside activities by the editorial employes which would compromise their obligations to objective reporting of the news.

"Like other newspapers, the *News* permits free-lance writing which is non-competitive. But as a matter of policy and by con-tract with the Newspaper Guild, *News* employes are specifically prohibited from using their connections with the paper 'to exploit in any way outside work or interest.'

"Staffers usually get advance guidance from their editors on what they can or cannot do. In the few instances where possible conflict of interest has arisen, the reporter has been asked to discontinue the outside activity, and, in every case, he has com-plied.

"The only example which *Newsday* cites of a *News* employe currently working for a government agency concerns Harry Schle-gel of our city staff. Since 1966, Mr. Schlegel has carried out part-time research assignments for the Joint Legislative Commit-tee on Interstate Co-operation. He took the job with the knowl-edge and approval of his superiors. The work is non-political: There is no conflict with his duties on the paper."

Newsday editor David Laventhol restated the paper's policy in a memorandum to the staff in December, 1969. The memo said: "An editorial staff member must not take part in anything that would compromise himself or *Newsday.* This is a broad area that would include official jobs, outside writing, loans, business trans-actions and political or civic activities . . ."

The center of most newsmen's outside political activity is the press room in the State Supreme Court Building in Mineola, where the county maintains offices for key governmental reporters from *Newsday,* the *New York Daily News,* the *Long Island Press,* two reporters for the *New York Times* (which also has a reporter in Suffolk), and assorted radio and television newsmen. (The *News* has seven full-time reporters assigned to Long Island, the *Press* about 24, and *Newsday* about 75.) "When a political job was available, the news spread like wildfire through the press room," a Republican source said.

The tradition of coziness between politicians and the reporters who work in the press room is a long one. In the early 1950s, then GOP leader and Nassau County Executive J. Russel Sprague handed out cash gifts of $50 to $100 to reporters and photographers at Christmas and election time. The practice was stopped in the mid-50s when a reporter for the now-defunct *New York Journal-American* began gathering information to write a news article about it.

Gene Turner, who on Oct. 6 succeeded Forrest Corson as executive assistant to the Nassau County Board of Supervisors at a salary of $30,000 and who previously headed the Hempstead Town public relations staff, said that he has referred reporters to Nassau County Republican Headquarters for political jobs. "I feel it's up to the reporter to make the moral judgment," Turner said. "And if he wants to work, the Republican Party is entitled to use him." This same view was reflected by officials of both parties, most of whom said they preferred to hire newsmen rather than public relations firms because newsmen did not charge as much, had a better knowledge of the area's problems and issues, and better contacts in the newspaper business.

Besides Turner, the party officials who steered reporters to political jobs included Nassau Democratic Party chairman Marvin Cristenfeld; former party chairman John F. English; County Executive Caso's press secretary, Robert Ryan; and Margiotta's press aide, Robert McDonald.

McDonald said, "Most of the guys we [the Republicans] hire, I grew up with in the press room. They come over and say, 'Is there anybody I can work for?' And then we put together a campaign . . . and we say, 'These are the guys [political candidates] we want you to work for.' You'd be surprised, in our circle, if you are not asked, if you don't get a candidate to work for, you feel like they are mad at you."

But many reporters have refused to become a part of this circle. One of them is *Long Island Press* reporter Bob Weddle. English said that while he was Nassau Democratic leader he tried to get Weddle to go to work for the party on the side and was refused. Weddle, who lives in Bellmore, said that he did not accept the offer from English and other offers which were made over the years because it did not square with his personal code of ethics. Another reporter, Roy Silver, the long-time Nassau correspondent for the *New York Times,* said the Democrats once offered him a part-time job with the Nassau County Bridge Authority. Silver said he checked with his editors and was told not to accept the position because "sometime we might have to do a story about the authority."

About half of the 18 newsmen uncovered in the survey held their outside jobs with the knowledge and consent of an editor at their newspaper. The others took pains to keep their outside jobs secret. Frank Krauss took more pains than most.

During the three years that Krauss handled public relations assignments for then Assemblyman Martin Ginsberg (R-Plainview) while also working at the *News,* Krauss persuaded Ginsberg to put his wife's name on a state payroll to conceal the fact that Krauss was working for the assemblyman. Krauss, 32, said he received $6,000 in state funds under his wife's name. "I felt it best that I keep it confidential," Krauss said in explaining why the name of his wife, Delphine J. Krauss, was listed on the payroll.

Mrs. Krauss' name appears under the job title "research counsel" on the payroll of the Joint Legislative Committee for Industrial and Labor Relations from Aug. 28, 1969, through March 31, 1970, at a salary of $2,500 and as an "assistant secretary" from Aug. 13, 1970, to March 31, 1971, for $3,500. Ginsberg, now a Nassau County Family Court judge, headed the health subcommittee of the joint committee during this period. Ginsberg, when asked why the job titles were listed in this manner, said: "They were just the positions that were available." Krauss said the money received under his wife's name was for public relations work he did for Ginsberg from late 1968 to 1971. "My wife didn't do anything," he said. Krauss wrote at least one story for the *News* about Ginsberg while holding the two jobs. Krauss left the *News* to become the press spokesman for North Hempstead Town in 1971.

Krauss, who is now a partner and vice president of Howard Public Relations Ltd. in Port Washington, said his duties for Ginsberg included writing news releases and brochures for his 1970 reelection campaign and writing publicity releases on Ginsberg's activities on the health subcommittee. "Some people might say it is an abuse [of taxpayer's money] to use a JLC payroll for a guy's personal advertising," Krauss said. "But how else can a guy get known?" Ginsberg said that under Krauss' direction his public image was molded as a legislator who specialized in areas such as retarded children and the handicapped.

Ginsberg said that another *Daily News* reporter, Bernard Rabin, also worked for him under an arrangement similar to Krauss'. He made the statement after he was shown payroll records stating that Rabin's wife, Miriam Rabin, was paid $1,210 as an Assembly clerk for the first five months of 1971. Asked if Rabin had worked for him, Ginsberg replied: "The answer is yes . . . he handled my public relations—he put out campaign releases and wrote photo captions."

Ginsberg said that Rabin previously worked for him from 1966 through March, 1969, and was paid, under his wife's name, about $1,500 a year. Rabin, a *News* employe for 18 years who formerly worked out of Nassau County and now covers the Queens and Brooklyn courts, said his wife worked for Ginsberg and was paid "a lot less" than $1,500 a year. Told about Ginsberg's account that Rabin actually did the work, Rabin said: "That's one reason I wouldn't work for these guys—these politicians have big mouths."

Official minutes of the Long Beach Urban Renewal Agency show that Rabin was paid $1,500 a year as the agency's public information officer for three years—Jan. 9, 1967, to Jan. 1, 1970. Former Long Beach City Manager Foster Vogel, who also served on the urban renewal agency during this period, said he had recommended Rabin for the job of writing newsletters and press releases about the agency. Rabin, however, said that Vogel, the minutes and agency members were all mistaken. He said his wife had the job. "I spoke to them [city officials] about the job but I couldn't do it," Rabin said. "I didn't have the time, and I didn't want to do anything where there might be an odor or anything."

The practice of reporters working for politicians has not gone entirely unnoticed. Last year, Huntington GOP leader Alexander Brandshaft formally complained to the *Daily News* that the Republicans were getting no exposure in the *News* because Huntington Democratic Town Supervisor Jerome Ambro had Grover Ryder, the *News'* Nassau bureau chief, on the town payroll for $6,000 a year.

Ryder said the management at the *News* felt that there was no justification for Brandshaft's complaint, but asked him to give up the town job nevertheless. "They said, 'We have to be as clean as a hound's tooth,' " Ryder said.

Ironically, Brandshaft has also had a reporter in his camp. In 1967, when Ryder was handling Ambro's campaign to unseat incumbent GOP Town Supervisor Quentin Sammis, the *News'* Long Island bureau chief, Bill Butler, was working for Sammis. (Both reporters said they worked without pay.) Brandshaft was the GOP co-leader in Huntington in 1967.

Sammis was defeated in that race and Ambro, the new town supervisor, gave Ryder a $6,000-a-year town public information job in January, 1968. Ryder said that he tried to keep his relationship with Ambro professional. "Ambro wouldn't try to get me to get anything in the paper because he knew I wouldn't do it," Ryder said. Ambro said he received no special treatment in the *Daily News* because of Ryder's town employment.

In 1969, Ryder replaced Butler as Long Island bureau chief for the *Daily News,* which put him in the position of helping to decide what was worth printing in the paper on a given day and assigning reporters to cover it. One *Daily News* reporter who asked not to be quoted by name said: "Ryder was in a direct conflict on the Ambro thing because he assigned reporters to cover Ambro's press conferences." Ryder said, "Most of the people in the press room didn't even know I worked for Ambro. I have never called another reporter [from another paper] concerning Ambro." Reflecting on the whole situation of reporters' taking outside political work, Ryder said: "Some reporters do it with integrity; some do not. I think there is a very fine line there. It would perhaps be better that nobody did this."

A newsman who recently said he had had second thoughts about his outside political work was Richard Wettereau of Manhasset, night city editor at the *Press.* Wettereau said he had received $50 to $100 a week from the North Hempstead GOP for 10 years—1959 through 1968. During that same period, he was the North Shore beat reporter for the *Press* and wrote stories on North Hempstead, Glen Cove and Oyster Bay. "I gave it up because it just didn't fit right with me," he said. "There was nothing illegal or immoral about it, but I thought it was jeopardizing the position of unbiased news."

Some of the reporters who did accept jobs did not want to write stories about candidates who employed them, and frequently "traded off" with other reporters. Tony Panzarella, who worked 10 years as a *Long Island Press* reporter before taking a job early this year as administrative assistant in the Nassau County Parks

Department, said he relied heavily on other reporters to get stories placed for his candidates. "I'd give them a [press] release and ask them to do what they could," said Panzarella, who was on Assemblyman Kingston's legislative payroll for $100 a week and who said that he earned $10,000 a year extra from his outside work. Conversely, Panzarella was not likely to say no when another reporter asked him for a similar favor. He admitted that he frequently accommodated his reporter friends on other papers by writing stories in his paper based upon press releases these reporters had prepared for their candidate.

Harry Schlegel is the assistant city editor for political and city hall assignments for the *Daily News.* Several reporters on the paper's Long Island staff pointed to Schlegel's political job as justification for their taking outside work. For a five-year period, he has been paid $54,316.34 in state funds. Since 1966, Schlegel, of 14 Kingsbury Rd., Garden City, has been on the state payroll as a research director for the Joint Legislative Committee on Interstate Cooperation, whose chairman is Sen. John Marchi (R-Staten Island). Marchi said he had asked Schlegel to take a leave of absence to help in Marchi's 1969 primary fight against Mayor Lindsay for the Republican mayoral nomination.

Schlegel said that former *Daily News* Editor Harry Nichols, now deceased, had given him permission to take the Marchi committee job originally but refused his request for a leave of absence to work for Marchi's campaign. "The boss [Nichols] said he wanted me around here to coordinate the campaign coverage," Schlegel said. As an editor, Schlegel helped decide what aspects of the campaign should be covered and directed a staff of reporters who wrote about the various issues.

In addition to this, Schlegel wrote eight news stories under his own byline about the Marchi-Lindsay mayoral campaign, including an interpretative article on June 19, 1969, on the computer analysis of the vote after Marchi beat Lindsay for the nomination. "I may have written [the Marchi-Lindsay stories], but it was on the assignment of my boss who knew I was working for Marchi," Schlegel said. "What could I tell him? That I wasn't going to write them? That would be insubordination."

Another editor in a position similar to Schlegel's was Arnold Friedman, of Floral Park, assistant managing editor of the *Long Island Press,* who was working for Rep. Seymour Halpern (R-Jamaica). Congressional payroll records show that Friedman was paid $11,755.68 for 13 months' work for Halpern spread over 1967, '68 and '69, while Friedman was employed as night news editor responsible for the selection of news that went into the *Press'* Queens edition.

Friedman, asked if he had ever handled Halpern stories, said, "I don't recall anything specifically, but if I did I never let my professional integrity be compromised." Halpern, who is retiring this year, said that he paid Friedman to "help in relation to speeches, committee testimony, newsletters [to constituents] and in-depth writing."

Articles about Halpern that appeared in the *Long Island Press* would normally be handled through the Queens-edition desk. Gene Turner, who was a combination copy editor-rewriteman on the Queens desk under Friedman before going to work for the Town of Hempstead, said, "He [Friedman] never asked me to give any favorable treatment to Halpern. I only handled them [Halpern assignments] routinely like any other story."

Turner said that his knowledge of the Friedman-Halpern business arrangement made him feel that it was nothing "out of the ordinary" to work an outside political public relations job. "In April, 1966, I moved from Queens to Uniondale," said Turner, who was earning about $10,000 a year. "I had two kids and a brand new house and I was worried about it. I called my friend Bob Ryan and said, 'Hey, I need some extra money,' because at the *Press* [salary] I could hardly carry my house." At that time, Turner had never heard of the man Ryan recommended. "Ryan said, 'There's this young legislator in Uniondale named Margiotta who needs some help,' " Turner recalled.

Turner was put on a state payroll and earned $500 for putting out newsletters for Margiotta and sending out a poll to his constituents. Turner said that he worked in Margiotta's 1966 campaign "as a gratis thing" without pay and took a full-time public relations job with the Town of Hempstead that same year.

Turner said he did not notify the *Press* management of his work for Margiotta. "I just chose not to," he said. "I felt they might say no for some obscure reason even though there was obviously no conflict." Turner said that none of Margiotta's stories came through the Queens-edition desk.

Panzarella said that he also kept all his outside public relations accounts secret except for $3,200 he earned last year for writing releases for *Catholic Charities.* Panzarella's record of outside public relations work dates back to the mid-1960s, when he earned $62 a week for handling press affairs for the Hicksville School District. More recently, Panzarella was on the legislative payroll of State Sen. Ralph Marino (R-Syosset) as a research assistant and said that he was paid $2,000 for four months' work in 1969 or 1970. From July, 1970, until last April, Panzarella was on Kingston's legislative payroll for $100 a week. In 1969, Panzarella was paid $300 by the Nassau County Republican Committee for writing press releases for a slate of Republican city council candidates in Long Beach.

Panzarella said there was no conflict in his dual jobs. "My office didn't even know that their [Kingston's and Marino's] press releases came from me," he said. "I never put a story in my typewriter concerning any of my accounts." However, the *Long Island Press* in October, 1970, carried a series of articles written by Panzarella that analyzed the campaigns of Nassau candidates, including Kingston and Marino.

Reporters were not the only source of help sought by political campaign workers. Former *Newsday* night photo editor William F. Sullivan was paid cash to help see to it that pictures of certain politicians received special treatment at *Newsday*. John Goertler, who was campaign photographer for Supreme Court Justice Sol Wachtler during his close but unsuccessful 1967 campaign to unseat Nickerson as county executive, said that he had paid Sullivan $200 cash to see to it that pictures of Wachtler and other Nassau GOP candidates were brought to the attention of the night city desk, where final decisions were made on which pictures would be published in *Newsday*. Wachtler said he was not aware of the Goertler-Sullivan arrangement.

Goertler said: "I gave the money to 'Sully' to make my job that much easier. It's tough to get a picture out of the darkroom to the night desk. If it never got past the photo editor [Sullivan], how could it get to the desk?" Sullivan, who lives in Merrick, said that when Wachtler's people brought in press releases with pictures attached, he would "take them out to the desk." He said he could not remember the exact amount of money he received. "It was $20 here, $50 there—there wasn't anything steady about the payments."

Newsday assistant publisher Stanley Asimov said that *Newsday* was unaware at the time of Sullivan's activities in the Wachtler campaign. However, Asimov said, in February 1968 the paper's management learned from several members of the photography staff that Sullivan had been paid by Oyster Bay Republican candidates to handle photography for the 1967 town campaign. Asimov said Sullivan was warned and given a second chance because he had 18 years of service with *Newsday*. But when Sullivan took administrative action the next day against some of the photographers who had spoken out about him, Asimov said, he was fired.

Sullivan said he could not recall how much he received in the Oyster Bay campaign, but Long Beach City Manager James Nagourney, a GOP publicity man at the time, said he put Sullivan on his payroll for two months before the election at a salary of $200 a week. Nagourney was managing the campaign for then Councilman Ralph J. Marino (now a state senator) against the late Michael Petito, then the Democratic Oyster Bay supervisor. "I made shots for whoever was running on the town ticket, not just Marino," Sullivan said. "I worked through Nagourney; for four or five jobs a week you'd get a weekly thing [payment]. It [the photography] was for the weeklies. Any of the stuff I did for them never got in *Newsday*."

Sherman Phillips of the *Press* is paid $10,997 as a registration supervisor at the Nassau County Board of Elections. He was hired to do public relations and promote mobile voter registration July 29, 1963, by English, who in addition to being Democratic leader was then a commissioner of elections. Phillips was the *Press'* night police reporter until last July, when he became a district reporter responsible for covering the North Shore from Great Neck to Roslyn. Phillips, who often wrote stories in the *Press* about the Board of Elections, said that he was never faced with the prospect of having to write a story about a Democratic politician who had gotten entangled in an embarrassing incident with the police. "If the thing came up, I'd do a story," he said. "There was never any conflict."

Richard L. Miranda, a reporter who left the *Press* Jan. 3, 1971, to become the $20,500-a-year press secretary for Hempstead Town Supervisor Alfonse D'Amato, said he averaged $2,000 a year from political jobs during his 12 years as a *Press* reporter. He said he worked for both Democrats and Republicans. "There was never a point in my newspaper career that I wasn't working for someone on the side," Miranda said. While with the *Press,* Miranda said, he primarily covered the police and district court in Nassau.

In 1963, while working for a group of insurgent Republicans in North Hempstead, Miranda said he spent more money on expenses than he was paid. Afterward, Miranda said, he worked for then State Sen. Norman Lent on two of Lent's legislative committees for an 18-month period in 1966 and 1967 and was paid $5,000 in state funds. In 1967, Miranda said, he also was paid $2,000 for working in the unsuccessful campaign of Democrat Patrick J. Purcell against GOP Supervisor Robert Meade in the Town of North Hempstead.

Later, Miranda worked six months as the press assistant to Assemblyman John Kingston (R-Westbury) and said he was paid $2,200. At the request of Robert Ryan (then head of Hempstead Town's public information department), Miranda went to work in 1969 as the public relations director for the Hempstead Town Local Development Corp. for a salary of $400 a month. He said he held the job with the corporation, which operates the Freeport Industrial Park, for almost two years.

After working in D'Amato's campaign for reelection as town tax receiver and after D'Amato had been designated to move up to supervisor because of the election of Presiding Supervisor Ralph Caso as county executive, Miranda was asked by D'Amato if he would like to be D'Amato's press assistant. "I was flabbergasted," Miranda recalled. "I never knew if I would fit into government—I had been on the other side so long."

A reporter for the *Daily News* who now specializes in transportation news, Frank Mazza, of Glen Head, was the only newsman of the 18 who declined to discuss his outside activities. Mazza worked for a number of Democratic campaigns over the years, including the Glen Cove City Council race of 1967, in which Mayor-Supervisor Andrew J. DiPaola was elected to office for the first time by the slim margin of 147 votes. The Glen Cove Democrats paid Mazza $2,020 for writing publicity releases and articles for a campaign newspaper. "We never used his position to get favorable news in the *News,*" former city Democratic Leader Vincent Suozzi said.

On Sept. 15, 1966, Mazza's byline appeared on a story in the *News* about a candidate he was working for, Edward B. Joachim, an Old Westbury attorney. The article identified Joachim as the Democratic candidate in the 17th Assembly District and detailed how Joachim had tipped off the district attorney's office to a Long Island call-girl ring.

Records show that Mazza was paid $5,000 in 1970 as a public relations consultant for the Nassau Coliseum Inc., a county agency, and that the Nassau County Democratic Committee gave him $500 in 1967 for publicity work. County Democratic Leader Marvin Cristenfeld said the party had used Mazza's services a number of times over the years. "I've called Frank from time to time and asked him if he was available to work [in a campaign] and then put him in touch with the candidate."

In the 1964 campaign that brought the downfall of Assembly Speaker Joseph Carlino (R-Long Beach), Hank McCann of the *Press* wrote the publicity releases for winner Jerome McDougal Jr. McDougal, a former first vice president of the Nassau County Democratic Party, described McCann as "a good, two-fisted, four-fingered typewriter man" whom he paid $600 a month—a total of $2,400 to $3,000—for writing press releases during the campaign. McCann, now the *Press'* news editor and previously editor of the paper's Sunday magazine for 13 years, denied that he had made that much money. "My recollection is that I was paid $60 a week, which would be $240 a month," McCann said.

McCann said that he wrote television and entertainment columns for the Sunday magazine while working for McDougal and that he did the political work with the approval of his management.

Two of the earliest political activists among area reporters were the late Ben White of the *Daily News* and the late Richard Prussin of the *Press.* White, a reporter who scooped the world on the sex transformation of Christine Jorgensen, was on the Nassau Democratic Committee payroll in 1961, according to former Democratic Leader John English. "He [White] was as responsible as anyone else for Nickerson's winning the election [for county executive]," English said. "He was a key policy adviser." English said White often referred to him reporters who were interested in taking on party assignments. After Nickerson's election, the county executive in 1962 recommended White for a $7,500-a-year public relations post at Meadowbrook Hospital, now the Nassau County Medical Center. White held the Meadowbrook job until his death in 1963. A former *Newsday* city editor, he worked for the *News* on Long Island from 1946 until his death.

Prussin, a long-time *Press* reporter who died in 1968, was on the payroll of the Joint Legislative Committee on Mass Transportation, headed by the late State Sen. Edward Speno, from 1958 to 1965. Prussin was credited by Speno aides with playing a major role in the development of Speno's national auto safety program.

Also among the early moonlighters were former newsmen Ryan, who is now County Executive Caso's public relations director, and McDonald, who is County GOP Leader Margiotta's press secretary.

Ryan recalled that his first outside political job was in the late 1950s while he was a reporter for the *Long Island Press.* He said that he and Stanley Pakula, currently the public information officer for the Town of Islip, shared a $500 fee for writing publicity releases for the Glen Cove Democrats. Pakula, who handled a number of political campaigns while working as a reporter at the *Press* from 1960 to 1963, recalled that the Glen Cove job was in 1961. In any event, after leaving the *Press* to work for the *New York Herald Tribune* in 1961, Ryan also did campaign work for a seven-man slate of Republican candidates running for office in Huntington Town. Ryan declined to say how much he was paid for the Huntington campaign.

McDonald, a long-time friend and associate of Ryan's, worked at the *News* 13 years before going to work for Margiotta in March, 1969. In 1965, shortly after Ryan had left the *Tribune* to work for Caso and while McDonald was still with the *News,* the two submitted a public relations proposal to the Nassau-Suffolk Regional Planning Board, but the package was rejected. McDonald was paid $6,000 in 1968 as the publicity agent for the Mitchel Field Development Corp., an agency set up by the county to plan the development of the former air base. The *News* published a story announcing that McDonald was going to work for Margiotta and mentioned the fact that he was the "public relations consultant" to the Mitchel Field agency.

JURY PROBING GINSBERG USE OF FUNDS

A grand jury in Albany will begin an investigation next week into whether former Nassau Family Court Judge Martin Ginsberg illegally used public money to help pay for campaign publicity.

The jury will begin hearing testimony on Thursday, the same day that Ginsberg is scheduled to be sentenced on his recent perjury conviction in Nassau County. Ginsberg's attorney, John Sutter, called the new investigation the work of overzealous prosecutors and said he was confident that Ginsberg would not be indicted.

The Albany inquiry concerns Ginsberg's activities as a state assemblyman, a post he held before he received his judgeship in 1972. The witnesses subpoenaed include Bernard Rabin and Frank Krauss, whom Ginsberg has said wrote campaign releases for him while also working as reporters for the *New York Daily News*. Also ordered to appear are Rabin's and Krauss's wives, who were placed on state legislature payrolls and received payments totaling $7,210.

The grand jury will try to determine Ginsberg's role in arranging those payments and whether the wives actually did any work for the legislature, sources said. If the jurors decide that the money represented payments for Rabin's and Krauss's campaign work, the sources said, Ginsberg might be indicted on larceny charges.

Ginsberg's arrangement with Rabin, Krauss and their wives was disclosed by *Newsday* in an article published in October, 1972. In that article, Krauss was quoted as saying that his wife, Delphine, did not perform any state work in exchange for the $6,000 in state money she received during 1970 and 1971. Rabin's wife, Miriam, was paid $1,210 in 1971. The 1972 article said that Ginsberg had acknowledged arranging the state jobs for the two women.

Rabin, who still works for the *News,* could not be reached for comment yesterday. Krauss, who has left the paper to go into full-time public relations work, said that he would cooperate with the Albany probe. Sources said the Albany district attorney probably would grant Rabin, Krauss and their wives immunity in return for their testimony. Also subpenaed yesterday was Pete Bowles, one of two *Newsday* reporters who wrote the 1972 article.

At the time of that article, no official action was taken against Ginsberg. But the issue was revived in December during Ginsberg's Nassau County trial on extortion, bribe-receiving and perjury charges. The prosecution introduced the articles as evidence in an attempt to rebut the testimony of Ginsberg's character witnesses. Shortly afterward, sources said, the Albany district attorney's office began making inquiries on the matter and decided to start an investigation.

Ginsberg was convicted on one perjury count and faces a maximum seven-year sentence. Albany County's chief assistant district attorney, Daniel Dwyer, said he expected the grand jury there to reach a decision next week on whether to indict Ginsberg.

New Ginsberg Charge Reported

Former Nassau Family Court Judge Martin Ginsberg, convicted of perjury in December, has been indicted by a grand jury in Albany, sources close to the case said yesterday. The grand jury has heard testimony concerning allegations that Ginsberg illegally used public money to help pay for campaign publicity.

Ginsberg reportedly is ill in a hospital and could not be reached for comment. His lawyer, John Sutter, refused to comment.

Ginsberg was convicted in Nassau Dec. 27 of lying to a county grand jury about a $7,500 payment he received in 1970 from a tow-truck operator seeking county towing privileges. Ginsberg was given an unconditional discharge.

The Albany grand jury inquiry concerned Ginsberg's activities as a state assemblyman, a post he held before he received his judgeship in 1972. The investigation centered on Ginsberg's role in placing on state legislative payrolls the wives of two *New York Daily News* reporters, and on whether the wives actually did any work for the legislature. Ginsberg has said that the two reporters wrote campaign releases for him.

Daniel Dwyer, Albany County's chief assistant district attorney, said yesterday that the county grand jury had handed up four sealed indictments and had been discharged. Dwyer refused to say whether any of the four indictments involved the Ginsberg inquiry. However, other sources said the former judge had been named.

With Ginsberg now ill in the hospital, the unsealing of his indictment may be delayed. Normally, a sealed indictment in the county is opened when the individual named in it appears in Albany for arraignment, Dwyer said.

The Albany grand jury heard testimony Feb. 13 from Bernard Rabin and Frank Krauss, who Ginsberg has said wrote campaign releases for him while also working as reporters for the *Daily News,* and from their wives, who were placed on state legislature payrolls and received payments totaling $7,210. Another witness was Pete Bowles, one of two *Newsday* reporters who wrote an article in October, 1972, that revealed the arrangement between Ginsberg, Krauss and Rabin.

It was learned during the grand jury inquiry that the grand jury was looking into possible charges of second- and third-degree grand larceny and official misconduct.

In the *Newsday* article, Krauss was quoted as saying that his wife, Delphine, did not perform any state work in exchange for the $6,000 in state money she received during 1970 and 1971. Rabin's wife, Miriam, was paid $1,210 in 1971. The article said that Ginsberg had acknowledged arranging for the state jobs for the two women. Krauss, who has left the *Daily News* to go into full-time public relations work, said yesterday that he and his wife were granted immunity in return for their testimony. Mrs. Rabin said that she and her husband, who still works for the *News,* also were granted immunity.

At the time of the *Newsday* article, no official action was taken against Ginsberg. But the issue was revived in December during Ginsberg's Nassau County trial on extortion, bribe-receiving and perjury charges. The article was introduced into evidence by the prosecution in an attempt to rebut the testimony of Ginsberg's character witnesses. Shortly afterward, sources said, the Albany district attorney's office began making inquiries on the matter and decided to begin an investigation.

GINSBERG DENIES LARCENY CHARGES IN ALBANY COURT

Former Assemblyman and Nassau Family Judge Martin Ginsberg pleaded innocent yesterday in Albany County Court to six charges of grand larceny and official misconduct for allegedly using state funds to pay for private campaign publicity.

Until this weekend, Ginsberg had been hospitalized for depression for about two weeks at South Oaks Hospital in Amityville. He was brought into the courtroom in a wheelchair, and one court observer said his face was ashen and his eyes vacant. "He looked like a cadaver, totally devoid of expression," the observer said.

As the court clerk read the first count in the indictments, Ginsberg replied in a low voice, "Not guilty, so help me God." His
attorney, John J. Sutter, leaned over and spoke briefly to him, and
to each of the remaining five counts Ginsberg replied only, "Not
guilty." He also was accompanied by his wife, Joan, and a cousin,
Irving Elfus.

The indictments charge that Ginsberg placed the wives of two
New York Daily News reporters on state legislative payrolls while
he was an assemblyman, but they actually did not work. Ginsberg
has said that the two reporters wrote campaign news releases for
him. The allegations first were printed in *Newsday* in 1972. At the
time Ginsberg acknowledged arranging the state jobs for the two
women.

Ginsberg was convicted in December of lying to a Nassau
County grand jury about a $7,500 payment he received in 1970
from a tow-truck operator seeking county towing privileges. He
was given an unconditional discharge in that case last month.

The three counts of official misconduct allege the same set of
facts as the grand larceny indictments. Conviction on these counts
could mean a maximum of one year in jail and a $1,000 fine or
a fine twice any gain to Ginsberg.

Sutter said that Ginsberg, who refused to talk with reporters,
was "shocked and numb" over the charges.

Ginsberg denies both the allegation and, if true, that they would
constitute a violation of the law, Sutter said. Albany County Judge
Arnold W. Proskin released Ginsberg without bail and gave Sutter
45 days to file motions. No trial date was set.

The indictments to which Ginsberg pleaded innocent yesterday
grew out of an Albany County grand jury investigation that began
after the allegations concerning the reporters were brought out in
testimony in his trial last year.

Specifically, Ginsberg is charged with two counts of second-
degree grand larceny in excess of $1,500, in which it is alleged that
he placed Delphine Krauss, wife of former *Daily News* reporter
Frank Krauss, on the state payroll, but that Ginsberg benefitted
by "the work, labor and services rendered by Frank Krauss." The
counts cover the 1969 and 1970 fiscal years. If convicted, he faces
up to seven years in jail on each count.

He also is charged with one count of third-degree grand larceny
exceeding $250, which alleges the same set of events involving

Miriam Rabin and her husband, Bernard Rabin, who still works for the *News.* Conviction could bring a maximum of four years in jail. Neither the reporters nor their wives were charged in the indictments. Each was given immunity from prosecution in exchange for their testimony.

The Patronage System

One of the most valuable kinds of investigative reporting examines not just one scoundrel but an entire institutional system. The following articles, reprinted here with permission, from a *Chicago Tribune* investigation of fat in the city budget show the importance of comparing one locality with another. The articles also indicate the voluminous research that could be undertaken by enlisting the cooperation of the Better Government Association and the services of its enthusiastic volunteers.

The entire investigation took four reporters about fourteen weeks to complete. Although only certain sections of the city budget were sampled, the stories revealed a pattern of vast waste. According to *Tribune* Task Force Director Pamela Zekman, the Chicago budget was compared to that of five or six other cities. The reporters checked, for example, the cost per mile to paint the lines on highways in different cities. They also did things like get up at 4:30 A.M. to tail city work crews. "A lot of people think investigative reporting is romantic and dramatic," Zekman said. "The truth is that it's drudgery. There is nothing more boring than reading budgets or cruising streets looking for a work crew."

The series, by Pamela Zekman, William Crawford, William Gaines, and Daniel Egler, opened on November 24, 1974 with a detailed and, we think, effective illustration in everyday terms of just how much $91 million is. William Crawford's interview, published November 30, 1974, with an "irate payroller" shows how effective a reporter can be when posing as someone else, in this case a fellow patronage worker. The article also demonstrates the success of letting an interview flow freely in print without the interruption of descriptions or explanations. The closing article, by William Gaines and Daniel Egler, which also appeared on November 30, 1974, shows the very limited results that an investigation, even one as thorough as this, often brings about. In spite of all the hard work, the articles had little substantive effect. Six months after the investigation was published, Mayor Daley was re-elected by a landslide. "Sometimes nothing happens," said Zekman. "You learn to live with that. You don't always topple a President."

$91 MILLION WASTED BY CITY

A burned-out light bulb on the Michigan Avenue bridge is guaranteed to draw a crowd—of city payrollers.

Changing that one bulb requires:

A city electrician to climb up and remove the outer globe.

Another electrician to unscrew and replace the bulb.

A third to hold the scaffold and shoo away pedestrians.

A fourth to stand by in case his coworkers need tools.

A city foreman to supervise the four.

The half-hour job observed Oct. 30 cost Chicago taxpayers $24.33 based on the salaries of city electricians.

Is it any wonder, then, that Chicago has to pay an average of $37.43 a year to maintain each of the city's 230,000 streetlights with crews ranging from three to five men while Milwaukee, for example, gets by with two-man crews at half the cost?

The changing of the bulb is a graphic example of waste totaling more than $91 million uncovered by the *Tribune* Task Force and the Better Government Association in Chicago's first billion-dollar budget. The investigation dealt with just nine bureaus of three major city departments.

The padding of work crews with extra payrollers, a fact of life in every city department, is the result of the patronage system, in which jobs must be found to reward loyal precinct workers.

At least a fourth of the city's 43,000 employes are hired this way and carried on the payroll as "temporary appointees." This is a device to avoid Civil Service regulations, and investigators found "temporaries" who have been on the job for years.

If $91 million in wasted taxpayers' money is a difficult statistic to imagine, think of it as about 21 times what the Purolator thieves made off with last month in the biggest theft in American history.

Brought down to grass-roots level, at a time when many Chicagoans are trying to set aside some Christmas money, one year's waste in the city budget amounts to $91 for every single household in the city.

Divided by 365, the annual waste in the city budget comes to better than a quarter of a million dollars a day, every day of the year.

Part of that money, $317,684, is spent to wash street signs. That's 33 cents a sign to do what officials in six other major cities say they leave to the rain.

James McDonough, commissioner of streets and sanitation, explained that rain cannot wash the dirty signs because "some rain is dirty." To which an astonished Bruce Hicks, meteorologist and rainfall specialist at Argonne National Laboratory, replied, "I've never heard anything like it!"

Each year the City Council votes to spend more than a billion dollars of hard-earned tax money on items like this, listed in a document that specifies funds allotted according to performance standards that are physically impossible to meet.

Nearly $100 million of waste, tucked into the pages of the ponderous budget, was verified by Task Force and B. G. A. investigators, who found widespread loafing and overstaffing.

They visited or surveyed 15 comparable communities from coast to coast to assure they had accurate and fair comparisons.

Here is a cross-section of their findings:

The Chicago Fire Department wastes $22.8 million a year on short workweeks and using able-bodied, highly paid firefighters as switchboard operators, guards, and maintenance men or to support such pet projects of the commissioner as the department's troupe of clowns.

The Water Department wastes $15.3 million on padded payrolls and outmoded facilities which are as much as 20 years behind cities such as Detroit, Indianapolis, St. Louis, and Gary, which have joined the computer age.

The Bureau of Sanitation wastes $18.1 million a year with an army of street sweepers and garbage men who bring the cost of keeping the city clean to three times what Milwaukee—with the same climatic conditions—pays for the same job.

The Bureau of Sewers, presided over by 27th Ward Democratic Committeeman Edward Quigley, wastes more than $9.6 million —more than two-thirds of its annual budget—thru use of inefficient machinery to provide positions for the greatest number of patronage workers.

The Bureau of Streets, which pays one group of its 3,000 patronage workers $6.66 an hour to climb stubby ladders and wipe the
dust off street signs, piles up a staggering $22.9 million in waste
out of an annual appropriation of $57.3 million for street mainte-
nance.

A study of the $3.9 million 1974 budget of the Water Collection
Division underscores the widespread misspending and overstaffing found during the Task Force-B. G. A. investigation.

That budget will increase to $4.2 million in 1975 if the mayor's
recommended appropriations are approved.

The department is staffed by $14,246-a-year water meter read-
ers who hold what some payrollers call "the plum job of City
Hall"—a job that is costing taxpayers $1.3 million in waste in
1974.

Tho the annual salary might not seem attractive, the job leaves
ample time to pursue other careers for many of the city's 120
meter readers.

Their salaries will increase to $15,672 under the 1975 budget
request.

"It's the real laugher," a former meter reader said of the job.
"It's a part-time job with full-time pay."

It costs $1.23 every time a meter is read in Chicago, the highest
rate of any city with comparable conditions.

Milwaukee spends 75 cents for the same job, and Indianapolis,
which has a privately owned and operated water company, spends
only 27½ cents.

In Detroit investigators found that the combined services of
reading, billing, inspecting, and maintaining water meters cost
$5.06 a meter a year. The cost in Chicago for the same operations
is $12.88.

"I can't believe one city can be two times as efficient as another," said Chicago Water Commissioner Richard Pavia in response to that statistic. "You simply can't compare the costs to
determine efficiency."

Investigators also compared the division's efficiency by examining the yearly workloads of meter readers in various cities.

In Milwaukee a meter reader reads 25,108 meters a year. In the
same year a Chicago rate taker reads 12,543 meters, about half as
many.

A computation of the number of annual meter readings divided by the number of rate takers shows how badly Chicago readers perform each day.

In Chicago, readers read an average of 48 meters a day, compared with 71 in Detroit, 98 in Milwaukee, 148 in St. Louis, and 150 in Indianapolis.

If Chicago meter readers were as efficient as Milwaukee's, it would need only 45 men—instead of the 94 now reading Chicago's 165,000 meters.

That would cost only $640,000, or less than half of the $1.3 million taxpayers now are paying for the service.

Pavia maintains that the workload for each of the 94 rate takers is programmed to take eight hours, with 90 minutes allocated for daily paper work.

The number of reading assignments varies depending on the route, he said.

Surveillances and interviews with former and present meter readers, however, contradict Pavia's claims that the men are given a full day's work load.

"I gotta read 30 meters a day. I can cover those 30 stops in an hour, and then I quit. I'm thru for the day," said Lenard Litviak to an undercover reporter posing as an interested car buyer at Ben's Auto Sales, 5858 S. Western Av., where Litviak can be found hawking cars after 1:30 P.M.

"Ya know, sometimes when I'm really feeling lousy, I won't even get outta the car and read the meters," Litviak said. "I just drive by the house and guess at it, write anything down."

Heading the army of meter readers is Edward Nihill, 76, the $28,764-a-year superintendent of water collection and a long-time Democratic machine politician.

Nihill insists that his six supervisors adequately police loafing, and claims a meter reader "is never without supervision for more than three days."

But Litviak says he's never been subjected to such supervision: "Nobody watches you, no one," he said. "I've got to check in twice a week and that's the end of it."

Nihill said his supervisors check on men by leaving notes tacked to meters scheduled for a reading. If the note isn't picked up, they know the men aren't working.

"We want to try to increase our efficiency," Nihill said. "I'd like to catch some of these guys you're talking about."

One of them is Harry Zimmerman, a former 23rd Ward precinct captain who was at his Maxwell Street shoe store at 1 P.M. Sept. 20.

On Oct. 11, Zimmerman read meters for only one of four working hours. He began the day with a 90-minute coffee break across from City Hall, stopped at a bank, and then spent 20 minutes conducting shoe business.

Paul Huebl, 24, is a self-employed "security consultant" when he's not reading water meters. On Oct. 16 he told a reporter seeking his services, "If I worked full time, how would I find time to go out and be an investigator?

"So I got an after-school type job [reading meters], a job for a couple hours a day. I sandwich the two in real nicely."

Sam Catanzaro, 2430 W. Eastwood Av., runs S & S Office Machines, Inc., a repair service at 5403½ W. Diversey Av. Catanzaro guaranteed "around-the-clock service" to a reporter inquiring about having typewriters repaired.

All of the meter readers later denied that their outside activities interfere with their city jobs.

Pavia said the combining of outside employment with meter reading assignments, as documented by the *Tribune* and B. G. A., is forbidden.

"I would consider [the moonlighter] unethical, irresponsible, improper, and certainly not the kind of person we want on the payroll," he said.

He said readers who are able to complete day-long assignments in a few hours are "either not doing their jobs right or there is something badly amiss in the amount of work demanded of these men."

Chicago's billion-dollar budget is churned out each year by Budget Director Edward Bedore, who says he accepts without question the statistics used by department heads to justify spending.

"That's the responsibility of department heads," Bedore said.

Asked what his responsibility is, Bedore said his personal half-million-dollar budget includes a staff of nine persons earning salaries totaling $104,786 to conduct "personnel utilization studies."

The team, headed by Richard Moorehouse, is charged with conducting surveillances of city workers to identify loafers and pinpoint overstaffing.

Last year it claimed credit for 228 suspensions, but no discharges.

"It is our responsibility to see that every city employe does his job," Bedore said. "The mayor has gone on record as saying that he doesn't condone anything but a day's pay for a day's work."

Irate Payroller Blasts System Costing Millions

[The City Hall patronage system is costing taxpayers millions of dollars a year in unnecessary jobs, with at least one-fourth of the city's 40,000 employes working as payrollers. A precinct captain who holds one of those jobs unwittingly gave a *Tribune* Task Force reporter who infiltrated the ranks of the Democratic machine this account of how the system works.]

"I'm a clerk in streets and sanitation. I don't do anything for a living!"

In one sentence, the life story and everlasting complaint of a Chicago patronage worker.

"I work one hour a day and sit on my duff the rest of the time. I twiddle my thumbs. But, that's the problem. I want to work. I want a job where I can work eight hours a day. Just like all those other guys in the department. We work one hour and then kill time the rest of the day."

Lenny Locuss, a Democratic precinct captain in the 48th Ward and City Hall payroller, is venting his anger and frustration at the system.

There are at least 10,000 Lenny Locusses on the city payroll. They hold useless and unnecessary jobs awarded them for getting out the vote at election time and fight a daily battle to better themselves. But they stay on an unending treadmill to keep those Democratic votes coming in, election after election, so they can hang on to what they've got.

The system, padding the city payroll with unnecessary workers to keep that ready-made army of doorbell ringers and precinct workers at battleready, is costing Chicago taxpayers millions in wasted money every year.

Locuss, 6354 N. Hermitage Av., moonlights as an entertainer

Reprinted, courtesy the *Chicago Tribune*.

in a North Side cocktail lounge, strumming a guitar and telling gags on weekends to augment the salary from streets and sanitation, a job he hates but fears losing.

At the moment he is entertaining a one-man audience, William Crawford, a fellow precinct worker who joined Locuss on Mayor Daley's payroll by helping the 48th Ward make a good showing Nov. 5. Crawford is a *Tribune* reporter who infiltrated the patronage army's ranks.

"How can a guy live on $750 a month? Tell me, will ya? I have to hold down two jobs, working until 5 A.M. on weekends to survive. For four years I've been asking Marty to get me a better job, and he does nothing."

Marty is Martin Tuchow, 48th Ward Democratic committeeman, and the man to whom Locuss and Crawford are indebted for their City Hall jobs.

"For three years he's been promising me a higher paying job, and nothing happens," Locuss continues.

"All I want is a nice, quiet little job driving a little truck for the Park District. The Park District has these little trucks, and they're easy to drive, and you don't do nothing and the pay is good. That's all I want.

"Christ, I work my precinct. I pay guys out of my own pocket!"

Locuss was a captain in the 50th Ward, and his original sponsor was County Commissioner Jerome Huppert. Dissatisfied with his lot, Locuss moved to the 48th Ward, where he is now a co-captain of the 22d Precinct under Tuchow, also a county commissioner.

"You know what the spike, the nail, of the Democratic organization has been?" he asks Crawford. "You know why we been successful year after year? I don't have to tell you. It's the money. You buy the votes.

"But, I ask you, how the hell am I going to buy a vote when I'm being paid $750 a month? That's $150 a week after taxes. That's why Tuchow has got to realize I need a better job.

"Come election day the battle commanders are going to be saying, 'Sure, I'll come out and vote, but where's my bottle of wine?' And the colored and the Puerto Ricans—Jeez—they'd vote this country right out of business. They don't care, just as long as you give them a few bucks. That's what made the Democratic Party great—and I can't do it with the lousy job I got."

At a subsequent meeting during a coffee break Nov. 15 in the

Bismarck Hotel, Locuss continues the conversation as tho it had never stopped:

"Tuchow wants to know how you did in your precinct before he'll consider you for a job, but how we gonna do good unless we got a good paying job to go along with the expenses of an election? You tell me."

Locuss sips his coffee and continues: "I happen to be sponsored by a man in the chair right now. You know Jerome Huppert? He's committeeman in the 50th, and he hasn't done [bleep] for me! He's worse than Tuchow.

"He gets up there holding a big poster of himself and he points to it and says, 'See that? Look at it. Take a good look at it, because that's the man we're electing next time around. Look at that face, and don't you forget it.'

"Now, what kind of talk is that? What are we, kids? You know, he's got a large Jewish population in his ward, and you don't tell Jews too much. . . .

"I went to Huppert and asked him for a job. He gives me a job. He says you'll be working at a pumping station. I'm supposed to be happy. About what? About driving from the extreme North Side to 9500 south? I get in the car and I drive down there. It took me an hour.

"So I get there and I pull in and I walk in this big place, and there's people coming and going all over the place. . . .

"Next thing I know, I'm descending these stairs and I walk thru these two huge—I mean, gigantic—doors, and there's these little men coming and going with hard hats on, water engineers or something.

"I go there, thru this long hall, and I come to this huge vat, three times the size of this room. A big round thing. I'm standing there all dressed up, coat and tie, and I look down into this filthy tank. I don't know, the water slowly runs out of it and there's this green slimy [bleep] all over the inside.

"Some guy comes up to me and tells me to put on this rubber suit and climb down into this huge tub and take a hose and squirt off the slime. I mean, what the [bleep]! And the job only pays $650 a month.

"I was so [bleeping] mad, I was swearing all the way back to Huppert's office.

"I walked in and he was writing and didn't even look up at me. I said to him, 'That's a job? It costs me $30 a month just to get there. Tell me, would you take the job?' He says, 'What's the matter, you don't like it?'

"But, the thing that really makes me mad is, he just keeps on writing. Not even looking at me. So, I tapped on his shoulder and I said, 'Look at me when I talk to you. Would you take that job?' He didn't say nothing!

"Anybody who'd pay for his job has got to be crazy."

Crawford reminded Locuss he'd been told he would have to pay "dues" for his City Hall job.

"Oh, yeah," Locuss replied. "You got to sell tickets to the dinner, and maybe take out an ad in the magazine. What they do is, they assess you so much, depending on how much you're making—$200 at $500 a month, $300 at $600 a month, or whatever it is."

Crawford: "I got to get back to work. Going back?"

Locuss: "No. . . ."

---

3 METERMEN SUSPENDED BY CITY FOR MOONLIGHTING

Richard Pavia, commissioner of water and sewers, announced Friday that three water meter readers have been suspended "indefinitely" for failing to register outside jobs with the department.

He also said allegations that city workers have profited from the sale of landfill are under investigation.

The action resulted from a *Tribune* Task Force and Better Government Association investigation which detailed $15.3 million wasted in the water department and $9.6 million wasted in the Bureau of Sewers.

While attacking the investigation for making "faulty comparisons" and using "inaccurate statistical data," Pavia said:

"There's always room for improvement in every governmental operation and the department of water and sewers will continue to work for improvements."

The three meter readers suspended are Sam Catanzaro, owner of S. & S. Office Machines, Inc., 5403½ W. Diversey Av.; Harry Zimmerman, owner of Zimmerman's Shoes, 801 W. Maxwell St.; and Lenard Litviak, who spends his afternoons hawking cars at Ben's Auto Sales, 5858 S. Western Av.

Reprinted, courtesy the *Chicago Tribune.*

Tribune and B. G. A. investigators found the three working their second jobs during hours when they should have been reading water meters.

Pavia claimed that all three denied they had told *Tribune* reporters they could complete their reading assignments in as little as three hours.

He said the actual average load for readers is 66 meters, not 48 as claimed by the *Tribune,* tho the *Tribune* figures were obtained by dividing the number of meters read in a year by the number of working days by the 93 meter readers Pavia said were on the payroll.

The investigators also found city water distribution crews selling dirt to Riverdale Builders Inc. in south suburban Calumet City tho Pavia claimed the landfill was provided free and was a "bargain" for the city.

"No checks, okay. Cash only," warned Ray Schapendonk, a truck driver for the department, when approached by investigators posing as interested landfill buyers.

Investigators observed city trucks hauling dirt to the site of River Oaks Estates from water main excavations at 93d and State streets and 91st Street and Wabash Avenue.

As much as $500,000 could have found its way into the pockets of city workers during the five years the *Tribune* was told the operation had been in existence.

Pavia also said it would cost $15 million to automate electric pumping stations and $28 million to convert steam-operated stations, as has been done at least 20 years ago in other cities.

When asked about the cost earlier, Pavia had said each pumping station would require a separate study so there was no figure available for the conversion.

He said studies are under way to consider the use of diesel or gas engines in the steam stations which "would permit partial automation without sacrificing the existing reliability under the natural gas-electricity energy systems."

Pavia also charged the per mile figure of $3,321 for maintaining Chicago's sewers was actually $2,671. Investigators, however, also included costs of inspections as are done in other cities. He admitted he had "no way of immediately knowing" if costs for other cities cited by the *Tribune* were incorrect.

He maintained that if the recommendations were carried out, 85 per cent of sewer services would be eliminated.

The Hoffa Case

The following story, written by Fred Girard and researched by Ralph Orr, Peter C. Gavrilovich, Peter Benjaminson, and Tom Hennessy, is one of many *Detroit Free Press* reporters wrote about the 1975 disappearance of former Teamsters Union President James R. Hoffa. The article was published on August 10, 1975 and is reprinted here with permission. We have included this example of thorough investigative reporting to illustrate the need for caution and the occasional unreliability of sources.

The story seems to prove that the blood found in a car belonging to the son of a Mafia figure implicated in the case was human blood, and not fish blood as the driver of the car claimed. An executive of the firm that packed the salmon is quoted as saying its carton was "leak-proof." The manager of the car wash where the driver of the car said the fish blood was washed off is quoted as twice denying that any such car was washed that day. Two uninvolved retail fish merchants are quoted as saying that such a salmon would not bleed much, if at all. Only the driver of the car, and the friend to whom he was delivering the fish, are quoted as saying that the fish bled. At the end of the "fish" portion of the story, a source is quoted as saying that "If [the blood] turns out to be human blood, somebody's in trouble."

The reporters who prepared the story were energetic in their pursuit of those involved in the fish delivery and of expert, uninvolved witnesses. No one seemed to be lying. The case for the fish blood actually being human blood looks very strong in this story, which led the paper on the Sunday it was published. Unfortunately, later that day, a source "close to the investigation" revealed that lab tests had indicated that the blood was indeed fish blood and not human blood.

Nothing at all is apparently wrong with the reporting, except for the probability that those who packed the fish or others in the business would be reluctant to admit that their packages occasionally leak and that salmon may bleed heavily. Every source has his or her biases, however, and this story holds together well. But the conclusion it inadvertently supports turned out to be the opposite of the truth. *Caveat investigator.*

FBI SEIZES HOFFA CAR

Bloodstains Found on Seat

Just Fish, Foster Son Declares

FBI agents investigating the disappearance of former Teamsters President James R. Hoffa seized a car belonging to the son of a major Mafia figure early Saturday morning, and sources said bloodstains were found on the front seat.

The FBI will have the blood analyzed to learn if it is of human or animal origin.

The *Free Press* reported earlier that the car, owned by Joe Giacalone, was driven by Hoffa's foster son, Charles (Chuckie) O'Brien, on the day Hoffa disappeared.

O'Brien, in a phone interview from West Memphis, Ark., where he is staying with his wife, told the *Free Press* Saturday that the bloodstains came from a "40-pound salmon" he was delivering to the wife of Robert Holmes Sr., another Teamster official.

The pre-dawn seizure of Giacalone's car was one of two major developments in the Hoffa case in less than 24 hours.

A U.S. Justice Department spokesman Saturday confirmed earlier reports that the entire Hoffa matter will go before a federal grand jury.

Giacalone is the son of Anthony Giacalone, one of three men the Hoffa family believes Jimmy Hoffa was going to meet on July 30, the day he disappeared.

O'Brien said Saturday the salmon had been delivered by Bucks Air Freight from Seattle. He said the fish, a gift from Teamster Vice-President Arnie Weinmeister, had been packed in a plastic bag surrounded by ice, and the bag placed in a cardboard box sealed with plastic tape.

O'Brien said the ice was beginning to melt, so he agreed to deliver the fish to Holmes' wife, Vi, in Farmington Hills.

O'Brien said blood was leaking from the box.

"When I first picked up the box I didn't notice," O'Brien said, "and I got blood all over my pants and shirt and everything. I don't know why I didn't put it in the trunk—I should have, I guess, but I put it on the floor in the back instead."

A salmon weighing 16½ pounds was sent July 28 from Arnie Weinmeister, a Teamster official in Seattle, to Holmes at the Teamsters' office on Trumbull Avenue.

The fish was packaged by Pacific Fish Co. of Seattle. Al Halela, manager of Pacific's retail operation, told the Free Press the fish was "whole and gutted" and said it was shipped in a "waxed-type carton" that was "leak-proof" and "odor-proof."

According to Halela, filament tape was used to seal the package and the fish itself was surrounded by a frozen gel and placed inside a plastic liner.

Halela said it was not likely that blood would come from the package and said a freshly caught 16½-pound salmon would not bleed enough to fill half a teacup. "It'll drip blood a couple of times, that's all," Halela said.

The fish was shipped by Airborne Freight Corp., a firm with offices in Seattle and Romulus.

Jim Loftus, operations supervisor for Airborne in Romulus, said the fish was delivered to the Teamster headquarters on Trumbull at 11:35 a.m. on July 30, about three hours before Hoffa was last seen. He said it was signed for by Carol Davis, apparently a Teamster employe.

O'Brien said the blood also leaked onto the floor and a kitchen counter at the Holmeses' house, as well as puddling on the back floorboard of Giacalone's 1975 maroon Mercury, which O'Brien had borrowed to make the trip.

Mrs. Holmes, interviewed at her home, said that the fish had been gutted but that there was still a lot of blood.

"When he brought it in, it was dripping with blood, and I had dripping blood in the garage, in the hallway and in the kitchen," she said.

She said she did not notice if there was blood on O'Brien's clothes.

O'Brien said he removed blood from the car with a paper towel, then drove it to Jax Kar Wash at 31500 Grand River in Farmington.

There, O'Brien said, he showed attendants the blood on the floor and "asked them if they could clean it up for me before it dried and started to stink."

Joe Spitz, manager of the car wash, said, "No way, no way did anybody come out and ask us to get blood off the seat of a car."

O'Brien, told what Spitz had said, responded that he had a Jax Club card, which entitles cardholders to wash jobs every day for one yearly payment.

"If he'll just check his records, he'll see I was there on that Wednesday," O'Brien told the *Free Press.*

Spitz, contacted again, said the FBI already had checked his records for that day, and "there was no way we recorded a Mercury or anything like that."

Spitz also said a check of the car wash's records did not turn up O'Brien's name.

Two Detroit area retail fish merchants reached by the *Free Press* Saturday agreed that if there were any blood at all in a fish sent the way O'Brien said the salmon was sent, there would not be much.

Samples of the blood found in the car will be analyzed at the FBI's Washington laboratory.

In addition, two FBI specialists flew from Washington to Detroit to dismantle the car and take samples of fibers, dust and other material in the car to be sent back to Washington for analysis.

"They'll strip that car down to the chassis and pack everything off to the lab in Washington," the *Free Press* source said.

One source told the *Free Press,* "If that turns out to be human blood, somebody's in a lot of trouble."

The FBI questioned O'Brien closely last Wednesday as to his exact movements on the day Hoffa disappeared. O'Brien's movements, as he described them to both the FBI and the *Free Press,* would place him close to the Machus Red Fox restaurant at Maple and Telegraph in Bloomfield Township, where Hoffa was last seen.

It was learned from persons Hoffa spoke to just before going to the restaurant that Hoffa believed he was to meet Giacalone, Detroit labor consultant and ex-convict Leonard Schultz, and former Teamster Vice-President Anthony (Tony Pro) Provenzano of Clifton, N.J.

All three men have denied that any such meeting was planned.

Neighbors of the younger Giacalone say five or six FBI agents showed up at Giacalone's apartment, 24000 E. Jefferson in St. Clair Shores, at 3 A.M. Saturday to impound the car.

An FBI spokesman said the agency would have no comment on

the seizure until Monday afternoon.

The *Free Press* also learned that the FBI acquired a second search warrant from U.S. Magistrate Barbara K. Hackett on Friday, when the warrant for Giacalone's car was obtained. The target of that warrant was unknown, but a source said it had not been executed as of late Saturday.

U.S. Attorney Ralph B. Guy Jr. took the first step toward a grand jury probe of the Hoffa case late Friday when he authorized issuance of the first federal subpoena in the case, for records of telephone calls made from Hoffa's Oakland County home before he vanished 11 days ago.

The FBI requested the subpoena, Guy said.

"As the scope of the Hoffa investigation widens and more witnesses are questioned and some stories conflict, the FBI will need access to the grand jury to deal with recalcitrant or reticent witnesses," Guy said.

At least one figure in the case, Anthony Giacalone, reportedly has refused to talk to the FBI.

Putting the Hoffa case before a grand jury would enable the department to subpoena witnesses and have them testify under oath.

A witness who balks before the grand jury by invoking the Fifth Amendment to the U.S. Constitution—which specifies that no citizen can be compelled to incriminate himself—can be granted immunity from prosecution in exchange for his testimony.

He then can be cited for contempt of court if he refuses to testify.

It is questionable, however, that immunity would be granted to a person like Giacalone, indicted twice earlier this year by the federal grand jury handling Organized Crime Strike Force cases.

Giacalone was indicted in April on income tax and mail fraud charges and a month later on fraud charges in connection with Integrated Medical Services Inc., a plan to provide health care for the Michigan Conference of Teamsters.

There were indications that the Hoffa family has mixed feelings about the timing of the grand jury probe.

Hoffa's daughter, Mrs. Barbara Crancer, said the family would welcome a grand jury investigation.

"We're in favor of anything that might lead to our dad's return. And if this will help, we're all for it," she said.

But another family source said the decision to lay the mystery before a grand jury might be premature.

"I don't want to second-guess when everybody is trying to be so helpful, but my gut feeling is that the probe is too early," said the source, who asked not to be identified.

"I'm afraid it might shut off some leads in the case."

Index